ABC OF INFLUENCE

ABC OF INFLUENCE

Ezra Pound and the Remaking
of American Poetic Tradition

Christopher Beach

University of California Press

Berkeley / Los Angeles / Oxford

University of California Press
Berkeley and Los Angeles, California

University of California Press, Ltd.
Oxford, England

© 1992 by
The Regents of the University of California

Library of Congress Cataloging-in-Publication Data

Beach, Christopher.
  ABC of Influence : Ezra Pound and the remaking of American poetic
tradition / Christopher Beach.
    p. cm.
  Includes bibliographical references and index.
  ISBN 0-520-07527-7 (alk. paper)
    1. American poetry — 20th century — History and criticism.
2. Influence (Literary, artistic, etc.)   3. Pound, Ezra, 1885–1972–
–Influence. I. Title.
PS323.5.B38   1992
811'.509–dc20   91-3972
                                                                      CIP

Printed in the United States of America
9 8 7 6 5 4 3 2 1

for Joel Oppenheimer
1930–1988

CONTENTS

ACKNOWLEDGMENTS

This project began at Harvard University, and I wish to thank my advisers, David Perkins and Kathryn Lindberg, for their suggestions, comments, and editing in the early stages of the book's creation. I also gratefully acknowledge the generous support and guidance I have received over the past several years from both Helen Vendler and Seamus Heaney.

I owe a spiritual as well as a practical debt to several of the poets I was fortunate enough to meet in the course of this project. The late George Butterick was a source of inspiration in his dedicated service to Charles Olson and to the tradition at large; his death was a tragic loss for all those who value his work in the field. Robert Creeley has been of great service in providing personal insights into the tradition. Finally, I dedicate the book to Joel Oppenheimer, whose friendship, interest, and intelligence will be sorely missed.

I also wish to thank the Homer Babbidge Library at the University of Connecticut, Storrs, for the opportunity to examine unpublished materials in its Olson archives, some of which have been used in the book. I also acknowledge the kind help of Malcolm Woodfield and Joseph Lease, both of whom read portions of the manuscript and made valuable suggestions in the course of its revision.

Finally, I thank my wife, Carrie Noland, for her love and support, for her acuteness and rigor as an editor, and for the many brainstorming sessions to which she has been subjected in the course of my writing this book.

Earlier versions of three of the chapters in this book have been previously published: chapter 2 appeared in *ELH* 56 (1989); chapter 6 in *American Poetry* 6 (1988); and chapter 9 in *Contemporary Literature* 32 (1991).

ABBREVIATIONS

For the convenience of the reader, unless otherwise noted, works originally published separately are cited from their author's collected volumes as abbreviated in the text and listed in the References.

ABC	*ABC of Reading,* by Ezra Pound
AI	*The Anxiety of Influence,* by Harold Bloom
AV	*Allen Verbatim,* by Allen Ginsberg
BB	*Bending the Bow,* by Robert Duncan
C	*The Cantos,* by Ezra Pound
CD	*Content's Dream,* by Charles Bernstein
CE	*Collected Essays,* by Robert Creeley
COCC	*Charles Olson and Cid Corman: Complete Correspondence, 1950–1964,* volume 1, edited by George Evans
COEP	*Charles Olson and Ezra Pound: An Encounter at St. Elizabeth's,* edited by Catherine Seelye
COIP	"Charles Olson and the Inferior Predecessors," by Marjorie Perloff
CON	*Contexts of Poetry: Interviews, 1961–1971,* by Robert Creeley
CORC	*Charles Olson and Robert Creeley: The Complete Correspondence,* edited by George Butterick
CPD	*The Collected Poems,* by Edward Dorn
CPO	*The Collected Poems,* by Charles Olson
CT	*Composed on the Tongue,* by Allen Ginsberg
FC	*Fictive Certainties,* by Robert Duncan
GW	*Ground Work: Before the War,* by Robert Duncan
H	*Howl: Original Draft and Facsimile,* by Allen Ginsberg

I	*Interviews,* by Edward Dorn
LE	*Literary Essays,* by Ezra Pound
LO	*Letters for Origin,* by Charles Olson
MM	*A Map of Misreading,* by Harold Bloom
MT	*Myths and Texts,* by Gary Snyder
OF	*The Opening of the Field,* by Robert Duncan
P	*Poems, 1960–1967,* by Denise Levertov
PR	*Poetry and Repression,* by Harold Bloom
PW	*The Poet in the World,* by Denise Levertov
PZ	*Prepositions,* by Louis Zukofsky
QG	*A Quick Graph: Collected Notes and Essays,* by Robert Creeley
S	*Slinger,* by Edward Dorn
SA	"Staying Alive," in *Poems, 1968–1972,* by Denise Levertov
SL	*Selected Letters, 1907–1941,* by Ezra Pound
SP	*Selected Prose, 1909–1965,* by Ezra Pound
SR	*The Spirit of Romance,* by Ezra Pound
SVH	*The Special View of History,* by Charles Olson
SW	*Selected Writings,* by Charles Olson
SZ	*S/Z: An Essay,* by Roland Barthes
V	*Views,* by Edward Dorn
WS	*Wallace Stevens: The Poems of Our Climate,* by Harold Bloom
YC	*The Years as Catches,* by Robert Duncan

I suppose if we should take to talking politics to each other I would disagree even more actively than all those others who have disagreed, but there has been no one living during my life time who has been as generous or as pure as you toward literature and toward writers. Nor anyone less generously thanked.

I know of no one who does not owe you a debt.

George Oppen, letter to Ezra Pound

INTRODUCTION

This book looks at the development of a tradition of American poetic writing that found its primary source in the ideas and practices of Ezra Pound. I focus my study of a "Pound tradition" on the two decades following World War II. The poets writing in this postwar tradition—most importantly, Charles Olson, Robert Duncan, Robert Creeley, Allen Ginsberg, Denise Levertov, and Gary Snyder—recurred to Pound in forming their sense of poetic inheritance and in establishing their own poetic theories. The tradition can be roughly defined as including those whose lives and work were directly related to Black Mountain College and the journals *Black Mountain Review* and *Origin*, to Duncan and the San Francisco countercultural movements, and to later descendants of these.[1] Not only were these poets directly influenced by Pound's writing but they also believed strongly in the importance of a tradition originating in the experimental, Modernist mode Pound represented. They promoted Pound, and to a lesser extent William Carlos Williams, as an essential counterforce to T. S. Eliot and to the "New Critical" poetry sanctioned by the Anglo-American academy. I am excluding from this book poets such as Robert Lowell, whose use of Pound, though significant, was not central to the way in which he defined himself culturally, historically, and institutionally as a poet. Nor do I treat the work of John Berryman, W. S. Merwin, Galway Kinnell, or Charles Wright, all of whom made interesting use of

1. A representative, but by no means comprehensive, list of these poets would include Edward Dorn, Jonathan Williams, Joel Oppenheimer, Paul Blackburn, Ed Sanders, Larry Eigner, Michael Rumaker, John Wieners, Theodore Enslin, Jack Spicer, Philip Whalen, Diane Wakoski, Robert Kelly, Clayton Eshleman, Jerome Rothenberg, Clark Coolidge, and Michael Palmer.

Pound's work, yet whose primary affiliations lay outside the
poetic tradition discussed here.[2]

Pound's influence cannot always be differentiated from more
general values and poetic practices which he shared with other
founding poets of the tradition I describe. There are instances in
the work of Olson, Duncan, and others in which William Carlos
Williams and even Louis Zukofsky may be more significant or
direct influences than Pound himself. For Ginsberg, Pound serves
largely as a mediator of Walt Whitman's influence; for Creeley
and Levertov, he mediates the more apparent influence of
Williams. Nevertheless, as I argue in chapter 3, while Whitman,
Williams, and Zukofsky share a good deal of the credit for the
evolution of what I am calling the Pound tradition in the 1950s
and 1960s, it is Pound himself who is the major source of its
ideas and practices and the unifying link with the tradition's
predecessors.

I leave aside the value judgment of Pound's relative impor-
tance; my focus on Pound as a poetic predecessor is necessitated
by the constraints of time and space. It would be next to impos-
sible to trace in a single book-length study the various influences
exerted by Whitman, Pound, Williams, and Zukofsky—not to
mention H. D., George Oppen, and many other poets for whom
a convincing case could be made as forerunners of the tradition.
I realize that in focusing on a single figure I am to some degree
neglecting the influences of many other poets, both male and
female. Among women poets, it goes without saying that Emily
Dickinson is of tremendous importance to any twentieth-century
American tradition; how direct an impact she had on the writing
of this particular group of writers is open to question.[3] H. D.,

2. I am also not treating those poets for whom Pound's influence came
indirectly, filtered through the work of E. E. Cummings or Marianne Moore, for
example, rather than directly from Pound's writings. For a more general discus-
sion of Pound's influence on modern poetry, see K. L. Goodwin, *The Influence of
Ezra Pound.*

3. See Burton Hatlen's discussion ("Carroll Terrell and the Great American
Poetry Wars") of Dickinson's importance as a forerunner of the radical poetic
mode constitutive of the Pound tradition. See also my interview with Joel
Oppenheimer (103–4), in which Oppenheimer discusses the importance of
Dickinson for poets of his generation.

who played a significant role in the early life of both Pound and
Williams, was an important influence on both Robert Duncan
and Denise Levertov, and her work constitutes for both of them
part of the same Modernist legacy as the work of Pound and
Williams. But H. D.'s impact as a mediator of Pound's influence
is less discernible in the tradition as a whole than is that of
Williams or Zukofsky. Two other women poets—Marianne
Moore and Lorine Niedecker—also deserve attention in a dis-
cussion of this tradition. Moore's work contributed significantly
to the wider dissemination of Pound's ideas and practices in
American poetry; Niedecker was associated with Zukofsky and
the Objectivists. Neither of them, however, has been claimed as
a major predecessor by poets of the tradition as have Williams,
Zukofsky, or, at times, George Oppen.

Several critics have posited poetic traditions that share certain
elements with the one I discuss; each emphasizes different as-
pects of the Poundian legacy. Hugh Kenner describes a "vortex"
of literary and artistic influence centering on Pound in his Mod-
ernist phase, but he does not trace the further evolution of this
tradition in the work of postwar poets.[4] Marjorie Perloff has
also contributed significantly to our critical understanding of a
Poundian strain of experimental Modernism. But her examina-
tion of Pound's influence is almost exclusively formal and the-
matic; it does not address the social and historical factors affect-
ing the extent and mode of this influence or its rationale.[5]
Charles Altieri has defined an "objectivist" tradition, linking
poets such as Olson, Creeley, and Duncan in terms of how they
exemplify an "immanentist mode" of poetry.[6] And Laszlo Géfin
has written a study of the impact of Pound on what he calls the
"ideogrammatic" or "paratactic" method in poets such as Ol-
son, Duncan, and Snyder.[7]

4. Kenner, *The Pound Era.*
5. In her article "The Contemporary of Our Grandchildren," Perloff identi-
fies the legacy of Pound in several aspects of the work of later poets: Pound's
insistence on precision, his "musical" free-verse line, his use of translation as
poetic invention, and his inclusion of history in the poetic text.
6. Altieri, *Enlarging the Temple.* See also his articles "From Symbolist
Thought to Immanence" and "The Objectivist Tradition."
7. Géfin, *Ideogram: History of a Poetic Method.*

My purpose is not to trace the evolution of a particular stylistic trait or mode of writing, as Perloff, Altieri, and Géfin do, but rather to respond to the larger question of poetic influence in its social, historical, political, institutional, and interpersonal contexts. Reading later poets through the lens provided by Pound's Objectivism or his ideogrammatic method can indeed provide insight into certain directions taken by poets who follow him; but these ideas, however central to Pound and his followers, do not account for the full range of attitudes and practices exemplified by these poets. My own reading stresses the tradition's diversity rather than its homogeneity. I examine the range of ideas and practices defining the poetics of the Pound tradition both in the immediate context of the influence of Pound's writing and in the larger historical context of the communal poetics that developed out of this influence. In providing such a biographical and historical context, I intend to recreate the sense shared by these postwar poets of a self-defining project—one that had at its root the awareness of a relationship with, and a debt to, not only Pound himself but the entire generation of Modernism that preceded them. There is at present no full-length critical or historical work that adequately covers this ground. My book is intended to fill the need for an updated and extended focus on Ezra Pound as an influence, while also addressing the question of canon and tradition in American poetry and delineating a postwar poetic of anticonventional orientation.

As will become clear in the following pages, a study of Pound's influence would not be complete without an attempt to contextualize his poetry and poetic influence both within its historical setting—the rise of Italian fascism, World War II and its aftermath—and within his own political and historical agenda. It is now well established that significant aspects of Pound's poetics—for example, his attempt to maintain an "absolute value" in the use of language and his promotion of a rigid and often authoritarian sense of cultural order—mirror fascist political beliefs.[8] But no critic has yet explored how the most

8. See, for example, Jerome McGann, "The *Cantos* of Ezra Pound"; Robert Casillo, *The Genealogy of Demons*; and Jean-Michel Rabaté, *Language, Sexuality, and Ideology in Ezra Pound's* Cantos.

radically experimental poetic writing in twentieth-century America could have derived from a poetics that reflects a fascist ideology. This book is, in part, an attempt to explain how such Modernist "guides to culture" as those provided by Pound have resulted in what Charles Bernstein has called "the present flourishing of a formally innovative, open, investigative poetry . . . unprecedented in its scale in American literature."[9]

What interests me in particular, given Pound's anti-Semitism and his embrace of Italian fascism, is that many of the most formally and politically radical postwar American poets have been drawn to his work. Why have writers as diverse as Charles Olson, Allen Ginsberg, Denise Levertov, and Gary Snyder, for example, claimed Pound as a predecessor of major importance? What have they found liberating in Pound's formal experimentation and in his use of political and historical referents? Although the direct influence of Pound's political and sociohistorical thought constitutes an important part of my discussion, the more interesting and complex issue concerns Pound's reception: how were the formal and political aspects of Pound's work combined in the operation of his influence on poets so clearly opposed to his political agenda?

The first two chapters provide, respectively, historical and theoretical overviews of the tradition. In chapter 1 I define the historical, canonical, and poetic contours of the postwar Pound tradition by exploring some of the issues that define a post-Poundian practice—most significantly, the question of tradition itself. The chapter provides a sense of the context in which Olson, Duncan, and other poets of the tradition wrote, and it examines Pound's influence and example in light of the alternatives then available to American writers. The chapter then examines briefly the range of Pound's influence as manifested in the work of Robert Creeley and Allen Ginsberg. Chapter 2 explores the way in which Pound's writings develop a model of influence and tradition that serves as an alternative to the Oedipal paradigm Harold Bloom has applied to a "Romantic Sublime" tradition. Because Bloom's model excludes from the poetic canon

9. Charles Bernstein, "Pound and the Poetry of Today," 638–39.

poets whose work does not display his particular brand of "revision," "misreading," or "poetic repression," Pound's paradigm can be seen as offering an alternative account that departs significantly from Bloom's own and that provides a different framework for understanding influence and poetic creativity. Chapter 3 enlarges the scope of the Pound tradition, analyzing the important contributions made by Walt Whitman, William Carlos Williams, and Louis Zukofsky.

Chapters 4 through 7 center on the two key figures in the Pound tradition: Charles Olson and Robert Duncan. Both find a central model in Pound's work, but they elaborate on Pound's practice in different ways. The first of the two chapters on Olson (chapter 4) sets forth his poetics of "historical method" and delineates ways in which his poetics embodies a sense of history and tradition differing from that of Pound. Chapter 5 examines a particular poem directly concerned with the question of Pound's influence—"I, Mencius, Pupil of the Master"—in light of recent critiques of Olson's relation to poetic tradition. Chapter 6 reads the work of Duncan in terms of two opposing poles: the Objectivist framework of a Poundian poetics and the Romantic impulses Duncan feels are repressed in Pound's work. Chapter 7 traces Duncan's developing sense of poetic form, a sense based in large part on Poundian examples of "collage" technique and the ideogrammatic method.

The final chapters move beyond the immediate scope of Pound's postwar influence to examine the way in which the tradition continued to develop among younger poets of the 1950s, 1960s, 1970s, and 1980s. In chapter 8 I examine the work of the contemporary poets Denise Levertov and Gary Snyder in terms of their Poundian inheritance and their sense of a shared poetics. Chapter 9 is concerned with the poetry of Edward Dorn and with the ways in which his work moves beyond the immediate influence of Pound and Williams while still participating in a poetics defined by them and by Olson. Finally, I conclude the book by addressing the current state of poetry within the Pound-Olson tradition in the work of Language poet Charles Bernstein.

●   ●   ●

An understanding of the Pound tradition, like that of any poetic tradition, depends on a broader theory of the nature of influence. I therefore pose in the course of this book several theoretical questions concerning the model of influence suggested by the work of Ezra Pound and his impact on later poets. Two of these questions are fundamental to this project. What is the nature of influence in general (and in what sense does the notion of influence describe the cycle of literary reception and production)?[10] What ideas did Pound express that might be formulated as a theory of influence and tradition? I also pose the more technical questions of how influence is to be identified, what importance it may have for an understanding or appreciation of an author's work, and how it relates to the formation of a literary tradition or canon. I respond to these questions by contrasting Pound's model of influence with other models that have contributed most significantly to my own discussion.

The most fundamental form of literary influence is that which transpires in the act of imitation. Influence as imitation assumes that literary "decorum" results from attempting to duplicate the formal, stylistic, and thematic achievements of one's predecessors. The model writer can be a living teacher who passes on techniques or ideas to a younger student or disciple or an admired author from a previous era. In *The Mirror and the Lamp* M. H. Abrams traces the idea of imitation in English literature, from Sir Philip Sydney's adaptation of Aristotle's *Poetics* to the work of eighteenth-century writers such as Alexander Pope and Samuel Johnson. Abrams finds wide acceptance for the classical notion of art—one based on a faith in the universality of customs, beliefs, and ideals and on a relatively stable aesthetic order.

---

10. In *Influence in Art and Literature* Goran Hermeren identifies three levels on which artistic and literary influence takes place; we can categorize these levels as the historical/sociological, the receptive, and the creative/imaginative. In other words, we must take into account a writer's historical and sociological relation to another writer, the reaction as reader to that other writer's text, and the creative or imaginative use to which that previous text is put in producing the new work.

In "Tradition and the Individual Talent," T. S. Eliot redefines the process of influence in somewhat more reactive terms. Eliot likens the process to a chemical reaction in which the mind of the poet acts as a catalyst on the various combined substances that he or she finds—that is, the body of works making up the literary tradition. For Eliot, a constant interchange exists between the poet and the past: a mutual dependence in which the poet uses tradition to help create a new work while in turn using that new work to alter the entire structure of the "existing order." Even though much of the poet's work must take place on a deliberate level, much also involves "a passive attending on the event." The poet uses tradition as an escape from his or her own "personality," from the temptation to express subjective emotions. What takes place in any successful work of art, according to Eliot, is not a personal or emotional "sublime," a search for novelty or originality divorced from a "sense of the past," but a process of "depersonalization" in which the writer surrenders to "something more valuable"—namely, the entire pantheon of the tradition within which he or she is working.[11]

Eliot's essay stresses the importance of the poet's choice of a tradition; the poet must remain "conscious of the main current, which does not at all flow invariably through the most distinguished reputations." The greatest poets are those who remain balanced in their use of the tradition, focusing neither on one or two "private admirations" nor on a particular historical period. The writer should neither become "traditional" in the sense of "following the ways of the immediate generation before . . . in a blind and timid succession," nor "conform" to the standards of the past. The poet's reputation will ultimately be "measured," however, by his or her ability to "fit in" to the canon of past literature; thus tradition remains for Eliot a relatively stable entity, a limited and canonical set of texts and practices. Pound himself was very aware of the limitations placed on the poet by

11. T. S. Eliot, "Tradition and the Individual Talent," in *Selected Essays*, 37–45.

Eliot's sense of tradition.[12] As John Guillory argues, noting Eliot's later substitution of the term "orthodoxy" for "tradition," Eliot's writings advocate a strictly defined reformation of the canon that was in large part responsible for the critical hegemony of the New Criticism.[13]

Claudio Guillen reorients the study of influence by replacing the notion of a relationship between an individual poet and a tradition with the idea of a broadly defined "experiential" or "aesthetic" process. In *Literature as System* Guillen argues that literary influence is only one of many artistic or intellectual experiences that affect the formation of a poet's mind and may have little or no bearing on the poem in terms of textual similarities or parallelisms. Guillen's argument opposes a rigidly deterministic understanding of influence—such as that implied by the agonistic poetic history of Harold Bloom—according to which a direct cause-and-effect relationship exists between one text and another, or material "flows" from one text to the next. The poem, according to Guillen, is the "displacement" of various literary and nonliterary influences, which themselves are consumed and forgotten in the process of artistic creation. The predecessors of the new poet are important mainly in supplying a poetic "vocabulary" with which the new poet can work. Guillen's theory posits two distinct levels of influence: "genetic function," or the generalized impact of one writer's work on the creative process of another, and "textual function," or the local parallelisms and echoes of one writer's work in another's. Guillen's model stresses neither an emulative relation to a predecessor nor an antagonistic one; instead, artistic creation is viewed as a necessary bridging of the "ontological gap" between "unformed" experience and newly formed experience in the finished work.

---

12. While Pound shares with Eliot the desire to replace the dominant poetic legacy of Milton and the Romantics with the work of formerly neglected lyric poets, Pound's sense of canon revision as a fundamentally idiosyncratic and iconoclastic practice places him in a different relation to tradition from that of Eliot. See my comparisons of Pound and Eliot in chapters 1 and 2.

13. Guillory, "The Ideology of Canon-Formation."

Northrop Frye's archetypal paradigm extends Guillen's sense of influence as a multilayered aesthetic process. Frye posits that literature is passed down through certain genres, figures, situations, and even linguistic or formal configurations rather than through contact between one artist and another. Frye's approach obviates the necessity for historical or biographical evidence. It entails studying, for example, not the influence of Homer on Pound and Pound on Olson but of the epic form on *The Cantos* and in turn on *The Maximus Poems* or of a particular mode of nature poetry on American poets from Whitman to Snyder. Frye claims for the work of art an autonomy from the "unconditioned will of the artist."[14] In the study of literary history, according to Frye, "there are much bigger critical problems involved than biographical ones." Thus, Frye's archetypal approach also questions the conventional notion that literature is a process developing in time. The "converging patterns of significance" he sees in great works of art make us wonder "if we cannot see literature, not as complicating itself in time, but as spread out in conceptual space from some unseen center."[15]

In the past twenty years, literary theorists have moved beyond the limited claims of Guillen and Frye for a depersonalized notion of literary influence in positing a concept of "intertextuality"—the language one text shares with many others. Indeed, the idea of intertextuality can be seen as posing a radical challenge to the concept of an individual influence from one poet's work to that of another. Julia Kristeva first adopted the concept from the work of Mikhail Bakhtin on the "dialogic" or "heteroglossic" structure of the European novel. Kristeva defines the "intertext" as a "crossing of words (texts) where we read at least one other word (text)": "Any text is constructed as a mosaic of

14. "The poet's task is to deliver the poem in as uninjured a state as possible, and if the poem is alive, it is equally anxious to be rid of him, and screams to be cut loose from his private memories and associations, his desire for self-expression, and all the other navel-strings and feeding tubes of his ego" (Frye, "The Archetypes of Literature," 19).

15. Ibid., 20–21.

quotations; any text is the absorption and transformation of another."[16]

According to Kristeva, modern poetic texts have a tendency to "absorb and destroy at the same time other texts in the inter-textual space," thus becoming in themselves a space for what she calls the discursive "cross-junction":

> The poetic practice which links Poe-Baudelaire-Mallarmé provides one of the most striking examples of this *alter-jonction*. Baudelaire translates Poe; Mallarmé writes that he will take up the poetic task as a legacy of Baudelaire, and his first writings follow the trace of Baudelaire. In the same way, Mallarmé translates Poe and follows his writing; Poe himself departed from De Quincey. . . . The network can be multiplied, but it would always express the same law: the poetic text is produced in the complex movement of a simultaneous affirmation and negation of another.[17]

Kristeva's theory of intertextuality, though it may give the initial impression that *all* texts overlap or intersect, is really not as radical a formulation as the subsequent adoption of her terminology by Roland Barthes and others may suggest. While she speaks of an overdetermining "law" of textual multiplication and reduplication, she also suggests that a writer such as Poe, Baudelaire, or Mallarmé makes at least a partially conscious choice to translate, "follow the trace of," or "depart from" the work of a previous author. In some respects, then, the process of textual absorption and rejection Kristeva identifies in her delineation of a Romantic-Symbolist tradition approximates the process of influence I describe within the Pound tradition.

Barthes, taking further Kristeva's notion of the literary text as a "mosaic of quotations," has advocated reading all texts outside the context of their "filiation" to sources and influences:

> Every text, being itself the intertext of another text, belongs to the intertextual, which must not be confused with a text's origins: to

16. Julia Kristeva, *Semiotiké: Recherches pour une sémanalyse,* 95. (My translation.)

17. Ibid., 196. (My translation.) There is no adequate way of translating the term *alter-jonction* from the French; it is clear, however, that it entails the coincidence of two or more texts in the formation of another.

search for the "sources of" and "influence upon" a work is to satisfy the myth of filiation. The quotations from which a text is constructed are anonymous, irrecoverable, and yet *already read:* they are quotations without quotation marks.[18]

To attempt finding the "author" of the text is for Barthes to deny that the author can reenter the universal intertext only "as a guest." Even though Barthes accurately assigns elements of a text to the cultural discourses from which they are drawn, he does not adequately explain through what agency the author chooses, orders, and juxtaposes these elements into a comprehensible and unique form. Would not the directives by which these elements are ordered be provided by a tradition or an influential predecessor?

Michel Foucault launches a similar attack on the notion of influence as it participates in the models of traditional historicism and in the concepts of tradition, development, evolution, "spirit of the age," oeuvre, and book. In *The Archaeology of Knowledge* he argues that these categories create a false sense of historical unity and continuity and should be replaced with certain "discursive formations." These would operate outside the bounds of historical time within a field of "rules of formation": "One may be compelled to dissociate certain oeuvres, ignore influences and traditions, abandon definitively the question of origin, allow the commanding presence of authors to fade into the background, and thus everything that was thought to be proper to the history of ideas may disappear from view."[19] Foucault maintains that "different oeuvres, dispersed books, that whole mass of texts that belong to a single discursive formation—and so many authors who know or do not know one another, criticize one another, invalidate one another, pillage one another—meet without knowing it and obstinately intersect their unique discourses in a web of which they are not the masters, of which they do not see the whole, and of whose

18. Barthes, "From Work to Text," 77.
19. Foucault, *The Archaeology of Knowledge,* 38.

breadth they have a very inadequate idea."[20] Thus, Foucault posits something like an intertextuality, although he defines the sharing of textual material more generally in terms of systems of discourse rather than as a more locally defined mosaic of quotations.

Barthes's universal (inter)text and Foucault's discursive formations are challenging alternatives to a personal and historical understanding of influence. They can be used to describe a large spectrum of the phenomena affecting literary production; in particular, they provide a rubric for examining questions of cultural discourse from a wider perspective than does a more narrowly defined study of an individual influence. The understanding of poetic influence reflected in this book is informed in part by the intertextual paradigm; Bakhtin's theories of novelistic discourse are especially useful in thinking about the techniques employed by many of these poets. Readings of *The Cantos* and of later poetry in a similar mode can also be profitably informed by Barthes's idea of "codes" or by Foucault's discursive formations.[21] Indeed, it would be next to impossible, having once considered the implications of such theories, to return to discussion of influence based solely on the identification of sources, echoes, or allusions or to maintain that a writer's social or historical context can completely account for the various manifestations of literary influence.

Nevertheless, although reading Pound and other poets in his tradition in terms of a theory of intertextuality can be fruitful, the theory's shortcomings merit attention, particularly in regard to literary history and reception. Although it is true that the syncretic mode of poetry adopted by Pound and his successors is one in which the poem is composed of, suggested by, or generated from the confluences of other discourses, these do not appear randomly in the poems discussed here. I do not propose

20. Ibid., 126–27.
21. See, in particular, my discussions of Edward Dorn in chapter 9 and of Charles Bernstein in the Conclusion. Rabaté, *Language, Sexuality, and Ideology,* briefly suggests the relevance of Barthes's "codes" to *The Cantos.*

as a model for the Pound tradition a poetics of aleatory process; rather, I advance one in which the poetic and nonpoetic discourses that enter the text are for the most part selected and coordinated according to well-defined aesthetic, philosophical, or ideological criteria. If I am not fully satisfied with the intertextual model, it is because I believe that some degree of historical and biographical specificity is necessary to provide a literary understanding that is incommensurate with the more totalizing and less locally applicable construct of the poem as intertext. My aim is to address not only a work's textuality and its relation to other texts and discourses but also the more local and particular dynamic of its historical production and reception. By examining the role of the poet-as-reader in the transmission of literary texts—first as passive addressee, then as active critic, and finally as creative producer of new texts—we can better understand the extent to which the historical, social, and interpersonal details of a work's reception determine its influence on other writers.[22]

The component of reception in literary influence necessitates a reemphasis on the historical dimension of the literary process. It is extremely likely, for example, that a writer will become a greater influence at times when political, social, historical, geographical, or educational conditions favor a positive reception of his or her work. Factors exterior to the text itself may in many cases play the greater role in determining what author or work will be influential at a given time. A poem is not simply what exists textually (part of an intertext); it is also a product of other elements that poets themselves do not and cannot ignore: history and tradition, authors and books. For this reason, much of our interest in literary production remains within the realms of literary history, archival research, and bibliographical scholarship.

22. See, for example, Hans Robert Jauss, *Towards an Aesthetic of Reception*. Jauss writes, "The historical life of a literary work is unthinkable without the active participation of its addressees. For it is only through the process of its mediation that the work enters into the changing horizon-of-experience of a continuity in which the perceptual inversion occurs from simple reception to active reception, from unrecognized aesthetic norms to a new production that surpasses them" (19).

Jerome McGann describes some of the dynamics involved in a historical reading of literary works.[23] Tracing the decreasing popularity and prestige of historical, textual, and bibliographical criticism throughout this century, particularly during the past thirty years, McGann argues convincingly for a reintegration into literary criticism at large of historical methods now increasingly relegated to the work of "textual scholars." McGann observes that a text's historical reception and the critical task involved in interpreting that work are inextricably linked. Critical work on a text, even that which seeks to isolate it from any social or historical context, necessarily becomes part of the text's history. In many cases, a conflictual relationship exists between the social and historical experience of an author and that of subsequent contexts in which his or her work is published and read. Because poetry is in large part a "social act"—an experience that cannot be conceived "outside of history and specific social environments"—it also entails a relationship on the part of the poet to "all human history (past and future)." The publication of authors' statements about their own work is also, like the publication of poems or works of fiction, a "social event in [its] own right," always contributing to and modifying the receptive history of those works.[24]

Among the models of influence just discussed, the one that most clearly provides for both the social and the aesthetic dimension of literary production is Guillen's: the displacement of various types of experience in the process of artistic creation. In the tradition beginning with Pound, each of the central poets adopts his or her metaphor or metaphors to describe that process: Pound's notion of vortex, *paideuma,* or ideogrammatic method; Olson's sense of the poetic process as an "autoclytic multiplication" or series of creative accidents; Duncan's idea of the poem as cell or collage; Snyder's theory of "interconnectedness," "riprapping," or "knot of turbulence"; and what I call

23. See, in particular, McGann, *The Beauty of Inflections.*
24. Ibid., 21–22.

Dorn's "migratory" poetics. All these metaphorical constructs are related conceptions of the poetic process and the role of influence in it: this process is constituted not in reference to a narrowly defined literary tradition or canon but in the various textual and extratextual sources that are brought together and assimilated within the fabric of the poem itself.

1 THE POUND TRADITION

But the things Pound turns you on to are *groovy*. . . .
he has like a big influence on me.
> Allen Ginsberg, in Jane Kramer, *Allen
> Ginsberg in America*

The wonder to me is, that, say, I can take yr premises,
can learn so precisely from you, and just because I do,
just because of it, I am able to make a verse which
remains distinctly my own.
> Robert Creeley, *Charles Olson and Robert
> Creeley*

At a moment of acute personal and spiritual crisis in his *Pisan Cantos,* Pound evokes as his sole means of salvation a "live tradition" to be gathered "from the air":

> What thou lovest well remains,
> > the rest is dross
> What thou lov'st well shall not be reft from thee
> What thou lov'st well is thy true heritage
> . . . .
> But to have done instead of not doing
> > this is not vanity
> To have, with decency, knocked
> That a Blunt should open
> > To have gathered from the air a live tradition
> or from a fine old eye the unconquered flame
> This is not vanity.
> > > (C, 521–522)

Christine Froula points out that Pound's identification of the "minor" English poet Wilfred Blunt as the vessel of artistic tradition allows him to "[bypass] the great Romantics to affirm a minor lyric tradition."[1] Although this assessment is generally accurate, Pound's "live" tradition is not a mere anthology of minor lyric poetry. What Pound proposes as a usable tradition of poetry is really a vortex of diverse poetic and artistic practices

1. Froula, *A Guide to Ezra Pound's* Selected Poems, 236–37.

that can be rediscovered and resynthesized in new directions by new writers and that are constantly leading toward a new sense of "culture"—"a live paideuma and not a dead one" (*SP, 393*). In his essay "Prefatio aut Cimicium Tumulus," first published as the preface to his 1933 *Active Anthology,* Pound chastises T. S. Eliot for supporting the notion of an already existing culture that "does nothing to prepare a better culture that must or ought to come into being" (*SP, 393*). Eliot, Pound claims, relies on culturally formed "taste" rather than actively seeking a greater diversity of poetic modes or traditions, and he does nothing to encourage an "appetite for the unknown best, or for the best still unread by the neophyte." Eliot's gesture in "revising" the poetic canon consists of little more than using Dryden as a "good club wherewith to smack Milton" (*SP, 390*).

For Pound, it is a question not so much of replacement as of augmentation. Tradition must be more than a sense of poetic inheritance provided by the available stock of writers within a given culture; it must indicate a web of shared poetic practice woven through the writings of poets from all ages and cultures, a nonlinear pattern of poetic writing. Pound comments, "After all, Homer, Propertius, Villon, speak of the world as I know it, whereas Mr. Tennyson and Dr. Bridges do not. Even Dante and Guido with their so highly specialised culture speak part of a life as I know it" (*SP, 390*).

It was Pound's more idiosyncratic, iconoclastic, and interactive sense of tradition, rather than Eliot's notion of tradition as orthodoxy, that appealed to postwar American poets such as Charles Olson and Robert Duncan. They and other poets of the 1950s and 1960s saw in Pound's poetry and concerns an alternative model of literary Modernism to what they considered the more rigid and hierarchical set of values and expectations represented by Eliot and the New Criticism. Olson and many of the other poets who followed Pound in the postwar era saw the schools of T. S. Eliot and W. H. Auden as inhibited by the restrictive value judgments made by critics within the academy. They felt alienated from what they considered formalized and tightly controlled verse, which relied on subtle effects for its impact rather than proposing any radically new conception of poetry itself. Poets of the Pound tradition felt themselves to be part of a movement representing a "new poetry," one generated by an altered conception of the poet's relation to phenomenological and artistic experience.

Robert Creeley, Allen Ginsberg, and Robert Duncan helped to delineate this sense of a new tradition in the decade following World War II. Creeley defined his tradition in opposition to the dominant poetry of the time: that of Allen Tate, John Crowe Ransom, Elizabeth Bishop, Robert Lowell, and Randall Jarrell. His countertradition—that of Pound, Williams, H. D., Zukofsky, George Oppen, and Charles Reznikoff—attracted to it younger poets who were "dissatisfied with the Ransom and Tate school" (*CON,* 14). Ginsberg, incensed by what he saw as the neglect by academic critics of Pound, Zukofsky, and "the other rough writers of the Whitmanic, open tradition in America," located himself within a tradition of "Whitmanic adhesiveness" that he felt connected his generation with that of its Modernist predecessors (*CT,* 93). Duncan identified the same postwar movement more specifically as one "deriving its music from the ground Ezra Pound had given us in his theory and practice forty years earlier [and] . . . from the composition by phrase which Pound had advanced to the high art of The *Pisan Cantos*."[2]

The year Duncan identified as the beginning of a new poetic sensibility, 1950, was marked by the publication of Olson's "Projective Verse," the "postmodern" manifesto largely responsible for defining the context of postwar Poundian poetics. In his essay, Olson invoked Pound and Imagism—"the revolution of the ear . . . the trochee's heave" (*SW,* 15)—of forty years earlier. Olson's essay not only represented a significant watershed for a radical postwar poetic consciousness; it also signaled the return to prominence among younger American poets of the long expatriated, American Modernist Pound. The events of the preceding four years—Pound's arrest and incarceration by the U.S. Army in Italy, his much publicized arraignment and trial, the

---

2. Duncan, "The Lasting Contribution of Ezra Pound," 23.

publication of his *Pisan Cantos*, and the controversial Bollingen Award of 1949 — all resulted in Pound's name being far better known in American literary circles than it had been throughout the 1930s and early 1940s. Now every writer who knew Pound — along with many who did not — was forced to come to terms with often ambivalent feelings about Pound the man as well as Pound the poet. Opinions were sharply divided.[3] Pound himself remained as active as one in his position reasonably could have. He continued to produce new Cantos and other writings, to meet with aspiring poets, critics, and followers of various kinds, and to disseminate his ideas by whatever channels he could find. It was the time of a remarkable resurgence of interest in Pound's work and in that of his contemporary Williams and his American predecessor Whitman.

It was largely within the context of these developments that the early 1950s saw the birth and development of a "new American poetry," a poetry of "open-form" composition that was in direct opposition to the more formal verse of the "establishment" poets writing in the New Critical tradition.[4] Epithets such as "establishment poetry" and "academic verse" must be judged as only partially accurate; not all poetry written by academics in these years conformed to this mode, nor did all poets outside the academic establishment write according to the

3. Many, if not most, of the articles written on Pound in the late 1940s and early 1950s deal primarily with his political status rather than with his poetry per se. For examples of this kind of criticism, see O'Conner and Stone, *A Casebook on Ezra Pound*. C. David Heymann, *Ezra Pound: The Last Rower,* is a more recent biography emphasizing Pound's political situation.

4. For further discussion of the new academic poetry and its relationship to the Pound tradition, see Burton Hatlen, "Carroll Terrell and the Great American Poetry Wars." Hatlen locates the emergence of American academic poetry in the 1930s, chiefly among the disciples of John Crowe Ransom, admirers of Eliot, Stevens, and Robert Frost, who "achieved a virtual hegemony over the way poetry was taught in American universities from 1940 well into the 1960's." Hatlen sees the work of this school of poets as in direct opposition to "experimental" Modernists like Pound and Williams and as a retreat into a conventional and formal verse in which "the impulse to press against the limits of language and the conventions of poetic discourse gives way to a ritualized reenactment of traditional poetic gestures." For a less partisan discussion of the general climate of American poetry in the 1940s and 1950s, and especially of the dominant role played by New Critical methods and assumptions, see James Breslin, *From Modern to Contemporary,* 10–52.

precepts of Pound and Williams. Nevertheless, the work to which Olson, Duncan, and others objected was a verse primarily written, promoted, and defended by professors of a relatively closed and well-defined academic / literary world. As such, it was a poetry doubly unattractive to writers who either by their own choice or through the neglect of academic critics were working outside mainstream academic circles—poets such as Pound, Williams, Zukofsky, Olson, the Beats, and many poets of the New York and San Francisco schools.

The late 1950s marked the second phase of the same movement. Ginsberg's *Howl* (1956) introduced postwar open-form poetry to the larger reading public, as did Donald Allen's anthology, *The New American Poetry* (1960), which helped define a context for the forty-three poets represented in it. Various journals and small presses, many of them run by the poets themselves, took on the role of publishing this experimental poetry.[5] The poets included in the Allen anthology saw in the work of establishment poets a reactionary desire to return verse to inherited forms. Duncan, for example, wrote that poets who "once had dreams and epiphanies, now admit only to devices and ornament" and that "taste, reason, rationality" were the ruling forces of the day, blocking out "the darkness of possibilities that controls cannot manage."[6] In his discussion of the "conventional" critic Elizabeth Drew, Duncan deplored the narrow-mindedness of those he felt were oppressing the "open" practices of Pound and Williams, finding in these critics "an imposing company of arbiters and camp followers . . . commandos of quatrains right! and myrmidons of the metaphysical stanza" (*FC*, 94). Ginsberg was even more outspoken in his

5. In addition to Cid Corman's *Origin,* which first appeared in the spring of 1951, the most significant journals included Creeley's *Black Mountain Review,* Leroi Jones's *Yugen,* Gilbert Sorrentino's *Neon,* John Wieners's *Measure,* Ron Padgett's *The White Dove Review,* and Clayton Eshleman's *Caterpillar.* The most notable presses were City Lights Books in San Francisco, New Directions in New York, and Jonathan Williams's Jargon. James Laughlin's contributions as publisher/editor of New Directions deserve special mention. Both in his New Directions Annuals and in the publication of books by individual poets, Laughlin has been tireless in his efforts to promote and solidify the Pound tradition.

6. Quoted in Sherman Paul, "Clinging to the Advance," 9.

criticism of mainstream academic critics who he felt would stifle any originality in poetic expression and who displayed either "total amnesia" regarding experimental poetry or "complete incompetence" in understanding or evaluating forms of writings not sanctioned by the academy: "All the universities [have been] fucking a dead horse for decades and this is culture?! Yet prosody and conceptions of poetry have been changing for half a century already and . . . yet I have to listen to people giving me doublethink gobbledygook about why I don't write poems with form, construction, something charming and carefully made."[7]

Pound's standards, by contrast, were seen as a call for greater artistic freedom on several levels. Following Pound's example, along with that of Williams, poets could include subject matter and diction hitherto deemed unacceptable to poetry, they could derive new poetic forms from a sense of everyday speech, and they could emphasize in their work the previously neglected factor of the visual and aural qualities generated by the physical placement of the poem on the page. Pound's poetry was unpredictable and idiosyncratic rather than conventional. It was "momently recognized" (moving instantly, as Olson would have it, "from one perception to another") instead of determined by the impositions of conventional form, thought, and diction.

Pound's work foregrounded for younger poets the importance of understanding language and form beyond the traditional concerns of poetry (diction, tone, and rhyme) so as to encompass the structural, etymological, and sonic properties of language, as well as the implicit social and political structures language contains. Pound's application of ideogrammatic structure to Western poetry was of central significance, as were his introduction of the idea of the "tone leading of vowels," his use of accentual meters and musical structures as a means of "breaking the pentameter," and his direct quotation of heterogeneous registers of language in the poem. Equally important to later poets was Pound's idea of an "absolute value" in language—that is, an

7. Ginsberg to John Hollander, quoted in Kramer, *Allen Ginsberg in America,* 136–37.

"energy" or a "charge of meaning" within language that links it directly to an experience of the world and gives it a status independent of its existence within an arbitrary linguistic code.[8] Following Pound's logic, poets explored the idea of the "perfectibility" of language: the notion that an intensified and attentive "sincerity" in the use of words can function as a critique of the misuse of language in a society, a misuse directly related to the other problems that society may face.

During the 1940s, when poets of Duncan's and Creeley's generation reached their maturity, Pound and Williams appeared to many to be the only viable poetic models. Other choices of poetic forebears included a return to the Georgians (the worst kind of conservative and sentimental verse), the clever and highly formal poetry of the "Ransom-Tate nexus" (compared by Creeley to "antiques" made by "awfully-old-Southern-gentlemen"), and the loosely affiliated Modernism represented by Eliot, Moore, and Stevens, poets who seemed neither completely committed to the formal tradition nor part of the open tradition of Pound and Williams.[9] The poetry written in these various modes was seen by those who accepted the teachings of "Projective Verse" as not only stylistically retrograde but as incapable of encompassing a sense of contemporary social and political reality. Duncan, for example, contrasted the poetry written by Eliot and Stevens with that of Pound:

> The voices of Eliot and Stevens do not present us with . . . disturbances of mode. They preserve throughout a melodious poetic respectability, eminently sane in their restriction of poetic meaning to the bounds of the literary, of symbol and metaphor, but at the cost

8. Related to this conception of poetry as "language charged with meaning to the utmost degree" are Olson's notion of poetry as an "energy-transfer"; Gary Snyder's idea of a "knot of turbulence—or vortex of language"; and Allen Ginsberg's sense of an "exact language of description" in Pound's poetry.

9. See Creeley's interview with Charles Tomlinson in *CON*. Olson also argues that Eliot's work is not "projective" in the way Pound's *Cantos* are: "We are only at its beginnings, and if I think that the *Cantos* make more 'dramatic' sense than do the plays of Mr. Eliot, it is not because I think they have solved the problem but because the methodology of the verse in them points a way by which, one day, the problem of larger forms is solved. Eliot is, in fact, a proof of the present danger, of 'too easy a going on the practice of verse as it has been, rather than as it must be, practiced' " (*SW*, 26).

of avoiding facts and ideas that might disturb. Both the individual and the communal awareness are constricted to fit or adapted to the convenience of accepted culture.[10]

Pound's poetry differed from that of other contemporary models not only in the way it disturbed culturally accepted modes of expression but also in what it demanded of the reader—what Creeley called "an active involvement with what was happening in the given poem." Unlike poets such as Auden and Stevens, whose works were read in the academy of the 1940s either in terms of their irony and the rigor of their verse patterns (Auden) or in conjunction with vague discussions of aesthetic value (Stevens), Pound insisted "on precisely how the line goes, how the word is, in its context, what has been done, in the practice of verse—and what now seems possible to do" (*CE*, 27). It was not always easy, according to Creeley, to find acceptance for alternative models like Pound within the academic curriculum of the 1940s and 1950s:

> The colleges and universities were dominant in their insistence upon an *idea* of form extrinsic to the given instance. Poems were equivalent to cars insofar as many could occur of a similar pattern—although each was, of course, "singular." But it was this assumption of a mold, of a means that could be gained beyond the literal fact of the writing *here and now*, that had authority. It is the more ironic to think of it, remembering the incredible pressure of *feeling* in these years—of all that did want "to be said," of so much confusion and pain wanting statement in its own terms. But again, it is Karl Shapiro's *Essay on Rime* which is successful and Auden is the measure of competence. In contrast Ezra Pound, H.D., William Carlos Williams (despite the token interest as *Paterson* begins to be published), Hart Crane, and especially Walt Whitman are largely disregarded.   (*QG*, 42)

In many respects, Pound was an ideal model for Olson and other poets of his camp. Pound was the neglected poet, the renegade, "reformer," great experimenter, mentor, adviser, as well as the politically and intellectually disreputable "traitor."

---

10. Duncan, "The H. D. Book," II, 5, 341–42.

As a figure encapsulating all those qualities, Pound was attractive to a group of poets who sought an antiestablishment stance as well as a new means of poetic expression.[11] Pound was the great polemicizer who sought to "shake up the context" (Creeley) and "clear the ground" (Olson). He provided later poets not only with new "ground to walk on" (Ginsberg) but with convenient tags on which to hang their own stances. Pound's assertion that "poets are the antennae of the race," for example, was frequently summoned as an argument for a poetry relevant to the world of political, social, and economic realities. Poets with entirely different politics from Pound's own were often attracted to him; in many cases it seemed to matter less to these poets what Pound's politics actually were than that his work addressed political issues at all:

> To the young of that period he was often simply a traitor, an anti-Semite, an obscurantist, a money crank—and such courses in universities and colleges as dealt with modern poetry frequently avoided all mention of the *Cantos.* . . . The work we were otherwise given was, on the one hand, Auden—wherein a socially based use of irony became the uselessly exact rigor of repetitive verse patterns—or perhaps Stevens, whose mind one respected, in the questions it realized, but again whose use of poetry had fallen to the questionable fact of a device.   (*CE,* 25)

Ironically, it was the "historical method" of *The Cantos* as well as Pound's questionable political status that brought him to the attention of younger poets such as Olson, Creeley, and

---

11. Samuel Charters, writing of the "conscious, articulate underground in American poetry" (Olson, Duncan, Snyder, Ginsberg, Creeley, and others), describes the way in which the sense of political and artistic alienation these poets feel toward the American establishment makes Pound a congenial model: "Pound . . . had a strong political motivation and a definite artistic attitude [which] has been important in the background of the new American poetry. Pound's disappointment in western society finally led him to a confused acceptance of the government of Italy's Mussolini, which was certainly fascist, but—among poets—there has been little criticism. In a way his motivation was acceptable—stemming from a genuine idealism" (*Some Poems/Poets,* 14). Despite his renegade status, Pound did receive some attention from "mainstream" poetry journals of the 1940s and 1950s such as *Poetry, Hudson Review,* and *Partisan Review.*

Ginsberg just as he reached the nadir of popularity within the academic world. It was not until the late 1950s and early 1960s—with the further maturation and institutionalization of the "new" poets—that Pound became an acceptable model for young writers.

The 1960s were marked by important and well-attended conferences in Vancouver (1963) and Berkeley (1965) celebrating poetry by followers of Pound, Williams, and Black Mountain. The 1960s also marked the rediscovery by many younger poets of Objectivist writers from the previous generation: especially Louis Zukofsky, George Oppen, and the English poet Basil Bunting. Bunting's poem *Briggflatts* was published in 1966, and Zukofsky's *All: The Collected Short Poems* finally reached print in the mid-1960s, along with the first twelve books of the long poem *"A"*. A second and then a third generation of poets in the Pound/Black Mountain tradition also appeared, as Ginsberg, Creeley, Levertov, Snyder, and Dorn reached their maturity and as younger writers such as Clayton Eshleman, Robert Kelly, Jerome Rothenberg, and Diane Wakoski sought out the more established poets of the tradition as teachers and mentors.

Nevertheless, by the end of the decade what had seemed urgently radical in Pound's work ten or fifteen years earlier no longer seemed so: the force of the Pound tradition had dissipated, and its practitioners had been scattered. Olson, now the "old man" to a number of younger poets, died in 1970, and Pound himself passed away quietly two years later, far removed from the world of American poetry that his work had helped to create.

Pound, however, still provides the impetus for many of the experiments in contemporary poetry, not only in the United States but throughout the world. The manifestos of "concrete" poetry, for example, a movement that began in Latin America in the 1950s, credit Pound with important contributions: the concept of the ideogram as "spatial or visual syntax ... [and] composition based on direct—analogical, not logical-discursive—juxtaposition of elements" and the idea of a musical (contrapuntal or fugal) form of the poem.[12] More generally, the techniques of repetition, syntactic and semantic play, minimalist composition, juxtaposition of diction, and the increased mixing of poetry with other media are all outgrowths of Pound's work and ideas. American writers as diverse in their approaches to the poetic medium as Richard Kostelanetz, David Antin, Clark Coolidge, Jackson MacLow, John Cage, Barrett Watten, Susan Howe, Ron Silliman, and Charles Bernstein have all attempted to provide an enlarged critical vocabulary for dealing not only with the open poetic practices of Black Mountain and related movements but also with the projects currently taking place in such diverse areas as concrete poetry, oral and recorded poetry (sound poetry), various kinds of collage techniques, and Language poetry.

The various manifestations of post-Poundian poetry, from Olson in the early 1950s to Bernstein in the 1980s, all in some measure fall under the rubric of postmodernism, though as James Breslin and others have indicated, the idea of the postmodern in American poetry is highly problematic. In the most fundamental sense, all these writers are by definition postmodernist in coming after Modernists like Pound and Williams and in one way or another following, reacting to, or departing from these Modernist predecessors. In addition, they are part of a broader movement of experimental postmodernism in all the arts that took place in the 1950s and early 1960s.[13] In a still more specific context, they are postmodern in the sense suggested by critics such as David Antin and Charles Altieri, both of whom describe a postmodernism corresponding to the "field poetics" of Charles Olson and the Black Mountain school. Altieri, for example, defines postmodern poetry as that which is formally radical, constituted by "essentially phenomenological forms of imaginative activity," and resistant to "tastes fostered

12. Augusto de Campos et al., "Pilot Plan for Concrete Poetry," in Richard Kostelanetz, ed., *The Avant-Garde Tradition in Literature*, 257.

13. See Hal Foster's discussion of this "postmodernist break" in his introduction to *The Anti-Aesthetic*, ix ff.

by academic, pedagogical versions of the New Criticism."[14]
(I return to a more detailed discussion of the postmodern in
chapter 4.)

Olson, the first American poet to theorize the postmodern and
to use the term consistently, approached the change to a post-
modern consciousness as nothing less than revolutionary: it was
not to be seen merely as a technical or formal shift but as an
epistemological reorientation that would be all-encompassing in
its scope and far-reaching in its consequences. In time, poets such

14. Altieri, *Enlarging the Temple*, 22–23. In recent years postmodernism has
been largely aligned with Continental philosophy and literary theory or at least
conceived within the intellectual climate generated by the poststructuralist ideas
of Jacques Derrida, Roland Barthes, Michel Foucault, Jean-François Lyotard,
and other theorists. The degree to which this critical or theoretical postmodern-
ism has displaced practicing artists' versions of the same phenomenon should,
however, not obviate our use of a term that remains descriptively valid for
various movements in the arts, including poetry. As Rosalind Krauss remarks in
regard to "postmodern" sculpture, given that the term exists, "there seems no
reason not to use it" ("Sculpture in the Expanded Field," 39).

A glance at the list of names in Ihab Hassan's adumbration of postmodern-
ism(s) will suffice to demonstrate the range of assumptions and practices that
have been labeled "postmodern." As Hassan accurately remarks, "Indubitably,
these names are far too heterogeneous to form a movement, paradigm, or school.
Still, they may evoke a number of related cultural tendencies, a constellation of
values, a repertoire of procedures and attitudes. These we call postmodernism"
(*The Postmodern Turn*, 85). Hassan's desire to emphasize the "pluralism" of
postmodernism rather than apply any "rigorous definition" (167) of its param-
eters is a healthy one. Indeed, many of the schematic oppositions he himself
proposes between Modernism and postmodernism can describe differences be-
tween Pound and later poets—form/antiform, purpose/play, design/chance, hi-
erarchy/anarchy, logos/silence, centering/dispersal, selection/combination, phal-
lic/androgynous. Yet other categories he associates with postmodernism can
equally well apply to Pound: the work as process rather than as finished product,
techniques of parataxis and antithesis rather than of hypotaxis and synthesis, a
poetry of immanence rather than transcendence, and a basic orientation toward
metonymy rather than metaphor.

It is clear that to polarize Modernism and postmodernism in any absolute
sense is to oversimplify what is a highly complicated pattern of influence,
cross-fertilization, self-definition, and differentiation. Perhaps a more useful
hermeneutic tool is Hal Foster's division of postmodernism itself into two basic
manifestations: a "reactive" postmodernism that uses a repudiation of Modern-
ism to celebrate more traditional forms and practices and a "resistant" post-
modernism that "arises as a counter-practice not only to the official culture of
modernism but also to the 'false normativity' of a reactionary postmodernism"
(*The Anti-Aesthetic*, xi–xii). It is the latter postmodernism, one posed as a
resistance to the Modernist orthodoxy but not as a reaction to Modernism's
fundamentally experimental stance, that characterizes the work of the poets
treated in this book.

as Creeley, Ginsberg, Duncan, Snyder, and Dorn would come to share at least parts of Olson's postmodern vision. All these poets would enter into a complex dialogue (or polylogue) with Modernism, with Pound, and with the notions of textuality, influence, and tradition he had proposed.

I conclude this general overview of the Pound tradition by looking briefly at two writers who represent very different strains of postmodern American poetry and whose practices I do not have the opportunity to examine in separate chapters: Robert Creeley and Allen Ginsberg. Neither of these poets writes in a way that immediately identifies him as an heir to Pound, and both have been conventionally aligned with other predecessors: Creeley with Williams and Zukofsky and Ginsberg with Whitman. Yet both were profoundly influenced by Pound's writing and example, and both have been central figures in the development of the Pound tradition. Their participation in the tradition emphasizes two aspects of Pound's influence that I develop throughout this book. First, what these poets share with Pound and with each other is manifested less in terms of stylistic and formal resemblances, thematic echoes, or repetition of tropes than in the sense of a continuity of techniques, attitudes, and stances toward poetic practice and tradition. Second, the diversity represented by their different understandings of Pound and their equally different uses of his work is itself a salient characteristic of this tradition.

Creeley's importance in the Pound tradition rests largely on his place as an editor, a correspondent, and an advocate for Pound, Williams, Zukofsky, and the new poetry of the 1950s and 1960s. By the time Creeley began his correspondence with Olson in the spring of 1950, he had already decided that Pound and Williams together represented the central movement in American Modernist writing: "I do have the feeling, those two are almost: a common ground. . . . Not then, Joyce & Pound, Lewis, Eliot, et al. is/ always has been: Williams & Pound" (*CORC*, vol. 4, 72). In that same year Creeley wrote to Pound asking him for advice about a journal of contemporary poetry he

wished to start up. Pound advised Creeley to stick to a practical
format: to use as a base the work of the editor himself and
"about four others whose work could be depended on" and to
supplement that base with a "variant," the content of which
should be "as hogwild as possible" (*CE,* 506). Creeley's maga-
zine never got off the ground, despite his attempts to enlist the
support of both Pound and Williams, and he had to wait until
the first volume of *Black Mountain Review* in 1953 to put
Pound's ideas into practice. Creeley's magazine, which ran for
several issues, did establish itself on the "base" of a few central
Black Mountain poets, and it joined Cid Corman's *Origin* in
printing some of the more experimental poetry being written in
America at the time.[15]

As a Harvard undergraduate in the mid-1940s, Creeley had
discovered that an academic education would not in itself teach
him what he needed to know as a poet. His course on contem-
porary poetry at Harvard was taught by F. O. Matthiessen, a
professor who was unusually open to flexibility in the canon. But
when Creeley asked him why Pound's *Cantos* were not being
taught, Matthiessen replied "that he understood Pound's work
too poorly, that he felt Pound's political attitudes most suspect,
and that he could not finally see the value of the work in a course
such as ours was" (*QG,* 95).[16] Creeley himself found the form of
The Cantos "intimidating" at first, though he had already prof-
ited from Pound's critical writings and the shorter poems of
Personae. Learning to read *The Cantos* was unquestionably
difficult for a young and relatively unguided poet in the years
following World War II, but the "work" Creeley put into trying
to read Pound's poem expanded his own horizons. Creeley
identified in Pound's work technical "possibilities" of great im-

15. In a letter to Pound dated January 3, 1954, Creeley distinguishes the
format of his own journal from that of Corman's *Origin,* which he considers
"too loose." *Black Mountain Review,* he maintains, will follow Pound's sugges-
tion more closely in providing the constant of Olson and Paul Blackburn,
supplemented by the work of Irving Layton, Rainer Marie Gerhardt, Katue
Kitasano, and others. (Creeley's unpublished letter is in the Pound collection of
the Beinecke Rare Book and Manuscript Library, Yale University).

16. Creeley related the same story to me in conversation, emphasizing his
overall respect for Matthiessen as a teacher and critic.

portance to him and other young poets. Pound had made it possible for them to "find the character of our own intelligence" by means of a "preoccupation with how the poem is to be put on the page" (*CON*, 5).

It was in large part Creeley's discovery of Pound's Imagist and Objectivist precepts that led him to adopt what Charles Altieri calls an "immanentist poetics," one "stressing the ways in which an imagination attentive to common or casual experience can transform the mind." It was a poetic mode opposed to the Symbolist model predominant at the time, which emphasized an "abstract meditation on poetic structure and on the mind's dialectical pursuit of ideal unity."[17] Creeley was himself mindful of Pound's relation to Symbolism. As Creeley noted in an interview with Charles Tomlinson, Pound "has always been intent to make a very clear demarcation between a symbol which in effect exhausts its references as opposed to a sign or mark of something which constantly renews its reference" (*CON*, 15).

Creeley joined Olson as one of Pound's public advocates when in a 1952 letter to the editor of the journal *Goad* he defended his predecessor against what he considered unfair attacks in an article printed there. In the letter, Creeley listed Pound's most important contributions to modern and contemporary poetry:

> 1) 50 years of work. . . . Criticism. Translation. Hauling over into the English of at least 3 major areas of thought. 2) A principle of verse (kinetic) which has made, literally, the basic condition which now makes it possible for us to go on with it. . . . 3) A body of work . . . based, surely, on a man's actuality, on his own actuality, and isn't that what, precisely, poetry is supposed to be? (*QG*, 92–94)

In a 1969 essay called simply "Why Pound!?!" Creeley elaborated on the significance of Pound's poetry and ideas to the postmodern generation. Most important was what he called Pound's "insistent stance of an active . . . intelligence" (*CE*, 28). Pound's criticism in books such as *Make It New*, *ABC of Reading*, *Guide to Kulchur*, and *Polite Essays* taught Creeley that it

17. Altieri, *Enlarging the Temple*, 16–17.

was not a knowledge of the canon or of literary history that would make him a poet; rather, he would become a poet by virtue of a poetic intelligence and awareness made possible by repeated practice and experimentation and by a greater attentiveness to language, music, and rhythm. What Pound taught was a practical method of "how to write":

> Rather than tell me *about* some character of verse, he would give the literal instance side by side with that which gave it context. . . . This emphasis I feel to be present in all his work, from the rationale of imagism, to the latest *Cantos*. . . . Pound took the possibility of writing to involve more than descriptive aesthetics. . . . He moved upon the active principle of the intelligence, the concept of *virtu* . . . the experience of an energy, of ear and mind, which makes of language man's primary act.   (CE, 26–27)

From *The Cantos* Creeley also learned that locally defined formal considerations were not in themselves adequate directives in making a poem: the inclusive structure of *The Cantos* taught him that "the variousness of life is as much its quality as its quantity" (QG, 96). Creeley agreed with Pound that the "content" of a poem (its direct reference to events or objects in the world) should not be subjugated to formal or symbolic concerns. But if poetic form for Creeley was "never more than an extension of content," he would not go as far as Pound, or even Olson, in allowing content itself to sustain the poem. Creeley believed that the necessary balance between form and content in the poem could be achieved and apprehended only through the language used: "I mean then *words*—as opposed to content. I care what the poem says, only as a poem—I am no longer interested in the exterior attitude to which a poem may well point, a signboard. That concern I have found is best settled elsewhere" (QG, 32).

Although Creeley found fault with Pound for relying too heavily on the content or material in *The Cantos* rather than on formal concerns more intrinsic to the poetic process, he recognized the important example of Pound's use of various materials as an essential "building place" where the "particulars" of a poem's "reality" can be stored (CORC, vol. 4, 31). Creeley wrote to Olson of his admiration for Pound's ability to "go by feel," "by ear," or "by language" in the poem, instead of writing "mechanically." Rather than write sentimental poems that "plot the heart . . . like one would nail a butterfly to a board," Pound used words to convey "the sensing" of an object or experience; he shaped "the word round the thing" (*CORC*, vol. 1, 103). Pound also provided a sincerity in his poetry that acted as an important counterbalance to the predominantly ironic mode of poetry at the time and that was reflected in Pound's constant vigilance against the misuses or perversions of language:

> Pound, early in the century, teaches the tradition of "man-standing-by-his-word," the problem of *sincerity*, which is never as simple as it may be made to seem. The poet, of all men, has best cause and least excuse to pervert his language, since what he markets is so little in demand. . . . I think the poem's morality is contained as a term of its structure, and is there to be determined and nowhere else. (Pound: "Prosody is the total articulation of the sound in a poem.") Only craft determines the morality of a poem.   (*QG*, 32)[18]

This concern with craft runs throughout Creeley's writings; it and a number of related concerns having to do with form and measure all derive from the original tenets of Imagism and the later reformulations of Objectivism. Foremost among these concepts is the idea of poetry as "condensation"; Creeley's work, more than that of any other poet in the Pound tradition, maintains a sense of extremely condensed, often almost minimalist expression in keeping with the Objectivist equation *Dichten = condensare* (to write poetry is to condense) suggested to Pound by Basil Bunting. For Creeley, the idea of the poem as a "literal transmission" of experience manifests itself not in terms of a fluidity of language and image (as for Duncan) or in the variable patterning of an excited state of mind (as for Olson), but in the transcription of a highly cautious, controlled statement. Such a transcription or transmission is a celebration of language as

---

18. Creeley told me in conversation that as a New Englander he valued the sense of rigor and verbal "Puritanism" implied by Pound's stance. Perhaps the same explanation applies to Creeley's fellow New Englander Olson.

"speech" in keeping with Pound's *Cantos:* "The *Cantos* are, first of all, an incredible condensing, as speech is" (*QG, 94*).

Also of great importance to Creeley's work is Pound's sense of "measure"—of an exacting sense of metrical, syllabic, and sonic "weights and durations." Creeley's use of the short, often enjambed line shows most clearly the influence of Williams; but the tight, almost sculptural form of many of his poems as well as their attention to the sounds and rhythms of language owes a great deal to Pound. In his essay "I'm given to write poems" Creeley quotes several of Pound's statements from his "Treatise of Meter" at the end of *ABC of Reading*. Besides the idea of the weights and durations of syllables, Creeley views as Pound's most important injunctions those concerning rhythm as "form cut into TIME, as a design is cut into SPACE," and those showing an awareness of the poem's sonic possibilities—"the sound it makes" (*CE, 503*).

The poem of Creeley's in which Pound's presence is most clearly felt is "The Finger," written in the late 1960s. It is not unusual that only one of Creeley's poems shows such a direct relationship to his predecessor—after all, Creeley's characteristic voice is not one of allusion or quotation, like the voices of Olson, Duncan, and Snyder. As Creeley himself explains, this poem's allusions place it in the same relationship to Pound as *The Cantos* does to many prior works, which appear as single or multiple echoes within its overall structure.[19] Unlike Olson or Duncan, who return repeatedly to Pound's work as a model or source for their own poetry, Creeley uses this single poem— significantly one of his longest and most impressive works—as his poetic acknowledgment of Pound's importance.

Creeley had already decided by the time of his 1951 poem "Helas" that even though he was "impressed by Pound's authority in the language," Pound's poetic solutions were not viable ones for him. Creeley differed from contemporaries such as Olson and Duncan in not wishing to pattern his writing on

19. This is from my own conversation with Creeley in March 1990.

the "didacticism" of Pound's poetic project.[20] Even this early in his poetic career, Creeley had determined that he could not find in his own experience a certainty corresponding to Pound's "axe" of lucidity and "right reason"; his was to be a poetry for the "indefinite," without the firm "edge" of didacticism or authority.

Cynthia Edelberg reads "The Finger" as an epic descent, or *nekuia,* by a hero figure bearing some resemblance to the Odysseus persona of Pound's *Cantos.*[21] I read the poem as going even further in creating a full-scale mosaic of allusions to Pound. In the first lines of "The Finger," Creeley alludes directly to Pound's "So that," which ends Canto I and begins Canto XVII. Pound first uses the words to form a transition from the translation of the *Odyssey* into his own poetic project, and later he uses them to reintroduce the divine and metamorphic world of the earlier Cantos. Although on a smaller scale, Creeley's poem and volume enact a similar "timeless" journey: "that time I was a stranger, / bearded, with clothes that were / old and torn. I was told, / it was known to me, my fate would be timeless." The poem goes on to evoke Pound's early Cantos on several levels: in the images of light and blindness suggesting Pound's Tiresias and Homer in the first two Cantos, in the mythological figures of Aphrodite and Hermes, in the seabird imagery derived from the beginning of Canto II, and in the overall attitude of stately reverence.

> The quiet shatter of the light,
> the image folded into
> endlessly opening patterns—
>
> Had they faced me into
> the light so that my
> eye was blinded? At moments
> I knew they had gone by
>
> searched for her face, the pureness
> of its beauty, the endlessly sensual—
> but no sense as that now reports it.
> Rather, she was beauty, that

20. See the discussion in Cynthia Edelberg, *Robert Creeley's Poetry,* 162.
21. See ibid., 85–135.

Aphrodite I had known of,
and caught sight of as maid—
a girlish openness—or known
as a woman turned from the light.

I knew, however, the other,
perhaps even more. She was there
in the room's corner, as she would be,
bent by a wind it seemed

would never stop blowing,
braced like a seabird,
with those endlessly clear grey eyes.
Name her, Athena, what name.[22]

Creeley, however, cannot remain long in his mode of Poundian authority; soon the myth becomes modernized, as first a sense of Christian martyrdom and then a disturbing note of sensuality enter the poem. Creeley's "hero" dances an unheroic "jig" as he approaches the "goddess," now transformed into a fleshly woman with a "low, chuckling laugh." As Creeley's vision of feminine beauty moves further away from Pound's, the style and language follow: Creeley's more characteristic lines reappear, with their self-consciously awkward enjambments and halting punctuation. The rest of the volume returns to the scattered, fragmentary format of poems as "pieces," leaving behind the brief but powerful moment of Poundian certainty and transcendence.

Compared to Olson, Duncan, and Creeley, Allen Ginsberg was late in recognizing Pound as an important precursor. In a letter to Lionel Trilling shortly before the publication of *Howl* (May 1956), Ginsberg contrasted the "classicism" represented by Eliot and Pound with the "romanticism" of his own generation:

I think what is coming is a romantic period (strangely tho everybody thinks that by being hard-up and classical they are going to make it like Eliot which is silly). Eliot & Pound are like Dryden & Pope. What gives now is much more personal—how could there be now

22. Creeley, *Collected Poems*, 384.

anything but a reassertion of naked personal subjective truth—
eternally real? Perhaps Whitman will be seen to have set the example
and been bypassed by half a century. (*H*, 155)

But in the next month Ginsberg seemed to revise his opinion of
Pound; Ginsberg sent him the manuscript of *Howl* with a letter
that indicated his respect for Pound's judgment: "Please read at
least 1 page of the enclosed mss. Or 1 line for that matter so long
as you can judge the rhythm. These are all l-o-n-g lines, used in
various ways. I don't think nobody's tried this this way. . . .
Please let me know how the poems strike or affect you" (*H*,
157).

Pound did not reply to Ginsberg's letter, but he did send the
poem on to Williams with a typically cranky note: "You got
more room in yr house than I hv in my cubicle. If he's yours why
dont yu teach him the value of time to those who want to read
something that wil tell 'em something what they dont know" (*H*,
157). There is no indication that Ginsberg was aware of Pound's
reaction or, if he was, that it bothered him greatly; in any case,
Ginsberg's estimation of Pound's poetry continued to grow.
When he visited Pound at Rapallo in 1967, Ginsberg praised
Pound's poetry as "the best of its time" and stressed the impor-
tance of its impact on contemporary poets.[23] In his meetings
with Pound, Ginsberg not only praised Pound's poetry; he ac-
cepted Pound's anti-Semitism in *The Cantos* as part of a natural
"process of thought" and expressed agreement with Pound's
economic critiques, especially those concerning the very institu-
tions of banking and "usury" that Pound had attributed to
Jewish moneylenders and financiers.[24]

Two possible explanations for Ginsberg's reaction can be
proposed—one personal and one historical. By the time Gins-
berg met Pound, he spoke only apologetically about his work
and his anti-Semitic prejudice. Rather than having to deal with
the political, economic, and sometimes anti-Semitic "ravings" to

23. Quoted in Michael Reck, *Ezra Pound: A Close-Up*, 154.
24. Ginsberg credits Pound with "unmask[ing] and demystify[ing] the nature
of banks and money and currency" and with demonstrating "that the whole
money system is a hallucination, a shell game" (*AV*, 181–82).

which Olson and Duncan had been subjected at St. Elizabeth's, Ginsberg had only to counteract Pound's silence and depression and to try impressing on him the value of *The Cantos* and its importance to younger poets. And by the time of Ginsberg's poetic success (the late 1950s and early 1960s), the immediate mood cast over the United States by the acts of Mussolini and Hitler had subsided. In consequence, the antiwar sentiment and the critique of the capitalist system Pound provided were more attractive to younger writers than they had been a decade or two earlier.

Ginsberg rationalized Pound's statements against Jews in *The Cantos* as part of an overall structure of "humours . . . irritations and angers." Ginsberg explained that the uniqueness of *The Cantos'* form lay in the way Pound registered the state of flux of such "humours" in his life: "The *Cantos* were for the first time a single person registering over the course of a lifetime all of his major obsessions and thoughts and the entire rainbow of his images and clingings and attachments and discoveries and perceptions" (*AV*, 181). Pound's perceptions, Ginsberg claimed, were "manifest in procession as time mosaics": "His irritations, against Buddhists, Taoists, and Jews, fitted into place, despite his intentions, as part of the drama, the theater, the presentation, the record of mind-flux."[25]

Clearly, something of Pound's social and economic critique also informs Ginsberg's work, as it does that of Olson, Duncan, and others. The moral outrage Ginsberg expresses in a passage like the "Moloch" section of *Howl* matches Pound's own disgust at economic ills and misuses in the Cantos dealing with "Usura." Ginsberg's Moloch, like the figure of Geryon in *The Cantos,* is the monster of economic evil that leaves a trail of corruption and social devastation in its wake. Ginsberg's commentary on Pound's "Usura Cantos" indicates a conscious parallel with his own Moloch. In an essay entitled "Pound Contra Usura," Ginsberg adumbrates Pound's Canto XLVI, the one following his

---

25. Ginsberg, "Encounters with Ezra Pound," 13–14.

famous "exorcism of usury": "He goes into incidents and scenes from World War I, people making money on the war. . . . Speaking from the American experience, he says that when a small group of people get a monopoly on the physical issue of actual money, currency, then corruption enters our *polis,* enters into our government and into the conduct of economic and political affairs" (*AV,* 173–74). Ginsberg's own poem reiterates in more compressed form the same images: "unobtainable dollars," "the vast stone of war," "the crossbone soulless jailhouse and Congress of sorrows," and "the stunned government."[26]

Like Creeley, Ginsberg learned aspects of poetic technique from Pound, but the concepts he adopted from Pound's practice were in most cases different from those that interested Creeley. Ginsberg praised Pound both for his use of classical meter as an alternative to a standard iambic-based rhythm and for a "mystical ear" that allowed him to "hear gradations of vowel lengths that other people wouldn't notice" and to "balance vowels from line to line, work with vowels as a measure of the line as other people couldn't." Pound's "ear," Ginsberg felt, had enabled him to "make a new kind of American measure based on the approximation of classical quantity." Ginsberg saw this new measure as "a revelation . . . of the musical possibilities of the vowels," and he contrasted Pound's experimental metrics with those of his more conventional contemporaries, in whose work the musical possibilities and shades of meaning were subjugated to a controlling metrical structure (*CT,* 127). Pound's poetics—with its emphasis on sound, or "melopoeia"—foregrounded the vital connections among poetry, speech, and song.

In a letter to Richard Eberhart, subsequently published as *To Eberhart, from Ginsberg: Letter about Howl, 1956,* Ginsberg discusses his technique in parts of *Howl* and in "Sunflower Sutra." He provides an example from the final line of "Sunflower Sutra"—"mad locomotive riverbank sunset Frisco hilly tincan evening sitdown vision"—a line that he calls "a curious but

26. Ginsberg, *Howl and Other Poems,* 17.

really rather logical development of Pound–Fenollosa Chinese Written Character–W. C. Williams–imagist practice."[27]

If we examine this example along with similar lines from *Howl*—"backyard green tree cemetery dawns" or "teahead joyride neon blinking traffic light"—we find that Ginsberg follows Pound's practice in several ways. Ginsberg eliminates connectives of any kind, as if in a more radical extension of Pound's Imagist directive "to use absolutely no word that does not contribute to the presentation." The Pound-Fenollosa adaptation of the ideogrammatic method is apparent in the direct juxtaposition of elements taken as independent visual concepts that together form a coherent meaning. In *The Cantos* Ginsberg finds a technique based on an "attention to specific perceptions" and "descriptions of exact language" that serves as a model for his own writing (*AV*, 12). Pound's most vivid passages—such as "tin flash in the sun dazzle" and "Soapsmooth stone posts"—form "a sequence of phanopoeic images," a "praxis of perceptions manifested in phrasing" (*AV*, 13). Ginsberg refers to such instances as the poetic "transcription" of images into words. Ginsberg's lines, like Pound's, transcribe images directly through the use of "condensed perception concrete images" around which other thoughts or references can revolve. As in the haiku-like condensation of Pound's Imagist poems and the later ideogrammatic constructions in *The Cantos*, Ginsberg's poem eliminates the use of the simile, thus allowing complexes of images, or "thing-facts," to "jump together in the mind" (*AV*, 182).

Finally, Ginsberg's phrases reflect his interest in Pound's idea of the tone leading of vowels and in the musical, or melopoeic, possibilities of poetry. Ginsberg's choice of words in the lines just quoted are determined as much by their sounds as by the visual or mental image they evoke. As in the lines from Pound's "Usura Canto" that Ginsberg quotes—"or where virgin receiveth message / and halo projects from incision"—the vowels in Ginsberg's lines create a sense of internal melody. In the "Sunflower Sutra," for example, a pattern of "i" sounds sustains this

27. Ginsberg, *To Eberhart, from Ginsberg*, 27.

melody: "locomo*tive riv*erbank sunset *Fris*co *hilly tin*can even*ing sit*down *vi*sion."

The examples of Creeley and Ginsberg illustrate two of the directions in which Pound's poetics have been developed by the postmodern generation. They also demonstrate how Pound's sense of a live tradition continues to operate among the poets who follow him. Both Creeley and Ginsberg exemplify the impact of Pound's notions of technique, or craft; both adopt Pound's ideas concerning the ideogrammatic method and the condensation of language it entails; both reenact his attention to sound and poetic form; and both share with Pound a sense of poetry's social and political role. Yet the poetry that results can hardly be more different than in the case of these two contemporaries. What they demonstrate most obviously in their use of Pound is the synthetic, nonlinear sense of tradition contained in Pound's own project; Pound's work and ideas become part of a vortex of diverse influences including the jazz of Charlie Parker in the case of Creeley and the poetry of Whitman, Blake, Apollinaire, Lorca, and Williams (not to mention traditions of Eastern religion and meditation) in the case of Ginsberg. It is this incorporative poetic and its theoretical implications for influence and tradition that I explore in the next chapter.

2 EZRA POUND AND HAROLD BLOOM

Influences, Canons, Traditions,
and the Making of Modern Poetry

The history of fruitful poetic influence . . . is a history
of anxiety and self-saving caricature, of distortion, of
perverse, willful revisionism without which modern
poetry as such could not exist.
    Harold Bloom, *The Anxiety of Influence*

It is only good manners if you repeat a few other men
to at least do it better or more briefly. Utter original-
ity is of course out of the question.
    Ezra Pound, *Make It New*

As I argued in the last chapter, Pound's sense of a live tradition
was based on a fundamentally incorporative poetics that allowed
him to explore a radically expansive range of models and sources
for his own work. In excavating both the literary archives of
various languages, cultures, and traditions and the materials and
discourses of nonliterary disciplines, and in adapting as a pri-
mary poetic method the ideogrammatic juxtaposition of these
borrowings, Pound developed a mode of poetic composition that
would have a lasting impact on American poetic practice in this
century. Underlying Pound's poetic mode, and to varying de-
grees those of his descendants, is a model of influence in which
the poet consciously chooses literary predecessors and traditions
as well as traditions of social, political, historical, economic, and
scientific thought with which to interact in a freely defined
intertextual space. This model assumes an active, positive, and
mutually illuminating relationship between the poet's work and
that of both predecessors and contemporaries.

The dominant tendency in recent works on poetic influence,
however, has been to represent the relationship between poets of
successive generations as repressive and antagonistic. Walter
Jackson Bate's *The Burden of the Past and the English Poet*
characterizes the process of influence as one involving a need on

the part of the later poet to escape the overwhelming burden of past forms and accomplishments and to deal with the increasingly stultifying effects of an "accumulating anxiety" concerning the need for originality. The most prominent study of influence by a recent critic, which Harold Bloom has undertaken in several books starting with *The Anxiety of Influence,* takes its cue from Bate's "anxiety" but relies for its argument on metaphors and terminology taken from psychoanalysis rather than from history. Bloom suggests that the poet's literary production results from a struggle with a "strong" father figure with whom he must contend through a series of rhetorical steps representing various stages of the "repression" of his own poetic self and "misprision" of the work of a predecessor. Even if Bloom is extreme in his assertions about the agonism and defensiveness of poets, he does point out that the overt nature of a poet's relationship to a predecessor is not necessarily the same as his or her covert or unconscious use of that predecessor.

Of any model yet proposed for the operation of influence in English and American poetry, Bloom's is the most systematic, and for many critics and readers it has proved the most compelling as well. Although the interest of Bloom's revisionist and agonistic theory of influence cannot be disputed, its tacit acceptance by most critics and its currency in critical discourse since the mid-1970s has worked to the detriment of other models. It has become a commonplace of contemporary critical discussion to talk of the anxiety of influence or of poetic misreading or misprision. The assumed validity of such ideas has important consequences not only for the way in which criticism is written but for the broader ways in which poetry is read and canonized. Bloom's criticism has been instrumental in establishing a tradition of critical practice that is largely based on shared assumptions about the centrality of a particular mode of poetry: that of "lyrical subjectivity" or the Romantic Sublime. But Bloom's criteria and methodology have already been questioned by various groups whose work does not fit easily into such categories, including proponents of the literature of minorities and women. In the course of this book, I propose another tradition or mode of writing—the Pound tradition—that departs substantially from Bloom's agenda for poetic ascendancy.

Although the comparison of Pound and Bloom as literary theorists is a juxtaposition of writers with different historical and institutional perspectives, it is not as incongruous a comparison as it first appears to be. Pound does not propose a theory of influence in the way that Bloom and other academic critics do, but he does offer in his nonpoetic writings a relatively coherent view of the process of influence and of how such a process operates within his own poetics. Less self-consciously theoretical than the model provided by Bloom, Pound's writings are no less rigorous. Both Bloom and Pound in his role as critic provide highly rhetorical and somewhat impressionistic accounts of how influence can be seen to operate in the work of a given set of poets. In contrasting the models of Pound and Bloom, I am interested not so much in the actual or rhetorical merits of their theories per se as in the implications their ideas may have for questions of poetic affiliation and canonization.

Bloom's model of influence is in many ways directly opposed to that suggested by Pound and his poetic descendants. The work of Pound, Williams, Zukofsky, and the various practitioners of the "New American Poetry" has until now been largely excluded from the dominant canons of American literature, those supported by the New Criticism and by advocates of the American Sublime such as Bloom. Bloom's exclusion of Pound and his followers from the canon is motivated in part by their enacting of a different model of influence from that suggested by the work of their post-Romantic counterparts. Rather than feeling the "burden of the past" in relation to their predecessors, or engaging in a subconscious and quasiviolent Oedipal struggle with them, these poets resemble Pound in deliberately assimilating the texts and ideas of earlier writers into their own poetry. This is not to say that the overt statements and poetic practices of the Pound tradition are in all cases convergent; rather, I am arguing that Pound, Olson, and Duncan thematize the question of influence in their work in such a way as to foreground their relationship with or debt to their predecessors, rather than repressing or escaping these debts and relationships. I am also not denying the possibility of ambivalence, competition, or even unconscious resentment among these poets. Even though such feelings may (and at times clearly do) exist within this tradition, my readings emphasize what has been in recent years an overly neglected aspect of influence: the way in which a poet's acknowledged debt to a predecessor becomes a major determinant of the formal and thematic structures of a text or series of texts.

The idea of the Pound tradition as an opposing force to Bloom's Romantic tradition of poetry has broader implications as well. Not only does Bloom's model exclude poets who follow Pound directly; in applying it as a universal principle for modern poetry, Bloom neglects what many consider to be the most important and representative mode of twentieth-century poetry in the English language, certainly equal in importance to his own "tradition of the Sublime." All those works within what we may call the "experimental" tradition—that descending from the seminal Modernist models of *The Cantos,* Eliot's *Waste Land,* and the works of E. E. Cummings, H. D., Marianne Moore, D. H. Lawrence, and David Jones—fall outside the Romantic mainstream central to Bloom's theories.[1] Zukofsky, Bunting, and the other Objectivists as well as those not directly in the Poundian tradition but influenced by the open-form experiments of Pound and Williams—for example, Langston Hughes, Thomas Kinsella, Kenneth Rexroth, John Berryman, Robert Lowell, Kenneth Patchen, Sylvia Plath, Mina Loy, Adrienne Rich, Robert Bly, Amiri Baraka (Leroi Jones), Nikki Giovanni, and the various constituents of the Beats, the New York school, the San Francisco Renaissance, and all their various descendants—are excluded by virtue of both their techniques and their derivations from Bloom's canon of poets.

Wallace Stevens: The Poems of Our Climate is Bloom's ultimate statement of his faith in the American tradition he has constructed. Bloom pits Stevens (and to a lesser degree Robert

---

1. I use the term *experimental* advisedly, referring both to Bloom's own designation of Pound and Williams as "innovators" and to these poets' continued interest in *formal* experimentation as opposed to the (re)examination of linguistic or rhetorical structures that characterizes the major project of other Modernist traditions.

Frost, Hart Crane, and others), the "true descendent[s] of Emerson," against Pound, Williams, Eliot, and other experimental Modernists. Calling Frost, "rather than Eliot, Pound, or Williams . . . Stevens' true twentieth-century rival" (*WS,* 68) is purely a matter of opinion. But Bloom most clearly shows his critical predisposition when he presumes to assess Pound and Williams according to his Romantic criteria:

> I think that Stevens here ventures the crucial formula for American Romantic poetry, including even Eliot, Pound and Williams at their infrequent best: it must make the visible a little hard to see, which is one of the great achievements of Whitman and Dickinson, and of Frost, Stevens, Hart Crane after them, and is still the gathering achievement of Robert Penn Warren, Elizabeth Bishop, John Ashbery, A. R. Ammons, and our other distinguished contemporaries who maintain this major tradition of our verse.[2]   (*WS,* 15)

Notice the repetition of the word *our*; Bloom maintains a personal identification with this tradition, the American Sublime. Bloom's tradition is not only "American"; it is "pure." He will claim that "an 'influence' across languages is, in our time, invariably a cunning mask for an influence relation within a language" (*WS,* 20). If indeed it is a cunning mask, just who wears it, and why would he or she "cunningly" do so? Does Bloom contend that Eliot's use of Dante and Laforgue, Gins-

---

2. Also note that Bloom errs in his claim that "making the visible hard to see" is in any way part of the poetic of Whitman, Pound, or Williams. On the contrary, the Imagist/Objectivist tradition of these poets, which manifests itself largely in an openness to the visual and phenomenal world and to a phanopoeic awareness and representation of that experience, is involved with the project of doing just the opposite—making the generally *invisible* a little *easier* to see—or of dealing, as Williams puts it, not with ideas but with things. As D. S. Carne-Ross remarks, Pound's poetics are best exemplified by the image of the green grass tip in the *Pisan Cantos,* which is in itself an event, an exterior visual entity not assimilable to any metaphysical or symbolic construct. Pound's image "offend[s] against the ways we have been taught to read literature . . . the great principle of inwardness or internalization that has put us at the center of things and laid waste the visible world" (*Instaurations,* 214). See also Herbert Schneidau's discussion of Pound's "presentational" mode as essentially nonsymbolic (*Ezra Pound: The Image and the Real*) and his discussion of metonymy rather than metaphor as the controlling mode of Pound's poetry ("Wisdom Past Metaphor"). Related discussions can be found in Kenner, *The Pound Era;* Donald Davie, *Ezra Pound: Poet as Sculptor;* and Perloff, *The Poetics of Indeterminacy.*

berg's of Lorca and the Surrealists, and Pound's of Homer, Arnaut Daniel, Cavalcanti, Villon, Heine, Sappho, Catullus, Confucius, and many others are in some sense invalid? If so, what does such a statement say about the important developments in poetic practice that have come about as a result of such "cross-language" fertilization? Stevens may be, as Bloom claims in his "antithetical" reading, more indebted to Emerson, Whitman, and Dickinson than to Baudelaire and Mallarmé. But even if this is the case, Stevens is not representative of modern poetry in general, and many other American poets of this century have significantly developed their techniques through the process of reading and translating the work of poets in other languages.[3]

Bloom's analysis of Stevens's work leads us to examine more closely the larger critical assumptions on which his model of influence and consequently his canonization of modern poetry are based. Bloom throws a direct challenge to all who value Pound and the poets who follow his Modernist mode of writing; Bloom finds it relatively easy to dismiss Pound and Williams as merely "innovators" who "may never touch strength at all" (*MM*, 9). In other words, Pound, Williams, and all others Bloom deems like them are to be excluded a priori from the canon. It is not surprising, therefore, that advocates of the tradition of Pound and Williams and the constituents of Bloom's "camp" have little in common, either in their poetic "theories" and notions of the canon or in their poetic practices. Nevertheless, from a Poundian perspective it is worth engaging the questions Bloom's books raise and attempting to respond to Bloom's theory in terms of the poetics that Pound himself presents. Pound

3. Bloom's assessment of American poetry suggests that the American mind is entirely impermeable, solipsistic, and paranoiac, a view he seems in general to take. Pound, however, fought such American "provincialism," which he (and later poets in his tradition) saw as "the enemy." For discussions of the Modernist and postmodernist enterprise of translation as poetic (re)invention, see Perloff, "The Contemporary of Our Grandchildren"; and Kenner, "The Invention of the 'Other.'" Kenner writes, "Eliot himself invented an English Laforgue; Joyce invited a very odd kind of Homer, master of every expressive wile; Leishman and Spender re-invented Rilke; Kenneth Rexroth and Gary Snyder have synthesized alternate Japans. . . . Ethnopoetics has invented American Indian rituals" (241).

not only expresses an alternative view of influence and tradition to that of Bloom but also calls into question the very nature of a notion of influence that excludes particular poets or groups of poets from the canon by a hierarchical model of direct genealogical succession. Where Bloom's model is exclusive, Pound's model is on many levels inclusive and porous. Although Pound presented to later poets an "ABC of reading," a canon of what he considered great writers, he left it open for later writers to supplement and revise. As one example, Charles Olson repeated the Poundian gesture of incorporating into his work historical documents lying outside the poetic canon but relied on different historical periods and figures.

Built into the structure of Bloom's canon is a predisposition to privilege those poets whose "strength" is demonstrated by the Oedipal struggle they allegedly enact in their poetry. His insistence on the father / son relationship in describing influence problematizes, at least in theory, the inclusion of women poets in the tradition he considers. Bloom does consider women poets such as Emily Dickinson and Elizabeth Bishop to be part of his "line," though how they fit into the Oedipal equation is never explained. Pound, despite his often gender-specific language for describing poets (he refers to writers in general as "men"), does not stipulate for the poets of his tradition a particular sex or indeed any identity based on a particular kind of cultural discourse, in the way Bloom does. Bloom's adoption of the terminology of genealogy and "family romance" implies a certain uniformity of class, culture, race, and sex as well as of metaphysical and poetic disposition. Pound's tradition, notwithstanding his apparent sexism and anti-Semitism, represents a substantial number of women and Jewish poets.[4] In its eclecticism, Pound's tradition encourages diversity, rather than similarity, among its poets. Thus, Pound's idea of a deliberate and openly

4. Pound's tradition of writing has to include one of the primary poetic models to which he recurs, Sappho, as well as his contemporary H. D. and subsequent women poets such as Moore, Niedecker, Loy, Levertov, and Wakoski. Jewish poets who have participated in the Pound tradition include Zukofsky, Oppen, Reznikoff, Rakosi, Ginsberg, Oppenheimer, Jerome Rothenberg, and Charles Bernstein.

declared "derivation" from predecessors and an eclectic use of models and sources can be viewed as an alternative to Bloom's closed, hierarchical, genealogical, and agonistic paradigm.[5]

As I have suggested, Pound's poetics also depart radically from what has come to be the standard twentieth-century view, represented by Eliot's paradigm of "tradition and the individual talent." Pound differs importantly with Eliot's sense of tradition in advocating the use of "mutually foreign, antagonistic" influences as a means of transgressing the boundaries of any single literature; further, he encourages the writer to seek for models among practitioners of all disciplines: musicians, painters and sculptors, philosophers, politicians, anthropologists, economists, linguists, and scientists.[6] Whereas Bloom (and to a lesser extent, Eliot) would maintain the exteriority of other cultural and political influences, Pound considers them to be ineluctably pertinent. Pound encourages the poet, when seeking models among other writers, to distinguish "donative" authors—that is, authors who are not merely representative or "symptomatic" of their time and place but who bring something new to it, who can "draw from the air about [them] . . . latent forces, or things present but unnoticed, or things perhaps taken for granted but

---

5. Pound suggests on one occasion that *The Cantos* was written "between Kung and Eleusis" (*C*, 258)—in other words within a context defined by the juxtaposition of Confucian and Greco-Christian elements. But this comment, like many of Pound's attempts to describe the composition of his own epic, must be taken as only partially accurate and as vastly inadequate to the complexity of *The Cantos* as a whole. *The Cantos* is a constantly shifting structure defined more by the preoccupations of Pound at any given time than by any of the "plans" he or others proposed for it. The English, French, and Italian lyric traditions; events in contemporary Europe; Italian, Chinese, and American history; economic and political theory; movements in the arts; and various philosophical, anthropological, and biological concepts all play as great a role in determining the structure of the poem as do his stated models of Homer, Dante, and Aquinas. Thus, any attempt to assign to Pound's poetry an underlying tradition or canon is at best an oversimplification of his poetic process.

6. I do not mean to imply by this discussion that Pound's inclusiveness has no limits or that he admits into his canon any writer or thinker whatsoever. My contention is only that his model of influence and poetic creativity makes for a more flexible, less narrow, and less procrustean attitude toward differing traditions or disciplines than that contained in Bloom's paradigm.

never examined." Pound goes on to comment on these donative artists:

> His forbears may have led up to him; he is never a disconnected phenomenon, but he does take some step further. He discovers, or, better, "he discriminates." We advance by discriminations, by discerning that things hitherto deemed identical or similar are dissimilar; that things hitherto deemed dissimilar, mutually foreign, antagonistic, are similar and harmonic.   (*SP*, 25)

This passage suggests several aspects of Pound's idea of influence. As in Eliot's conception, the new writer will in some way have been "led up to" by the "tradition" of his or her forebears, but Pound's model differs from Eliot's in its emphasis on "discovering," on "taking steps further," rather than on merely "fitting in." While he agrees with Eliot that existing works form a complete order that is changed by the introduction of the "really new" work, Pound finds that Eliot's criticism—with its emphasis on "taste" and "commentation," rather than on "perception" and "elucidation," as a means of determining the literary canon—suggests a reader / critic whose engagement with past works is not sufficiently active. Pound wishes to replace Eliot's idea of literary "monuments" (a term that to Pound implies that past literature was merely a "series of cenotaphs" to be beheld by the reader) with "a zoological term" that characterizes works of past writers as "something living," something speaking "of the world as I know it." He also supplements Eliot's notion of "an ideal order of monuments" with the concept of "KRINO, to pick out for oneself, choose, prefer . . . to determine, first, the main form and main proportions of that order of extant letters, to locate, first the greater pyramids and then, possibly, and with a decently proportioned emphasis, to consider the exact measurements of the stone-courses, layers, etc" (*SP*, 390).

Pound seeks in past poetry for the "luminous detail" that will sum up succinctly and beautifully an entire period or culture. The method of luminous detail involves a mode of "seeing" clearly and of discriminating so that a few facts can replace either the multitude of facts or the "sentiment and generalization" in terms of which most people think. By "facts" Pound intends not only historical data but any instance of the application of art or of the intellect that can be discerned by a modern reader, viewer, or listener. The luminous detail is one of the "few dozen facts . . . [which] give us the intelligence of a period" and "a sudden insight into circumjacent conditions, their causes, their effects, into sequence, and law" (*SP*, 22–23). Perceiving the luminous detail requires a strength of conviction that presumably few artists have and therefore requires a "strong" practitioner, though not one with the same kind of metaphysical strength Bloom demands of his strong poets. In his essay "I Gather the Limbs of Osiris," Pound outlines what will be his lifelong attempt to pick up the lost strands of culture, the "classics" from any tradition that will give his own work "authority" and that will later provide the materials out of which he can construct the ideogrammatic formulas that make up much of *The Cantos:* "The donative authors, or the real classics, interilluminate each other, and I should define a 'classic' as a book our enjoyment of which cannot be diminished by any amount of reading of other books, or even—and this is the fiercer test—by a first-hand knowledge of life" (*SP*, 30).

Pound's belief that great literature should reflect lived experience as well as that found in books is central to his view of influence as a complex process involving a wide range of models and sources. For Bloom, however, influence consists in various types of misprision or creative misreading, each of which involves a slightly different rhetorical trope corresponding to a particular psychic state or phase of poetic engagement with a predecessor poet, a father figure whom the new poet, or "ephebe," must in some sense overthrow.

In *A Map of Misreading*, Bloom further delineates the theory outlined in *The Anxiety of Influence*, explaining in greater detail his central notions of "belatedness" and "revisionism." Belatedness is the feeling poets have of "coming after," of having to do again what has already been done by their "fathers." Whereas for Pound the most praiseworthy category of poets is that of "the inventors," those "discoverers of a particular process or of more than one mode or process" (*ABC*, 39), such invention or discovery is impossible in Bloom's schema, where all poets are essentially creative imitators (misreaders) of an earlier master's work. Poetic history is for Bloom "indistinguishable from poetic influence, since strong poets make that history by misreading one another" (*MM*, 5); thus the kind of innovation Pound sees in the rhymes of Arnaut Daniel, for example, can for Bloom exist only as a reaction to the language of a previous poet.

Instead of identifying poets according to a dichotomy of strong and weak, as Bloom does, Pound places poets in six categories according to the degree and type of their influence and contribution to poetic practice. After the inventors come the "masters," who combine the processes they invented and "use them as well or better than the inventors." These two categories, from which Pound claims all truly "essential" literature comes, are followed (though not necessarily in a chronological sequence) by the "diluters," by those who "wrote well in the general style of a given period," by the "belles-lettrists," and finally by "starters of crazes." Pound's typology is important in that it emphasizes concrete stylistic and technical developments in poetry rather than a more abstract notion of poetic "power" or sublimity. Pound's model also views influence as occurring less in a genealogical line of poets than as a continual and gradual distribution, a branching out of poetic practice to an ever larger group of writers. Rather than the gradual diminution of poetic power and sublimity seen by Bloom, in Pound there is a cyclical development in which each era produces one or two donative writers, who generate a new poetics and thereby give a host of other writers an opportunity to produce a "symptomatic" body of work (*ABC*, 39–40).

The state of all strong poets in Bloom's canon is by definition belated with regard to a history they must rewrite. "Revisionism" is this "rewriting," the continual reinterpretation of poetic history by poets attempting to make room for themselves. It is strongly connected to the way in which the canon is formed; the canon itself is determined not only by how previous poets are misread but by *which* poets are misread, which poets become the material for revisionist misreadings. For Bloom, literary history consists of a hierarchy of metaphysical relationships between the words and tropes used by different poets. Bloom intends by influence "not . . . the passing-on of images and ideas from earlier to later poets," but rather "only relationships *between* texts" (*MM*, 3). This assertion implies that a living poet cannot return directly to the text of a poet from a time far removed from his or her own, like Milton, but must read that poet through the misreadings of all other strong poets since. Bloom's revisionist literary history maintains that our only connection to our forefathers is through our fathers. The only exception to this patriarchal succession arises, for Bloom, when the living poet is stronger than his or her father and can pass over the predecessor's generation to an earlier one. In general, however, Bloom's interpretation of poetic history suggests a diminution of powers from Milton through the Romantics to "strong" Modernists like Yeats, Stevens, and Crane to even less "strong" postmodernists like Ashbery, Ammons, and Hollander. Bloom's genealogy of the American Sublime—a descendancy of Emerson to Whitman to Stevens—assumes the same pattern of decreasing strength.

Belatedness, then, seems to be a predominantly negative factor for poets, who are reduced to misreading ever weaker predecessors. Indeed, according to Bloom, modern poetry since Wordsworth is only rewriting. He says of "Tintern Abbey" that it "begins that splendidly dismal tradition in which modern poems intent some merely ostensible subject, yet actually find their true subject in the anxiety of influence" (*PR*, 57). For Bloom, "the meaning of 'Tintern Abbey' is in its relationship to Milton's invocations," and "the poem becomes, despite itself, an invocation of Milton" (*PR*, 56). Wordsworth's concern with his ostensible subject, the spiritual renovation of the poet through the power of nature, is only a "mystification" to hide his "real concern," that of the anxiety he feels about his predecessor Milton, who in the poem "counts for more than nature does" (*PR*, 81).

Bloom's theory is intensely deterministic in its assertion that "no poet can choose his predecessor, any more than any person can choose his father."[7] Pound's understanding of influence and tradition, by contrast, does away with the idea of belatedness, for the poet cannot be belated in a world of which he or she is an active and vital part and in which he or she can still have an impact through writing and teaching. It is for this reason that the strongest writer in Pound's canon, Confucius, was a politician and political philosopher, a man of the world as well as a poet. For Pound, being an important poet or thinker is not a matter of wrestling with predecessors (or rather, in Bloom's conception, the linguistic tropes of predecessors) but instead is a matter of wrestling with the new ideas and problems facing the world, nation, or community at a given time. The poet, like the political thinker or politician, cannot have a purely belated or recupera-tive role in his or her world because for Pound "all ages are contemporaneous" (*SR*, 6).

Implicit in the various correspondences and ideogrammatic linkages he sets up among different personae in *The Cantos* is Pound's rejection of an opposition between the "originary" and the belated. The poet—at least in the tradition of Pound and Whitman or Williams, Zukofsky, Olson, Duncan, Levertov, Sny-der, and Dorn—finds sources for his or her own work in areas outside the "poetic Sublime" or the psychic (metaphysical) trauma that would implicate the work in a binary latecomer / predecessor relation. Influence for these poets cannot take place, or at least would be meaningless, within a political and historical vacuum such as the world of psychotextual memory in which Bloom's poetic tradition exists. These poets' relationship to the past is not exclusively one of metaphysical "sadness" or nostal-

7. Bloom even goes so far as to link the idea of influence to that of sickness or disease, suggesting in his metaphor of influence as "influenza" that the poet can no more escape the all-consuming influence of a predecessor's work than he or she can avoid catching the flu. "If influence were health," writes Bloom, "who could write? Health is stasis" (*AI*, 95). Perhaps, but it might equally well be asked how, without the "healthy" infusion of "new blood" through the intro-duction of alternative poetic sources into the tradition, poetry could continue to exist or to develop. In Pound's poetics, as in Whitman's, it is the metaphor of health, rather than that of disease, that defines the poet's task. The poet must create a "clean" language to help cure the "ills" of society and to nourish the developing culture.

gia, such as Bloom delineates, but one that seeks to use the past, to make it relevant to the situation of the present.

Pound's relationship to past language is not one of belatedness either. His desire is not to recapture the linguistic power of past writers but to do away with the "crust of dead English, the sediment present in my own available vocabulary." Pound feels the need to "make [his] own language" not only "a language to use, but even a language to think in." He expects poets not to use the language of past writers indiscriminately but to study their "lingual inventions" to "sort out these languages and inventions, and to know what and why they are" (*LE*, 193–94). Pound's attention to the use of words goes beyond the terms of the verbal intertext that Bloom sees as controlling poetic language. For Pound, language must have its ultimate basis in something outside the boundaries of previous poetic texts if it is to be more than overused poetic cliché. Pound wishes to avoid the kinds of words and themes that "I and 9,000,000 other poets have spieled on endlessly" and cautions future writers to shun expressions of an inherited poetic language, such as "dim lands of peace" (*SL*, 37). Poetry, Pound admonishes, must be "as well written as prose" but should in effect be better than prose by virtue of its greater condensation and concreteness, the greater "charge of meaning" of a concentrated poetic language stripped of all unnecessary words.

Pound's requirement that language be kept "efficient" and "accurate" applies not only to poetry but to uses of language in other aspects of life as well. He stresses, for example, the importance of language in economics, where a misuse or misunderstanding of seemingly simple terms such as "money" or "usury" can lead to serious problems for society as a whole. In all uses of language, Pound seeks to avoid the verbal cliché by striving to find the "exact definition," or *ching ming,* the absolute and prime sense of a word that withstands the test of time as well as the various attempts to misuse or devalue it.

The question of the Sublime remains Bloom's central preoccupation in defining the trajectory of English and American poetry over the last two hundred years. In his book *Poetry and Repression* and after, the Sublime becomes a matter of a Freudian dialectic between an identification with ancestor poets, on the one hand, and a struggle with and transumption of these "mighty dead," on the other. The attainment of the Sublime depends on "the poetic equivalents of repression" in which creative freedom must first be repressed "through the initial fixation of influence" (*PR*, 27). Bloom sees Milton as representing the apex of a Sublime tradition in European literature; Milton first achieves what will be the predominant mode of English poetry from the great Romantics onward, the "post-Enlightenment strong poem." In this kind of poem, the Sublime is dependent on an absence, a "reliance on words apart from things" (*MM*, 87), that can be filled only through involvement with the past poets who haunt the poet's language.

Pound, who stresses a reliance on words only in connection with the things they denote, finds essential models in the work of Dante and the poets who led up to him, whose clarity and emotional directness celebrate the poet's unmediated involvement with the world. It is no coincidence that the canon of Bloom's Romantic Sublime and Pound's loosely defined canon hardly overlap at all (with the notable exceptions of Whitman and Robert Browning) and that the poet most central to Bloom's genealogy, Milton, also exerts what Pound sees as the most deleterious influence on English poetry. What chiefly interests Pound as a poetic mode is not the "rhetoric" of Milton and the belated Romantics, but "presentation," the way in which words are "objectivized" through exact descriptive terms for examined natural phenomena.[8]

---

8. Schneidau, *Ezra Pound*, shows how the presentational mode of poetry Pound adapted largely from the ideas of Ford Madox Ford—that of the "prose tradition in verse"—led to some of the most important formulations of what was to become Imagist, and later Objectivist, practice. Schneidau demonstrates how the idea of presentation of words is never far removed in Pound's mind from the visual sense, from the "visualization," as image or sculpture, that the precise word presented to be the reader implies. Language for Pound is importantly connected to a concrete, sensory framework. Pound resists the abstraction that he finds when language loses this focus, when "all metaphysical thought degenerates into soup."

Where Bloom's ideal is a poetry of "lyrical subjectivism" motivated by an anxiety about creative freedom and incorporating an active dialectic, Pound's is an "objectivity" reflecting a confidence in the powers of sensory awareness and poetic technique and stating a clear and unambiguous worldview unadorned by "rhetoric." Where Bloom views poetic language as highly figurative, rhetorical, and self-referential, Pound seeks a poetry that is free from rhetoricity, figuration, and other excesses of language and that contains no word that does not contribute directly to a literal and definitive meaning. For Pound, the language of poetry, as that of prose, should be active and forward moving rather than reversing, troping, and revising.[9]

In his *ABC of Reading,* Pound analyzes textual examples of the poets who provide an alternative to Bloom's post-Miltonic canon: Chaucer, Gavin Douglas, Arthur Golding, Mark Alexander Boyd, Marlowe, Donne, Rochester, Samuel Butler, Pope, George Crabbe, Walter Savage Landor, and Browning. He also lists authors (both English and French) through whom the metamorphosis of English verse in general may be traced: Villon, Thomas Campion, Robert Herrick, Edmund Waller, the Earl of Dorset, Edward Fitzgerald, Théophile Gautier, Tristan Corbière, Rimbaud, and Laforgue.

When he looks further afield, outside the realm of influences on English literature, Pound's choices seem equally idiosyncratic: he investigates the poetic legacies of the Provençal troubadours, of Sappho, Cavalcanti, and Heine, and of Confucius and Li Po. Pound and the other poets of his tradition (Whitman, Williams, and Olson, for example) would have found the claim that the poet cannot choose his or her own predecessors absurd. And Bloom's own inclusion of Whitman in the American Sublime seems to raise questions about the element of choice in critical as well as poetic reading. Although Whitman has been

9. Although the conception of a poetic language as unmediated relation to the real has been attacked on many fronts by recent critical theory, it is nonetheless important to recognize that this impulse toward the real shapes the poetic enterprise of the Pound tradition. Regardless of whether it is in fact possible to have an unmediated relation to the real, it is the *desire* to have it, and the conviction that it is possible, which determine the poem's construction.

consistently claimed by the poets of the Pound tradition as a poet of presence, a kind of projectivist forefather, Bloom sees him as the "greatest example" of the American Sublime, relying for this interpretation on what he claims are the "most sublime passages" in Whitman (*PR,* 248).

If we are going to admit this degree of conscious choice in a *critical* misreading, who is to say that an equal degree of choice does not take place in the readings of one poet by another? There is no reason Whitman cannot be both the great poet of the Sublime—father to Stevens, Crane, and Ashbery—and the originator of the "open-form" poetics that led to the work of Williams, Olson, and Ginsberg. The corpus of a poet does not represent a single unified whole, a consciousness to be wrestled with; rather, the corpus comprises a variety of forms, manifestations, moods, and personae, each of which represents a particular aspect of the poet's work. As my examination of Pound's own influence shows, his work contains a great diversity of topoi and modes of expression, each of which has a differing impact on the work of subsequent poets.

Pound's choices of models reflect an interactive engagement with poetic tradition and provide an always changing canon of poets to read and discuss. In his *Active Anthology* of 1933 Pound explains that his objective is polemically to challenge current critical assumptions. To do so he presents to the public authors capable of progressing further in their work, rather than those whose present and past work may be most highly regarded. Even his own current judgments are not absolute; he writes, "I expect or at least hope that the work of the included writers will interest me more in ten years' time than it does now in 1933."[10] Thus, Pound's canon is intended to be in a state of constant revision; he would not have sanctioned, as Bloom does, an existing order of Sublime talents whose works operates in a hermetic and self-referential aesthetic system. The vast array of writers who in their ensemble make up Pound's idea of literature represent a great diversity of talents, sensibilities, styles, genres,

10. Pound, *Active Anthology,* 253.

orientations, and traditions. Pound's writers are not united by any particular mode of discourse or by any modus operandi; their poems and books function as a body of work that displays for future writers and intelligent readers the many forms good writing can take.

For Pound, questions of the canon, tradition, and influence are of practical importance as well. Good writing can be learned, and that learning requires, along with a measure of "genius," a great deal of the discipline and hard work necessary to absorb the lessons of past writers. Writers of less than monumental talents are important to Pound not as writers struggling to the death to establish their own identities but as artists keeping alive a tradition of writing and, ultimately, a culture always in need of a body of literature to sustain and strengthen it. Pound views poetry from the vantage point of the artisan, always working to perfect his or her own art and to find standards by which the art of others can be evaluated.

Bloom, by contrast, treats such stylistic and technical concerns as irrelevant to the work of strong poets. Poetic influence in his Sublime tradition is not marked by any stylistic devices, visual echoes, sound patterns, or repeated images but rather by the *absence* of a previous poem, a "central poem of the imagination," which in Bloom's schema the ephebe must not have even read.[11] Bloom's idea of a total intertextuality without any concrete manifestation of the intertext can occur only in a tradition in which the "central" poets and texts are already implicitly accepted by the later poets.[12]

Pound's technical criteria work in just the opposite way, encouraging poets to read in a number of styles and traditions, to seek qualities Pound views as desirable in *any* poetry. Pound's

11. See *AI*, 70; and Bloom, *Kabbalah and Criticism*, 67.

12. Bloom's belief in an intertextual and exclusively literary framework for poetic influence seems in a sense to contradict his claim that such overt matters as literary style and technique are unimportant to later poets. Bloom differentiates between a writer's style as it is manifested in the surface level of poetic composition and the seemingly more profound impact of poetic themes, topoi, or tropes on later poetic texts. For me—and I am sure for Pound as well—such a distinction is untenable in most instances.

view of the role of translation as a necessary and creative exercise in developing poetic skills is a further indication of his conviction of the universality of art and culture, a conviction that was strengthened by his discovery after 1930 of Leo Frobenius and *Kulturmorphologie.*

Pound's concept of history emphasizes that the individual can be a causal historical factor, thus putting him in opposition to those who favor the notion of the zeitgeist as a dominant historical principle. Pound's vortex works across historical boundaries as well as within a given period; it forcefully suggests that the truly donative artist or idea not only resists the influence of the ideas and artists of his or her time (or that of his or her immediate predecessor) but is essentially separate from those ideas or artists, that zeitgeist.

Pound's artistic *paideuma,* unlike Bloom's poetic Sublime, cannot exist apart from the ideas informed by the larger struggles and movements that make up the political and historical "reality" of a time. Pound's ideal poet can certainly not afford to indulge in Bloomian "solipsism," even a "triumphant" one, for to do so is to deny that poetry has anything to do with the rest of the world. Nor can the poet sequester himself or herself from the work of contemporary writers and artists so as to preserve a solipsistic lyric voice. Pound's own tireless efforts on behalf of other writers of his generation as well as writers from the past parallels his conception of poetic tradition as a "handing down" of the essentials of culture through what he refers to as *Sagetrieb* (a drive to tell)—an oral tradition or "tale of the tribe."[13] For Pound, poetry is not "necessarily a competitive mode" as it is in Bloom's description of strong poets (*PR,* 7); nor is the "generosity" Pound displays toward different writers and traditions merely a matter of the "civility" of poetic and critical convention.

13. John Wain comments on Pound's practice: "[Pound] never sought to claim our attention for the promptings of his individual inner voice, but rather for something of value that he has found in Provencal, in medieval Italian, in Anglo-Saxon, in classical Latin or Chinese.... [He has] always sought to win our assent not simply to his own thoughts, but to the thoughts of other minds with whom he has been in resonance" ("The Prophet Ezra v. 'The Egotistical Sublime,' " 66).

Michael André Bernstein sees Robert Duncan and the other poets of the Pound tradition as sharing with Pound a trust in the communal aspect of art and experience:

> The sense of a poem's discourse as part of our linguistic common-wealth whose neglected resources it is the artist's task to make available again for communal appropriation underlies the references of a Pound or a Duncan. Because, for them, the world itself, both in its purely natural aspect and as an historical realm of human actions and perceptions, is seen as inherently significant, their poems enact rituals of rediscovery, celebrations of possibilities potentially available to everyone, rather than any private or autonomous transcendence.[14]

Bloom, however, seeks to deny not only that poetry can be understood in terms of its reference to "the world" but also that poems have any linguistic significance other than as markers of a relationship to other poems. His intertextual stance is most apparent in *Poetry and Repression,* which seeks to explore the relationship between the "text" and the "psyche." Bloom here posits a "reliance of texts on texts," which he claims literary critics have always understood but which poets themselves have attempted to cover up by pretending to look for truth "in the world":

> Unfortunately, poems are not things but only words that refer to other words, and *those* words refer to still other words, and so on, into the densely overpopulated world of literary language. Any poem is an interpoem, and any reading of that poem is an interreading. A poem is not writing, but *rewriting,* and though a strong poem is a fresh start, such a start is a starting-again.   (*PR,* 3)

Pound would not have accepted the notion that there is such a thing as an "overpopulated world of literary language"—that language has an autotelic existence or that every poetic act is merely a linguistic or rhetorical trope reusing and reinterpreting the words of another poem. Pound's interest in poetry is not primarily with relationships between texts—with misreadings and rewritings—but with poetic texts as concrete entities in their own right. Each poem has particular visual and aural qualities

14. M. A. Bernstein, "Bringing It All Back Home."

that give it a unique aesthetic presence. Reducing all texts to examples of intertextuality, to instances of shared poetic vocabulary, denies that the impact of one poet on another has largely to do with qualities that cannot be measured in terms of intertextual relationships between words: the overall sound or music of a line or poem, the visual presence of a poem on the page. A poem is not just composed of words that interact in a metaphysical or psychological realm; it comprises words in a specific physical environment, a "concrete" and "constructed" reality. In the tradition of American poetry begun by Whitman, the poem has been described in terms of such physical entities as leaves of grass, carved wood, or a living cell; a collage, machine, or vortex; a knot, pattern, or weave; a sculpture, stone, or fragment; a fugue, sonata, song, libretto, or canto.

The physical conception of poetry embodied in the names of the various movements of the twentieth century—Imagism, Vorticism, Objectivism, Objectism, Projectivism—runs counter to that of intertextuality as understood by Bloom, as do the ideas of craft and of *techne* central to many modern poets. In his discussions of other writers, Pound makes clear that "influence" is a highly complex matter having to do not only with shared language and poetic attitudes but with a wide range of technical and formal components that come into a poet's work from various sources. In general, Pound values purely "linguistic" or textual influence less highly than that which comes out of some shared experience of life or ideas. He is careful to caution others not to "allow 'influence' to mean merely that you mop up the . . . vocabulary of some one or two poets you admire,"[15] and he claims that the works of the greatest writers contain a "brew" of "life itself" (*SR,* 178).

Pound's use of quotation and of the materials of history provides us with another kind of intertextuality; his method foregrounds direct quotations of the utterances and writing of others, inviting them into a dialogic interrelation with him and his own writing. Thus, his version of intertextuality involves a

15. Pound, *Make It New,* 338.

chosen inclusion, rather than an attempted suppression, of the previous poet's discourse. The resulting engagement with another poet or thinker can be poetic, but it can also, as with the inclusion of actual historical documents and other writings (letters, journals), reflect on questions of ideology or stance. The world of language created in this way is not overpopulated; it is constantly renewed by the introduction of concepts from other disciplines and by the use of other languages and traditions that help the poet to "make it new."

Pound views the process of influence as involving the poet's active choice of sources, which he or she should openly proclaim.[16] Bloom's agonistic model presents an overly negative and conflictual picture of poets' relationships to their predecessors and to the past in general. Does a poet's relationship to the past have to be defensive, as Bloom suggests, or can it be the enriching source of poetic creativity that it has been for the poets of the Pound tradition? Although the patricidal model Bloom develops may carry a good deal of validity for certain poets, it accounts inadequately for those poets, such as Pound, who value their sense of poetic and personal ancestry. (It also leaves out, or at least misrepresents, important aspects of the work of a Romantic poet such as Wordsworth, who is often capable of paying direct and unambiguous homage to his predecessor Milton.) Even if personal histories and family romances *do* play a role, as Bloom suggests, in determining the relation of poets to their predecessors, the Oedipal configuration so predominant in Bloom's

16. In a letter to the French critic René Taupin (*SL*, 216), Pound demonstrates the extent to which he is aware of his own influences. When writing at another point to W. C. Williams, he answers Williams's charge that his work is a "parody" or "imitation" of Provencal and Italian poetry by arguing that his conscious imitation is no worse than Williams's supposedly "unconscious" one: "But what the French real reader would say to your Improvisations—'Voui, c(h)a j(h)ai deja (f)vu c(h)a c'est du R(H)imb(h)aud!!'—So much for your kawnscious or unkawnscious. I certainly never put up translations of Provencal as 'American' and Eliot is perfectly conscious of having imitated Laforgue" (*SL*, 226).

thinking about modern poetry is not the only one available for explaining such relations.[17]

Pound's belief in the impossibility of "utter originality" in poetry does not prevent him from finding and valuing examples of poetic innovation and discovery. A recognition of the importance of history—whether that of the poetic past or of the social, political, or economic past—is crucial to the development of the "documentary method" of *The Cantos,* which contributes to the startling newness of the work's vision and construction. *The Cantos* is throughout an example of brilliant formal and thematic innovation, but it is not interested exclusively in modernity or in a timeless status as pure experience. In *The Cantos* the preoccupation of Pound's earlier poetry with the idea of poem as pure, timeless act, as isolated "image," gives way to a more balanced aesthetic that can contain both the moments frozen in time characteristic of his shorter poems and the factor of temporal change, of movement through history.

Pound's epic makes a case for his view of the influence process in several ways. It demonstrates that the "greatness" of past writers does not hinder the potential for important writing by present writers and that the fact that a word has appeared in other contexts (within a verbal intertext) does not deny its unique "presence" in a new context. *The Cantos* demonstrates again and again how words can gain in value by being placed in a specific context and by being examined closely and "scientifically" in a new light. Poetic language is susceptible to historical forces and discourses, but it is also susceptible to pressure from the sensory world as experienced by the poet; the world can be rendered concretely in language through the modes of phanopoeia (the visual image) and melopoeia (sound or music).[18]

17. Two critics have recently provided evidence that Pound's personal and familial history was largely responsible for his positive relation to his predecessors and to the past in general. See Lewis Hyde, *The Gift,* and James J. Wilhelm, *The American Roots of Ezra Pound.*

18. The poetics of Olson and Duncan suggest other kinds of somatic stimuli through which poetry can also be generated. Olson derives units of poetry from the workings of the breath and the heart; Duncan includes all the organs, limbs, and muscles of the body in the poetic process.

Pound's *Cantos* constitutes not a poetry of "veiled imitation," not a "swerve" from or a "revision" of past models, but a nexus, a "vortex," of formal and expressive possibility derived from a plenitude of openly declared sources. In *The Cantos* the models and sources Pound inherits (as well as those he discovers) are allowed to retain their distinct identities yet at the same time to become part of a new creation, different from any of its antecedents. The ideogrammatic, collagelike structure Pound chooses for his epic relieves him of the need to "distort" or "caricature" his predecessors; the concatenation of voices and personae in his open-ended and monumentally allusive tale of the tribe releases him from the burden of poetic anxiety that would force him to transume his precursors in his own poem, which itself enacts a sublimity of a very different order.

3 EXPANDING THE POUNDIAN FIELD
Whitman, Williams, and Zukofsky

As we return to Whitman as a base, we return to just
such a poetic courage as the early Pound envisions in
those who would "exist close on the vital universe."
In Whitman there is no ambiguity about the source of
meaning. It flows from a "Me myself" that exists in
the authenticity of the universe.

    Robert Duncan, *Fictive Certainties*

One day Ezra and I were walking down a back lane
in Wyncote. I contended for bread, he for caviar. I
became hot. He, with fine discretion, exclaimed: "Let
us drop it. We will never agree, or come to an agree-
ment."

    William Carlos Williams, *Kora in Hell*

will you give yourself airs
from that lute of Zukofsky?

    Robert Duncan, "After Reading BARELY
    AND WIDELY"

The rediscovery of Walt Whitman by poets in the 1950s and
1960s represented a move toward a poetry that was more
"open" in its aesthetic and more blatantly American in its origin.
As such, this rediscovery served as a powerful response to the
then fashionable style of Anglo-American "academic" verse.
Whitman, along with Pound and Williams, represented the pos-
sibility of a greater creative freedom, the sense of making it new.
His poetry exemplified, in opposition to the formally closed and
emotionally cloistered poems of the New Critical mode, an
expansiveness, an inclusiveness, and a celebration of the world
of objective experience. Whitman's poetry not only anticipated
in many ways the poetic concerns of the postwar years; it also
served as a forerunner to much of the poetry of Pound and
Williams, who were seen by Olson, Ginsberg, Duncan, Creeley,
and Snyder as continuing the tradition of American poetry that
Whitman had begun.

Whether Pound would have placed himself in such a line is debatable. Despite an important involvement with Whitman in his own poetry and other writings, Pound had strong reservations about Whitman as a poet. Pound also rejected the notion of a purely "American" art, which Whitman's work represented to many other poets, finding such a label indicative of parochialism or sentimental and misplaced patriotism. In essays such as "Provincialism the Enemy" (1917) and "National Culture—A Manifesto" (1938), Pound argued against the idea that an "American culture" could exist that was not in tune with developments in Europe. The "pseudoculture" of America in the early twentieth century was for Pound "twenty years behind" that of its European counterpart. Pound considered the true American culture that of Jefferson and Adams, a "Franco-English" racial blend of "French ideation" with "the one English segment that ever threw off the tyranny of [its] conquerors" (*SP*, 164). Pound excluded from his notion of American culture a writer such as Williams, who was of partly Spanish descent. Williams, Pound claimed, was not American at all but "international"; it was not he or even Pound himself who had followed the American "line" of Whitman, but the New Englander Cummings, "Whitman's one living descendent."

If Pound was somewhat reticent about seeing himself as a Whitmanic poet, younger writers such as Duncan were not. Duncan found in Whitman's poetry a prototype of an Imagist use of language and of the relation of poetic language to the physical body, as implied by Pound's conception of logopoeia, phanopoeia, and melopoeia. Duncan also saw personified in Whitman the bias stubbornly held by Pound and Williams against abstraction in language and the need to "test language, as if many of its functions were unreal or unsound or unsavory, against a control taken, in mimesis of the empiricism presumed in the scientific method, from the observable 'objective' world" (*FC*, 163). As read by Duncan and others of his generation, Whitman was the instigator of many of the defining conceptions of a new tradition in American poetry, one opposed not only to the rigid self-control and "propriety" of the New Critical mode but to the dominant mode of all Western poetry, which Olson would define as the "nonprojective." Like Pound, Whitman was able to open a space for poetry that was not based on an imposed rationality of form or idea but that explored in unambiguous terms a direct relation of the poet to objects in the "vital universe," to sources of meaning that could be shared by poet and reader (*FC*, 191).

Duncan, Olson, and Creeley were at least partly correct in their assessment of Pound's debt to Whitman. At about the time that Pound was first formulating the ideas about poetry that in later manifestations were to have such a great impact on twentieth-century poetic practice, he was also preoccupied with his "spiritual father." Pound's 1909 essay, "What I Feel about Walt Whitman," expressed his feelings about Whitman in unusually positive terms:

> Mentally I am a Walt Whitman who has learned to wear a collar and a dress shirt (although at times inimical to both). Personally I might be very glad to conceal my relationship to my spiritual father and brag about my more congenial ancestry—Dante, Shakespeare, Theocritus, Villon, but the descent is difficult to establish. And, to be frank, Whitman is to my fatherland . . . what Dante is to Italy and I at best can only strive for a renaissance in America of all the lost or temporarily mislaid beauty, truth, valor, glory of Greece, Italy, England and all the rest of it.   (*SP*, 145–46)

As the title of the essay indicates, Pound could at this point only describe his "feelings" for Whitman rather than apply any rigorous critical standard to his work. The passage reveals Pound's complex and ambivalent relation to his predecessor, which Pound understood and honestly expressed. Pound recognized that although Whitman's dominant presence in American poetry made him a necessary "father" for Pound's own work, Whitman was a father that Pound—as well as an American nation in need of a dose of European "culture"—had in some ways outgrown. Whitman was the father whose presence at home was embarrassing to Pound, who had found a new realm of literature more suited to his own sensibilities. In comparison to the work of other writers, Dante in particular, Pound found

Whitman's work often "disgusting," an "exceedingly nauseating pill" that caused him "acute pain" when he read it. Nevertheless, he saw that it was a pill that had to be taken if he was to remain an "American" poet, true to the vital "sap and fibre" as well as the "crudity" of America.

Whitman was for Pound the quintessential "Uncouth American" who needed to be chastened, to have his broken wood "carved," to have his America "scourge[d] . . . with all the old beauty" of Europe. In *The Spirit of Romance* Pound compared Whitman, perhaps unfairly, to his "greater" European counterparts (both "fathers" of their own traditions) Dante and Villon. Though Pound never quoted a line of Whitman as evidence of these claims, he assumed his "cultivated" reader would agree with him that Whitman was less "perfect" and "convincing" than Dante, more self-complacent and less sincerely suffering than Villon. Pound provided both a poetic parody of Whitman's "Song of Myself" and a cutting commentary on Whitman's "horrible air of rectitude." Pound's youthful attitude toward his compatriot notwithstanding, he never forgot that he, too, was an American and as such could not forsake entirely the tradition of Whitman, who "is America." Pound realized in his later life and work that what Whitman had achieved, the "optimism and breadth of vision" Pound had satirized in his early writing, was a worthy poetic aim.[1] It was Whitman's lack of craftsmanship that Pound found hardest to forgive, though he did say, with some foresight, that "we have not yet paid enough attention to the deliberate artistry of the man" (*SP*, 146).[2]

The copossession of Whitman and Pound by many later poets suggests that the differences between them as artists were less

1. Pound attempted as early as 1913, in his essay about his relationship to America entitled "Patria Mia," to sum up the "American keynote" in Whitman's poetry: "It is, as nearly as I can define it, a certain generosity; a certain carelessness, or looseness, if you will; a hatred of the sordid, an ability to forget the part for the whole, a desire for largeness; a willingness to stand exposed. 'Camerado, this no book; / Who touches this touches a man.' The artist is ready to endure personally a strain which his craftsmanship would scarcely endure" (*SP*, 123).

2. Pound saw Whitman as an artist of "reflex," the first "honest reflex, in an age of papier-mâché letters" (*SP*, 110).

important to their reception than what they were seen to share. The poets of the following generation detected a homology both in their concept of artistic creation and in their vision of America. Pound's America, like that of Whitman, was one of democratic possibility and promise as well as one of virile and sometimes violent character—based as it was on the "real work" needed to overcome severe natural forces. Whitman and Pound shared a dislike for the genteel and effete tradition of Eastern intellectuals, which represented the other "America."

Pound differed importantly from Whitman, however, in refusing to extend his vision of democracy to his readership. He could not agree with his predecessor that "to have great poets, there must be great audiences too," nor would he see himself as one of the "mass," as Whitman had done.[3] Both Olson and Duncan were to criticize Pound for just this anti-Whitmanic attitude, for his inability to understand the increasing needs and demands of the masses, and for the resulting tendency to cling to an authoritarian order that could stand for "culture." Likewise, Williams chastised Pound for selling out to cultural "grand schemes" and for embracing the ready-made culture of Europe rather than trying to establish an art that would be more representative of his American origins.[4] Pound's "poem including history" is clearly not intended to be the history of the common man that Whitman, Williams, and, to a great extent, Olson envision in their work; nevertheless it is, as Ginsberg and others see it, the Whitmanic "song of myself," an open-ended and fluctuating record of "mind-consciousness."

3. Whitman, Collect and Other Prose, 521.
4. Williams, The Selected Letters of William Carlos Williams, 213–15, 227. Williams was very much concerned with the needs of his readership and with the direct social relevance of Paterson, for instance, to the common reader, to the masses. Pound, too, was interested in his impact on the masses in an indirect sense, in how he could affect society as a whole, but he believed that because relatively few people would really grasp his ideas, the principal target of his books and poetry should be a more "educated," even erudite audience that would be familiar with his many difficult or even obscure references. Pound's writing is marked by expressions of this attitude, such as "In aiming this manifesto at a few dozen men . . ." or "I do not expect one reader in 600 to believe me when I say . . ."

It should be apparent from this discussion that reading Pound through Whitman (or Whitman through Pound) raises important questions about the nature of the Pound tradition. Making Pound the heir to the most "American" of poets—as the later American poets who use Pound as a model have chosen to do—is clearly problematic. Even though Pound did inherit some portion of the legacy of Whitman, it was an inheritance heavily supplemented by the works of poets from different traditions, some of which strongly contradict the impulse of Whitman's poetry and his democratic stance.[5] But it is in the nature of a poetic tradition to define its models by what it needs to find in them. Just as Pound needed to be identified with Whitman to give him legitimacy as an American poet after World War II, Whitman needed Pound to make him a legitimate model in a more sophisticated twentieth-century America. In the revisionist reading of Whitman by the internationally literate generation of postwar American poets, the crude poetic persona and the provincial sense of culture that Pound had seen in him were no longer emphasized. Whitman came increasingly to be seen by the new poetic community as the direct precursor of two American Modernists: the more "provincial," yet dogmatically experimental, Williams and the culturally "sophisticated," yet unmistakably American, Pound.[6]

Despite his age (a year older than Pound), Williams displayed a sensibility that was to ally him more closely with the postmodernist generation of Olson, Duncan, and Creeley than with the "High Modernist" mind-set of Pound. As early as 1920,

5. Note, however, that this kind of eclecticism in the use of poetic models has been typical of the poets of the Pound tradition, thereby establishing a link between the practice of poets such as Ginsberg and Duncan and that of Pound himself.

6. Pound advocate Burton Hatlen argues forcefully for the separation of American poetry into two distinct traditions, both of which began in the nineteenth century: the "academic" poetry of a cultural mainstream and the "underground," "populist" tradition of Whitman and Dickinson, which in our century has led to Pound, Williams, and the poets descended from them. Although I concur to some degree with Hatlen's division, I see it as an oversimplification of what is in the case of Pound and other American poets a complicated "line" of descent.

Williams had in *Kora in Hell* accused Pound's writing of being too dependent on received notions of poetry and culture, calling him "the best enemy of American verse." For his part, Pound had sought to convince Williams of the necessity for European culture as an antidote to his naive idealization of America. Pound had also urged Williams to spend some time on the other side of the Atlantic so that he might "see a human being now and then" (*SL,* 173). Throughout the 1920s and 1930s, Pound's teasing and often patronizing attitude and Williams's rebellious feelings characterized their complex relationship, one involving a deeply founded friendship, a mutual sense of respect, and, at the same time, increasingly antipathetic political and artistic viewpoints.

In part, it was their differing responses to "Whitmanic" American poetry that accounted for their deep-seated differences in poetic and cultural orientations. Whereas Pound considered Whitman's presence as an American forebear of primary importance, Williams viewed the poetry Whitman wrote more clearly as a model for his own. For Williams, Whitman's work was a necessary statement against the "order" called for by formal poetry represented in this century by "the new Anglo-Catholicism" of Eliot and the later poets of the New Critical mode. Williams saw in the "structural innovations" of Whitman a verse that was "measure" (not merely "free verse") but that would be "one of more trust, greater liberty, than has been permitted in the past . . . an open formation."[7] Williams in 1939—like Duncan and Ginsberg some two decades later—saw Whitman as a liberating model through which to justify his own metrical experiments as well as a counterbalance to the rival "academic" tradition.

As Pound was adopting a vision of "culture" supported by his version of European history and civilization and by the propaganda of fascist Italy, Williams felt increasingly alienated from him and took a largely defensive position in response to Pound's criticism of Williams's work and his country. In a 1933 letter

7. Williams, *Selected Essays,* 212.

Williams accepted some of Pound's criticism but not his use of America:

> Fer the luv of God snap out of it! I'm no more sentimental about "murika" than Li Po was about China or Shakespeare about Yingland or any damned Frog about Paris. I know as well as you do that there's nothing sacred about any land. But I also know (as you do also) that there's no taboo effective against any land, and where I live is no more a "province" than I make it. To hell with youse. I ain't tryin' to be an international figure. All I care about is to write.[8]

By 1938 Williams's patience with Pound had been exhausted, and a vehement rhetoric had replaced the friendly tone of his earlier letters. "What the hell have you done that I haven't done?" he wrote Pound. "I've met a hell of a lot more of all kinds of people than you'll ever get your eyes on and I've known them inside and outside in ways you'll never know."[9] During the period from 1939 to 1946, the rivalry Williams had always felt with Pound developed into a complete intolerance for him. The relationship reached its lowest point in 1946, when on Pound's return from Europe Williams showed little interest in visiting him at St. Elizabeth's or in offering him support.[10]

By this time Williams was engaged in writing his own epic— *Paterson*. As the immediate mood of the war subsided, Williams turned from the sense of anger and betrayal he felt toward Pound to a recognition of the importance of his poetry. It is in the crucial period from 1947 to 1950, the same period during which an involvement with Pound by a new generation of poets instigated a revival of interest in Pound's work, that Williams was to write his most significant criticism of *The Cantos*. This criticism affirmed both Williams's own place in the Pound tradition and the resemblance of his sentiments concerning the importance of Pound's work to those of younger poets discovering Pound for the first time.

8. Williams, *Selected Letters*, 139–40.
9. Quoted in Paul Mariani, *William Carlos Williams: A New World Naked*, 413–14.
10. Williams writes in his *Autobiography* that his visits to Pound in the late 1940s were "not frequent" and that he was surprised more than anything by the failure of Pound's incarceration to change his political attitudes.

Williams had always recognized the importance of Pound's use of language and his poetic line, but at this point his praise of *The Cantos* included other areas as well: Pound's use of history to "make a world, an actual world—not 'of the imagination' but a world imagined"; his use of poetic "material"; his "superb ear" and the musicality of his verse; even the essential "truth" of most of what Pound said in *The Cantos*.[11] Just as Williams's later poems, including *Paterson,* contained the greatest poetic expression of his particular assimilation of Pound's poetic principles, the criticism of Pound's work that Williams wrote in the late 1940s and early 1950s was his most mature commentary on Pound's poetic practice. Williams's critical judgments and continuing poetic development were supported by the younger poets of the Pound tradition. In fact, Olson's "Projective Verse" helped Williams to articulate more clearly some of the directions his own poetics had been taking in the 1940s.[12] According to M. L. Rosenthal,

> Williams saw ["Projective Verse"] as an extension and clarification of his own vague but germinative idea of the "variable foot." Announcing that "an advance of estimable proportions is made by looking at the poem as a field rather than an assembly of more or less ankylosed lines," he linked the essay's importance to the fact that, as he puts it, "the reconstruction of the poem [is] one of the major occupations in our day."[13]

The wisdom of Williams's reappraisals of Pound's work, along with his support of Olson's manifesto, helped plant the seeds for a postwar Pound tradition. Williams's criticism of *The Cantos* reflected in large part his own interests in the field of poetics. His praise of the "music" of Pound's poetry, "the way

11. Williams, "Fistula of the Law," 11. See also Thomas Parkinson, "Pound and Williams," 164.

12. This fact has been well documented. To quote Sherman Paul: "During the 1940s, Williams tried repeatedly to state clearly his notion of a new measure; in 1948, at Seattle, he admitted that 'the fact that the project itself [a new world, made possible by a new science, requires a new prosody] . . . is not yet raised to consciousness, to a clear statement of purpose, is our fault,' and he may have printed part of 'Projective Verse' in his *Autobiography* (1951) by way of acknowledging that Olson had succeeded better than he had in doing this" ("Clinging to the Advance," 9).

13. Rosenthal, *The New Poets,* 142.

the words are joined in the common line," was concomitant with his interest in the idea of the poetic line as "measure," following the sequence of a musical phrase.

Williams stressed the importance of Pound's use of poetic "material" such as history and economics as a means to important social or political statement. "Money as we use it (usury) is our hell," Williams wrote. "[Pound's] poem happens to be true, true to the facts which, being overridden in the past, have continued to destroy us through the ages, bringing on wars." Williams also credited Pound with contributing importantly to the American poetic language, which was at war with that being spoken and written on the other side of the Atlantic and which "had burst the bounds of a narrow world and was spreading helter-skelter over a vast continent." The *Pisan Cantos,* Williams wrote, were written in "the most authentically sounding language . . . of our present day speech."[14] Williams saw in the language of these Cantos an integrity achieved through "a sense of reality in the words."

Although Williams and Pound never completely resolved their differences, younger poets of the Pound tradition were not greatly bothered by what they viewed as the largely superficial squabbling of their elders. It was Pound and Williams's joint legacy to younger poets, not their differences, that mattered. Olson saw the Objectivist techniques of Pound and Williams as harbingers of the "projective" stance of his generation; they had opened up the possibility of a "change beyond, and larger than, the technical" that would lead to "a new poetics." But Pound's Objectivism, which in Olson's terms represented the search for an objectification of experience that minimized interference by the subjective "lyric" ego of the poet, was a partial failure. Pound's Objectivism never reached the point at which the poet was in a "natural" relation to his experience of an object. Olson coined the term *Objectism* to refer to "a more valid formulation" of Objectivism suggested by his reading of Alfred North Whitehead. Objectism stood for "the getting rid of the lyrical

14. Williams, "Fistula of the Law," 10.

interference of the individual as ego, of the subject and his soul, that peculiar presumption by which modern man has interposed himself between what he is as a creature of nature and those other creations of nature which we may, with no derogation, call objects" (*SW*, 23–24).

Unlike Williams, whom Olson felt was more in touch with a realistic experience of social reality and whose "emotional system" was "capable of extensions & comprehensions the ego-system . . . is not," Pound tried to "break down" everything, including history, with the "beak" of his ego (*SW*, 82).[15] Yet although the "ego as beak" was to become "bent and busted" (in Pound's inability to achieve a workable solution to the political, historical, and formal problems of *The Cantos*), the only possible alternative, Williams's "localism" in *Paterson*, was also inadequate to Olson's needs. Olson criticized both Pound and Williams for failing to provide in their work a system of understanding that could be translated directly into action. (See chapter 4 for a more detailed discussion of Olson's relationship to Pound and Williams.) In a letter to Cid Corman, Olson explained that if Williams "gave us the lead on the LOCAL," Pound's "ragbag" was "one long extrapolation . . . on WILL," a call to "be political" (*LO*, 130). Pound came closer than Williams to satisfying Olson's need for a larger "context" by providing a notion of "process" based on a "politics" and engendered by acts of "will," even though the position from which Pound's view of history and politics was proclaimed — that of cultural elitism, political fascism, and ethnic prejudice — compromised its validity.[16] Pound provided the right impulse, "the BLAST instead of the STORY," even if it was often a "blast" in the wrong direction (*LO*, 129). Despite the overall social and political mood of the American poetry movement in the 1950s

15. Charles Altieri argues that the postmodernist critique of the Modernist "ego" was one of the most important factors in their rejection of the high Modernist aesthetic: "Pound and Yeats see the universal as viable only if the individual can so enlarge his or her imaginative capacities as to hold all abstractions or all history in a single image or set of images. For the postmoderns, on the other hand, the ego is not a thing or a place for storing and ordering experience; the ego is not a force transcending the flux of experience but an intense force deepening one's participation in experience" (*Enlarging the Temple*, 43–44).

16. See M. A. Bernstein, *The Tale of the Tribe*, 236.

and 1960s—one that favored the more accessible and politically attractive Williams over the often obscure, erudite, and politically suspect Pound—poets such as Olson, Duncan, and Snyder found Pound rather than Williams to be the more compelling model for their own poetic projects.

One poet who interpreted and applied Pound's ideas more literally than Williams did and who developed a system of poetics based on Pound's ideas long before Olson's "Projective Verse" was the intellectual leader and chief spokesperson for the short-lived Objectivist movement, Louis Zukofsky. Even though Pound and Williams can be considered the movement's sponsors, the Objectivists really consisted of a group of younger poets of the early 1930s: the Americans Zukofsky, Oppen, Reznikoff, and Rakosi and the English Bunting. The Objectivists were, as Laszlo Géfin points out, "the first group of American poets who attempted to make use of Pound's theories and to prove that his aesthetics offered new possibilities in poetic composition."[17] These poets were not well received by the academic community, and they labored in relative obscurity until the 1960s, when they began to be known by a small but loyal following composed mainly of younger poets of the Pound tradition. Zukofsky and the other Objectivists provided in their statements of poetics the first and still the most formally descriptive poetic theory based on his ideas, and they established in their own poetic practice further evidence of the uses to which Pound's poetic ideas could be put.[18]

Although less actively involved in the Objectivist movement than Williams, Pound was the major impetus behind the formation of the group and behind Zukofsky's own poetry, and

17. Géfin, *Ideogram*, 67.
18. Zukofsky's influence at Black Mountain was stronger on the younger poets than on Olson. Zukofsky was discussed at Black Mountain, but according to Joel Oppenheimer Olson spoke of Zukofsky as a "dead poet," as someone out of the past who no longer constituted an active force. Olson's reticence to discuss Zukofsky may be explained by an antipathy for his poetry or by a resentment of his increasing influence in opposition to that of Olson himself. After the "rediscovery" of Zukofsky in the 1950s and 1960s by Black Mountain poets Creeley, Oppenheimer, Dorn, Jonathan Williams, and Fielding Dawson, he began to attract a larger following.

Zukofsky's *"Objectivists" Anthology* was dedicated to him. Zukofsky greatly admired Pound's art and sought to put into practice many of his ideas. Zukofsky's relationship to Pound differed from that of Williams, however, in being almost entirely that of disciple to mentor. Zukofsky felt less need to distance himself from Pound than Williams had, and he adopted not only many of Pound's ideas but often his vocabulary as well in an attempt to establish a scientific poetics based on Pound's work. Zukofsky was the first poet to see clearly the fundamentally ideogrammatic structure on which Pound's *Cantos* was constructed, identifying as early as 1930 the way in which "Pound has not concerned himself merely with isolation of the image—a cross-breeding between single words which are absolute symbols for things and textures . . . but with the poetic locus produced by the passage from one image to another" (*PZ*, 134).

As acute as Zukofsky was in his criticism of Pound, the difficulty of his own poetry as well as the intimidating terminology of his poetics made his work less generally attractive and useful to other poets than that of Williams. Zukofsky's manifestos—"An Objective" and "Sincerity and Objectification"—are particularly dense documents that resist easy interpretation and application. Zukofsky defines Objectivism in terms of two concepts that have attained common usage in the Pound tradition: sincerity and objectification. Although most attempts to clarify their meaning have failed, it is possible to look at them as two stages in Objectivist poetry: sincerity is that quality present in all good poetic writing involving an "attention" to the details of experience and the honest reaction to that experience, and objectification is the ultimate and rare state of a poem conveying "the totality of perfect rest" (*PZ*, 13).

Pound's Imagist practice is clearly the basis for the Objectivist position, but while it shares with that of Imagism the notion of conveying the totality and energy of the object or experience, Objectivism places a greater emphasis on formal construction, on the sense of the poem as object. Zukofsky defines the aim of the movement in terms that have particular resonance for poets like Duncan and Creeley: the movement would consist of the

"desire for what is objectively perfect, inextricably the direction
of historic and contemporary particulars" (PZ, 12).

Duncan, the self-proclaimed "first of my generation" to read
Zukofsky along with Pound and Williams, attempts to describe
the way in which Zukofsky's Objectivism differs from Pound's
Imagist or Vorticist practice in *The Cantos*. Pound, Duncan
asserts, presents in his work a stream of consciousness in images
of light and water, radiation and flowing. Pound's is a moving
image that sweeps up particulars in the path of its emotional and
aesthetic energy. "Pound sees the condition of the modern mind
as a fractured stream," Duncan writes, "not as a construct."
Zukofsky, however, seeks a fully *attained* emotion that will be
"the product of a work, the poem a piece of work like a desk . . .
the prospect of constructing and attaining an object built up of
parts of 'emotion' in progress." As Zukofsky emphasizes in his
analogy of poetic craft with woodworking, the formal charac-
teristics of his composition will be more highly foregrounded in
a poem than they are in much of Pound's work. Form is not
opposed to artistic freedom in Zukofsky's poetry; rather, the
two impulses work together in what Duncan calls "the function-
alism of the modern style . . . to seek the essential in the working
articulation of the poem."[19] Objectivism's emphasis on sincerity
as a means of achieving form follows Pound's decree to reject
"abstraction," to "act upon particulars" as a way of avoiding
falseness or artificiality, and, in Carl Rakosi's words, "to present
objects in their most essential reality and to make of each poem
an object . . . meaning by this, obviously, the opposite of a sub-
ject, the opposite of all forms of personal vagueness."[20] The
sincerity of a poem and its level of "objectification" were seen as
the measures of the poet's craft. Thus, the first step toward
sincerity for the Objectivists was, as Hugh Kenner suggests,
"care for the single words" and often for the "little words . . .
like 'tree' and 'hill' " (and even smaller words such as "a" and

19. Duncan, "Reading Zukofsky," 424–25.
20. Rakosi, "A Note on the 'Objectivists,' " 36.

"the") whose semantic, syntactic, and sonic interaction with other words can be calibrated with mathematical precision.[21]

Zukofsky also contributed to the reception of Pound's work in two other ways: in making more explicit the musical analogy for poetic form and composition suggested in Pound's writings and taken up by, among others, Olson, Duncan, and Ginsberg; and in emphasizing the importance of "typography" as a "graphic representation of thought," a concept Olson developed further in "Projective Verse" (*PZ*, 17).[22]

With Duncan's support, Zukofsky became an important presence at Black Mountain, a "polar force" to Olson himself. In a sense, Zukofsky and Olson represented two sides of Pound's own work, each exemplifying tendencies that were anathema to poets in the other's camp.[23] Where Olson took on Pound's more grandiose poetic persona, proposing a "primordial, titanic, unaccountable spirit in poetry, beyond measure, where one could only take soundings and carry the compass in a boundless time and space," Zukofsky sought a poetry that enacted more rigorously the tenets of Imagism—the mathematical exactitude of a work "stripped to essentials" (*FC*, 213).

Robert Creeley was the poet at Black Mountain whose work was the most deeply indebted to Zukofsky's Objectivism. Creeley was introduced and "converted" to the work of Zukofsky by Duncan in 1955 and printed several of Zukofsky's poems in *Black Mountain Review*. Creeley subsequently wrote several articles on his Objectivist forebear and was instrumental in bringing him to greater recognition. While recognizing the differences between Zukofsky's art and Pound's, Creeley saw Zukofsky as following in the Poundian mode of attention to the interplay of sound, form, and meaning. Zukofsky shared with

21. Kenner, *A Homemade World*, 166.

22. Zukofsky's *"A"*, following *The Cantos*, takes the form of the fugue. Zukofsky defines the poem as "a context associated with 'musical' shape" (*PZ*, 16) and defines poetry as a function of "lower limit speech, and upper limit song"—a concise and evocative definition that appealed to later poets such as Creeley.

23. Duncan writes of Zukofsky and Olson: "Neither, certainly, could read each other at all. Devout followers of Olson must also have been puzzled by the importance Zukofsky had for Creeley and for me. And followers to the letter of Zukofsky can be found for whom he stands, even as against William Carlos Williams, as the one redeeming poet of his time" (*FC*, 213).

Pound "a particular sensitivity to the qualities in poetry of 'sight, sound and intellection' " (*QG*, 131).

Two poems from among those mentioned by Creeley demonstrate the aspects of Zukofsky's work that were most attractive to younger poets. One of Zukofsky's most impressive shorter poems, number 36 from the series *Anew* (1941), exemplifies many of the Objectivist qualities of his work:

> Strange
> To reach that age
>   remember
>   a tide
> And full
>   for a time
>   be young.[24]

Zukofsky's care for the sound of individual words and his sense of "form as measure" are both apparent here, as is the mode of strict "attention" to a given experience. All these elements combine to produce what Duncan calls an "emotion in progress," that intensification of direct experience leading to a state of sincerity. The poem enacts a tension between the movement toward stasis or completion and the reassertion of temporality and flux. This tension is reflected in the poem's graphic composition; the lines move backward and forward across the page, rotating around the centrally placed image of "a tide" — itself an embodiment both of constant change (toward death) and renewal.

The most important of Zukofsky's works for younger poets was the long poem *"A"*, an alternative to *The Cantos* and *Paterson* as a model for the development of the longer poetic form. Pound himself had admired Zukofsky's earlier work but found later sections of *"A"* too "mathematical," too far removed from "actual speech."[25] Duncan appreciated what Zukofsky had accomplished in his poetry: "In time we see that

24. Zukofsky, *All: The Collected Short Poems*, 106.
25. Duncan quotes Pound's notes to his *Active Anthology*: "One of my colleagues says he 'likes that mathematical use.' I think the good poem ought probably to include that dimension without destroying the feel of an actual speech. In that sense I like Zukofsky's earlier poem better than his later" (*FC*, 214).

increasingly *"A"* moves towards a speech specific to the poem itself, yet providing breakthrus [sic] of our common speech. . . . The 'feel' of actual speech has been enlarged to include in its range not only how we hear others talking but how others could talk" (*FC*, 214).

In tracing the evolution of *"A"*, we can fruitfully compare an early passage from section 2 (1928) with a later passage from section 22 (1970–73). The first passage, although it illustrates the clarity and immediacy of Zukofsky's vision as well as his precision of statement, is little more than an expanded Imagist moment:

> The music is in the flower
> Leaf around leaf ranged around the center;
> Profuse but clear outer leaf breaking on space,
> There is space to step to the central heart;
> The music is in the flower,
> It is not the sea but hyaline cushions the flower—
> Lifeforever, everlasting.[26]

The second passage achieves an intense formal compression through the use of five-line stanzas composed of five-word lines:

> Others letters a sum owed
> ages account years each year
> out of old fields, permute
> blow blue up against yellow
> —scapes welcome young birds—initial
>
> transmutes itself, swim near and
> read a weed's reward—grain
> an omen a good omen
> the chill mists greet woods
> ice, flowers—their soul's return[27]

Although my discussion just touches on the complexity in this passage, it is clear that Zukofsky goes beyond the original tenets of Objectivism in his interweaving of sonic, visual, and mental patterns and in his relative disregard for what Pound would have

26. Zukofsky, *"A"*, 7.
27. Zukofsky, *"A"*, 508.

considered clarity of statement. The characteristic reliance on a diction of precise images remains, as does the propensity for short, even monosyllabic words. But the poem's syntax (at least as traditionally understood) has been subordinated to other concerns: the free interplay of images; the musical effects of "tone leading" of vowels as well as various kinds of assonance, consonance, alliteration, and verbal repetition; and the mixing of registers of diction.[28]

Despite the continuing advocacy of poets such as Duncan and Creeley, the work of Zukofsky and the Objectivists was not recognized by the academy for more than a decade after the publication of Olson's "Projective Verse." This fact is hardly surprising given both the questionable academic status of Pound and his followers during these years and the radical departure Objectivist poetry represented from the poetic models taught in the age of New Criticism. It was not until the early experiments of the Language poets that Zukofsky became a seminal influence rivaling the importance of Pound and Williams.

Nevertheless, it was Black Mountain that provided the environment in which Zukofsky was first read and actively discussed and in which his influence contributed, along with that of Pound and Williams, to the postmodern poetic revolution of the early 1950s. As Black Mountain's rector and spiritual leader, Olson helped to form a new understanding of intellectual community, which included alternatives to canonical texts and authors. The Poundian vortex of writers, artists, and thinkers in various disciplines whose ideas Olson helped bring together embodied expanded possibilities for higher learning and allowed for an openness to traditions not prized by most institutions of Western academic thought.

28. The techniques adopted in Zukofsky's later poetry (such as the passage quoted from "A"-22) were to have their most pronounced influence not on the work of immediate descendants like Duncan and Creeley but on the later experiments of the Language group. See my discussion of Charles Bernstein in the Conclusion of the book.

4 HISTORY IN A CYCLOTRON

Charles Olson as Poet-Historian and the Model of Ezra Pound

> And why art is the only twin life has—its only valid
> metaphysic. Art does not seek to describe but to en-
> act. And if man is once more to possess intent in his
> life, and to take up the responsibility implicit in his
> life, he has to comprehend his own process as intact,
> from outside, by way of his skin, in, and by his own
> powers of conversion, out again.
>   Charles Olson, *Human Universe*

The next two chapters trace the evolution of Poundian poetics in the writings of Pound's most representative and influential descendant, Charles Olson. More specifically, I propose to outline the dynamics of influence within a tradition of historically based poetic writing. It is clear from my discussion of Pound's poetics in earlier chapters that one of its underlying principles is that of the "poem including history": of the poem adopting as its source and frame of reference not only poetic language and tradition but also a world exterior to literature whose social, cultural, and historical presence is in continual dialogue with the poet's aesthetic project. In this chapter and the next, I argue that in the act of revising Pound's poetics, Olson reiterates the Poundian paradigm of influence: a process involving the use of extrapoetic materials and the adoption of extraliterary stances. Because most previous studies of Olson have focused primarily on *The Maximus Poems* and have treated in some depth its relation to *The Cantos*, I focus my discussion on Olson's other writings: the prose essays in which he defines theoretically his own relation to poetic tradition and to the conventions of past literature and the shorter poems in which he most directly confronts that tradition, in particular "To Gerhardt, There, Among Europe's Things . . ." and "I, Mencius, Pupil of the Master."[1]

---

1. For studies focusing primarily or exclusively on *The Maximus Poems*, see Don Byrd, *Charles Olson's* Maximus; and Brian Conniff, *The Lyric and Modern*

Olson's understanding of the poetic process and the process of poetic influence and tradition was deeply informed by a broader understanding of history. Trained primarily as a historian rather than as a literary scholar and with no formal training as a poet, Olson displayed little interest in conventional discussions of literary issues or in attempts to define the poetic canon. Unlike Pound's approach to literary tradition—one marked by an intense engagement with the linguistic and stylistic features of poets such as Bertran de Born, Cavalcanti, Dante, and Villon—Olson's initial involvement with Pound and other writers was motivated primarily by a need to understand the historical and political consciousness underlying their work. In his 1946 essay "This Is Yeats Speaking," Olson commented on the psychopolitical situation of Modernists like Pound, addressing his own "postmodern" generation through the mask of Yeats. Olson proclaimed the Modernist "forerunners" to have been "out of phase" with the sequence of history and declared an "antithetical" stance for his generation, one that had to "hold the mirror up to authority, behind our respect for which lay a disrespect for democracy as we were acquainted with it" (*COEP*, 30).

If Olson's age, education, and literary background put him in a different sociohistorical "phase" from that of Pound, he shares with his predecessor the fundamental desire to locate himself in relation to the historical moments of previous poets and to understand the process of literary history as a manifestation of larger social or political forces. Both motivations run counter to a notion of poetic descent such as Bloom's, which attempts to separate the genealogy of poets from any reference to the historical events in which they are implicated. Olson's nonpoetic writings—as well as poems such as "A Lustrum for You, E.P.," "ABCs (3—for Rimbaud)," "La Preface," "La Torre," "To Gerhardt, There, Among Europe's Things . . . ," and "The Death of Europe"—reveal his need to deal directly with the historical

---

Poetry. The book-length studies by Robert von Hallberg (*Charles Olson: The Scholar's Art*) and Paul Christensen (*Charles Olson: Call Him Ishmael*) concentrate primarily on *The Maximus Poems* but give a fair amount of space to Olson's other poems as well.

reality embodied in his predecessors' works so as to define his own poetic stance. This reaction, whether accepting or rejecting, has its basis in, as Sherman Paul remarks, "history rather than spite or anxiety of influence."[2] As with Pound, influence for Olson is not only an interpersonal or a psychopoetic matter; it is a part of a more largely defined historical moment and signifies a rupture or continuity with the previous moment and its cultural matrix.

Central to Olson's poetic practice is his notion of the poet as historian. Beginning in the late 1940s and early 1950s, he took on the role of the literary or cultural historian Pound represented and of the historical researcher who seeks out the "elemental particles" that make up human life. These same materials became the building blocks for Olson's poetic project, which he had envisioned as early as 1945: "The need today is to make yourself a cyclotron to break down the matter into its elements. And it is that size of machinery because things are so dispersed and hidden today, as was the atom. It is true on all fronts: to get to the elements you must make yourself a huge hammer."[3]

Olson's metaphor of historical exploration is a radical reformulation of Pound's notion of the poet as archaeological archivist, whose task it is to sift through the rubble of past cultures for what Donald Davie calls the "imaginary museum." Olson's cultural and historiographical writings define a methodology capable of investigating and describing historical processes in ways that challenge Pound's more traditionally chronological system of periodization. Pound claims to represent all ages as contemporaneous; he seeks to understand the past, as he writes in *Guide to Kulchur,* not "in chronological sequence . . . but by ripples and spirals eddying out from us and our time."[4] To some extent, Pound succeeds in this endeavor; yet in the explicitly historical sections of *The Cantos,* Pound focuses on particular periods in Italian, American, and Chinese history, relying for his basic structure on a chronological sequence of historical events

2. Paul, *Olson's Push,* 9.
3. From Olson's notes, published in *Olson: The Journal of the Charles Olson Archives* 5 (1976): 19.
4. Pound, *Guide to Kulchur,* 60.

and on events in the lives of figures such as Sigismondo Mala-
testa and Thomas Jefferson. Olson seeks a historical methodol-
ogy that goes beyond Pound's in its radical dissection of inher-
ited systems and assumptions; above all, he wishes to examine
the archaeological data that provide an index to the daily lives of
people in past cultures. Pound's method is fundamentally that of
the nineteenth-century cultural archaeologist: he studies the cul-
tural archive for comparisons with, and supplements to, an
unfavorable present. Olson's method, exemplified by his work
on Mayan remains in the Yucatán, is in a more rigorous sense
that of the on-site archaeological researcher.[5]

Olson sees Pound as applying his methods only to what
remains within the "box" of historical time—Western civiliza-
tion since Homer and more specifically since the Renaissance. In
a 1953 appendix to his "Mayan Letters," Olson includes Pound
as one of the few authors who "applied [himself] to the study of
. . . history," but he criticizes Pound for his "admitted insistence
he will stay inside the Western Box, Gemisto, 1429 A.D., up"
(*SW*, 129). Olson wants to replace the "searchlight" Pound uses
in discovering his cultural *paideuma* with a "crowbar," a "ham-
mer," or even a "cyclotron," a more powerfully decentering
conceptual tool with which he hopes to "bust apart" the ossified
perceptions of Western culture and reach the "cutting edge"
where he will once again be in harmony with the "particulars"
of the world. Olson feels that Pound's efforts to redefine the
cultural archive are a useful beginning but that they do not go far
enough: "Cleanings, yes, but WE WANT SCOURINGS" (*COEP*, vol.
1, 92).[6]

---

5. In a letter Olson sent to Robert Creeley from the Yucatán, he outlines his
future plans to apply for Fulbright awards to do further archaeological digs:
"Next yr . . . to Yaxchilan; the next, to Iran, for similar gig!" Olson has ideas of
becoming a "professional" archaeologist and even considers taking "some job
with—o, say, Oriental Inst of Chicago, or, Kramer's U of P, to—go there and
look at other pots, other hooks & eyes" (*CORC*, vol. 6, 19).

6. As James Longenbach suggests, Pound's work may have forced him "to
think strenuously about the ontological status of history and the nature of
historical understanding," but I am skeptical of Longenbach's larger claim that
"the heart of Anglo-American literary modernism may be found in Pound's and
Eliot's attempts to negotiate between several conflicting types of historicism, and
discover a vitalizing attitude toward history" (*Modernist Poetics of History*, 12).

Various commentators have characterized the High Modernism of Pound, Eliot, and Yeats as a fundamentally reactionary mode in which history is viewed either as a factual source of "authority" or as part of a resurrected wealth of past knowledge needing only to be reclassified and reordered within the bounds of literary writing. In this context, postmodernism is Modernism's antithesis: it is associational, fragmented, random, and nonordered and represents history as "discourse" rather than as fact. To some degree, this opposition holds true in the case of Pound and Olson. If Pound defines *The Cantos* as a "poem including history," Olson seeks in *The Maximus Poems* a form that reflects more immediately the act of history itself. Pound's definition is essentially static; it implies a process whereby parts of history are inserted into, "contained" by, the poem. Olson's conception of "history as a verb" is active; it is always dependent on the reinterpretation of historical process by observer, reader, or listener. Olson's sense of history also frees it from a linear and causal understanding that is based on Western metaphysics and thereby dependent on ancient Greece, the source of modern Western civilization. To quote George Butterick, Olson's "postmodernist advance" beyond poets like Pound and Williams represents "a consciousness-change, a sense of sweeping anti-Westernism and de-rationalism, and a sense of the primordial as a value replacing previously dominant ones."[7]

Nonetheless, the notion of postmodernism as a reaction against Modernist models can be easily problematized in the case of Pound and American poetry: Ihab Hassan cites Pound's *Cantos* as one of the few points at which Modernism and postmodernism meet.[8] Pound's work is largely associational and fragmentary, engaging in what Hassan calls a "flirtation with incoherence," despite Pound's stated aim of "making it cohere." *The Cantos* is an ongoing and unending struggle to achieve form and coherence without formal and thematic closure. Pound is

---

For the most part, I concur with Olson that Pound's interest is more with specific historical figures and events than with historiography as discipline.

7. Butterick, "Charles Olson and the Postmodern Advance," 6.

8. Hassan, *The Postmodern Turn,* 34. Hassan also lists Dada, Surrealism, Joyce's *Finnegans Wake,* and the writings of Kafka.

fully aware of this aspect of his poetry: "Art quite possibly *ought* to be the supreme achievement, the 'accomplished'; but there is the other satisfactory effect, that of a man hurling himself at an indomitable chaos, and yanking and hauling as much of it as possible into some sort of order (or beauty), aware of it both as chaos and as potential" (*LE,* 396).

In reading Pound's quote after Olson's, we are invited to formulate a connection between Pound's "indomitable chaos," which must be "yanked and hauled" into ordered form, and Olson's "elements" needing to be broken apart by the violent means of a cyclotron. Unlike Pound, Olson is no longer interested in "dominating" a chaos but rather in exploring in painstaking detail the world around him. His metaphor is technological rather than personal and heroic; it suggests a "postmodern" process of fragmentation and reintegration rather than a Modernist ethos of masculine virility and physical force. Olson's conception is less concerned with control and order than with discovery. Yet despite their obvious differences, both quotes articulate a similar sense of violence in the interpretive and artistic act. Pound and Olson share an awareness that writing—or any form of creative endeavor—cannot take place before the writer or artist has first engaged in the laborious process of comprehending and assimilating the raw materials to be found in the surrounding world. Thus, Olson's postmodernism can best be seen not so much as a reaction against Pound's Modernist project but as an extension of the most extreme forms of Modernist practice.[9]

Olson's own use of the term *post-modern* does not refer primarily to a poetic context, or even to the context of literary history, but to a larger and more radical conception of an entirely new epistemology, "an alternative to the entire disposi-

---

9. As Fredric Jameson writes of the general relationship of postmodernism to High Modernism, "Radical breaks between periods do not generally involve complete changes of content but rather the restructuration of elements already given: features that in an earlier period or system were subordinate now become dominant, and features that were dominant now become secondary" ("Postmodernism and Consumer Society," 123).

tion of mind that has dominated man's intellectual and political life since roughly 500 B.C."[10] Olson's differences with early twentieth-century Modernism involve more than questions of poetic sensibility, style, or technique; they are inextricably linked to a reinterpretation of history and a different view of how best to appropriate history and historiography within a poetic praxis.

As much as Olson attempts to differentiate his historical consciousness from Pound's, his poetic is deeply indebted to the example of Pound as poet-historian. Even though much of Olson's later writing reflects a dissatisfaction with chronological "history" as a mode of relating to human experience, Olson should not be seen as antihistorical in any absolute sense. Instead, as Michael Bernstein suggests, Olson cautiously integrates Pound's notion of the "poem including history" into his own work.[11] Bernstein differs with Donald Davie, who cites Olson's criticisms of Pound's historical method as evidence that "Pound's disastrous career . . . will rule out . . . any idea that poetry can or should operate in the dimension of history."[12] Bernstein correctly argues that Olson's critique of Pound has more to do with the specific "materials" of history Pound examines than with the idea of historical poetry per se. Olson credits Pound with achieving in *The Cantos* a radical and necessary break with past poetic models; he has managed to "destroy historical time" in his poetry by adapting a "methodology" of "ego as beak" that allows him to cut through accumulated layers of historical exegesis to find the relevant or revelatory source.

Olson learned from several aspects of Pound's historical method: his treatment of specific "facts" of history and culture rather than abstract concepts as a means of arriving at a total cultural perception, or *Kulturmorphologie*; his ability to attach any concept, like that of *usura*, to a tangible or visible reality; and his interest in a record of oral history (the tale of the tribe). Olson also inherited Pound's distrust for the conventional writ-

10. Quoted in Butterick, "Charles Olson and the Postmodern Advance," 6.
11. M. A. Bernstein, *The Tale of the Tribe*, 239–40.
12. Davie, *Ezra Pound*, 244.

ing and teaching of history and his guiding belief in the need to examine primary sources and materials. It was through Pound that Olson was exposed to the ideas of two seminal historical thinkers: the cultural anthropologist Leo Frobenius and the economic historian Brooks Adams.

Yet despite the centrality of Pound's example to the development of Olson's historical poetic method, the practical reality of Pound as political and historical thinker became an increasing source of ambivalence for Olson. Olson found as early as his 1946 visits to Pound at St. Elizabeth's Hospital that his predecessor was "behind the times," a "cento man" with a "nineteenth-century stance." Olson wrote of Pound: "I think of the presence in his work of the worship for past accomplishments and a kind of blindness to the underground vigor of the present" (*COEP*, xvi). Olson's preference for "the underground vigor of the present," rather than for "the worship of past accomplishments," signaled a deep aversion to the use of history or literary tradition as a means of escaping or repressing a relationship with the present situation.

The impression of Pound that Olson took away from his visits was not principally that of a visionary poet, or even of the consummate artist and clear thinker Olson knew from Pound's writings, but rather of a misguided and sadly disillusioned man who was more preoccupied with economic theories than with poetry. Although Olson continued to view Pound's poetics as a central model, his experience of Pound as an anti-Semite, a fascist, and a traitor colored his feelings for Pound the poet as well and led him to reject aspects of Pound—aesthetic as well as political—that he could not condone or understand. Olson saw during his visits a "contradiction" in Pound and in his own curious involvement with this mentor: "The contradiction I am in here was exhibited all the time yesterday. Whenever Pound remained on the level of intellect and the creative he was dead right. . . . But wrong with the stink of death on all to do with politics and society" (*COEP*, 44–45). Olson's attempt at an explanation for the discrepancy between Pound the man and Pound the poet led him to speculate that "the only life he has lived is, in fact, the literary," so that "the verbal brilliance, delightful as it is, leaves the roots dry" (*COEP*, 97, 101).[13]

Nevertheless, Olson *had* been one of Pound's first and most vocal defenders at a time when such a position clearly represented an important (and potentially dangerous) engagement for a young poet.[14] As a politician turned poet who considered himself a fellow renegade from conventional society, Olson experienced at once an affinity for Pound, who always struggled to "keep his head above things, against the others, Eliot, Joyce, Lewis, Yeats even" (*COEP*, xvii), and a sense of disgust at Pound's political position, which Olson at first derided and later only pitied.

Olson identified Pound's failing not only as an individual one but more generally as a symptom of a tendency among writers and artists of the Modernist period to turn in their quest for a higher art to unacceptable political alternatives like fascism. Olson felt Pound and other Modernist writers had used "history" for their own ends: to build a case for the relative inferiority of the present state of civilization, an inferiority that could be rectified only by the establishment of standards of "culture" based on elitist models gleaned from the past. Pound's assignment of the "great men" of the past into a history divided into distinct periods and his explicit comparisons between these periods put an emphasis on chronology and causality that to Olson detracted from the immediacy of any truly engaged act. These comparisons created a hierarchical structure that failed to account for person or poet as he or she existed in the present environment. For Olson, it was the relevance of any historical

13. Olson at times criticizes the "gentilities" of Pound's literary method. Pound's genteel literary inclinations, Olson feels, often make his writing in *The Cantos* "more fine than strong" (*CORC*, vol. 2, 92). In his 1965 reading at the Berkeley poetry conference, Olson again differentiates his own concerns from what he sees as Pound's more "literary" agenda for poetry: "We're here to say something a hell of a lot more important than 'beauty is difficult' or than 'paradise is not artificial' " (*Muthologos*, 121).

14. Olson takes pride in the fact that he was one of the first to take a stand on the "Pound issue"—"on the record, Winter, 1945–46, THIS IS YEATS SPEAKING, in Partisan review, on the Pound case, (and not, notice, such late biz, as the Bollingen, but, the INDICTMENT, THE TREASON, the BIZ" (*LO*, 110).

moment to the "living present" that mattered, not "the passage of time and time's dreary repetition by monotony" (*SW*, 84).

Olson saw in Pound's attitude a desire to abandon the present, or "the only place where history has context" (*HU*, 137). Of course, Pound *did* attempt to update the past (to make it not only relevant but also analogous to the present situation) in books such as *Jefferson and/or Mussolini* and *Guide to Kulchur,* in his Dantean critique of modern civilization, and in his attacks on usury and economics in *The Cantos*. But for Olson, Pound's treatment of history (and thus his use of literary models, sources, and tradition) was compromised by a reliance on an "ego system" that prevented him from experiencing a present apart from the limiting and distorting optic of the past. Olson believed that Pound—either directly as cultural critic or indirectly through the guise of his poetic personae—had succeeded in attaching himself to the donatives of history, to the "grrreat men," so as to place himself directly in history. But Pound was able to triumph over time only by imposing his "ego position," a purely personal system of values that contradicted Olson's own sense of a communal relation to the world. Furthermore, Pound achieved his grip on the past through "nomination," by invoking predecessors, "intelligent men whom he can outtalk ... break[ing] all down to his equals or inferiors" (*SW*, 81). Although Pound's ability to "drive through ... time material" was admirable, his technique of "nomination" stood in the way, according to Olson, of "the ego as responsible to more than itself" (*SW*, 83). In other words, Olson suggested that history should consist not only of those "important" individuals with whom historians (and writers) have been concerned—Jefferson, Adams, Malatesta, Confucius, Dante—but with anyone or anything that is part of our past, the "*Z*'s and *X*'s" of the universe.

Pound's reliance on what Olson regarded as an elitist European "culture" bothered Olson particularly because Pound was an American who in embracing an almost completely foreign canon could be seen as turning his back on the cultural potential of his own land and people. In one of the letters Olson wrote to

Robert Creeley from the Yucatán, he praised Pound for having written "KULCH" (*Guide to Kulchur*) but criticized the political and historical consciousness displayed in much of Pound's other work. Pound's "19th century stance," his use of "culture" to attack "the State or the Economy," was nothing more than a self-satisfying "Bohemianism." Furthermore, the "materials of history" Pound found useful—classical civilization, the quattrocento, the Renaissance, eighteenth-century patrician America— were outmoded because their use was contrary to an understanding "that the substances of history now useful lie outside, under, right here, anywhere but in the direct continuum of society as we have had it" (*SW*, 83–84).

Olson's most trenchant critique of Eurocentric culture came in his review of Ernst Robert Curtius's *European Literature and the Latin Middle Ages*. Olson saw Curtius as contributing to "the historism plaguing all Europeans, and so the world, by proselytizing from the center," and Olson chastised him for the idea that "European culture, in contrast to all others, is an 'intelligible unit' of unique cast . . . apostolic and universal" (*HU*, 155). Olson would doubtless have associated Curtius's stance with that of Pound, who also privileged European culture over that of the Americas. Olson, however, preferred to follow Whitman and Williams in celebrating an America free from the time-bound cultural legacy of Europe and therefore capable of more vital artistic expression. As he had written several years earlier in *Call Me Ishmael:* "We are the last 'first' people." Olson commented laconically that even when Pound attempted to describe America, he showed no real understanding of its changing cultural potential: "What's shallow about [Pound's America] is the deadness of it, the 18th century lag in it, the moan for the lost republican purity, the wish to return America to its condition of a small nation of farmers and city-state patricians. . . . Pound can talk all he likes about the *cultural lag* in America . . . but he's got a 200 year *political lag* in himself" (*COEP*, 52–53).[15]

•   •   •

15. As mentioned in chapter 3, Williams served as an alternative to Pound in representing the "local" and embracing the present American scene. There is no doubt that Williams's later work modified Pound's influence on Olson in impor-

One of the poems in which Olson addresses most directly what he considers the fundamentally elitist position of Pound's writing is "To Gerhardt, There, Among Europe's Things, of Which He Has Written Us in His 'Brief an Creeley und Olson,'" written in 1951 and published in *Origin* the following winter. This poem, composed while Olson was living in the Yucatán, is an extremely important expression of his attitudes toward European culture in general and Pound in particular; Olson promotes the poem in a letter to Cid Corman as a poetic restatement—a "REMONSTRANDUM"—of the essay "Human Universe" (*COCC*, 241).[16] In his September 24, 1952, letter to Corman, Olson explains that the poem is an attack on Pound's "19th century act of 'epater les bourgeois,' the plain snottiness of same" (*COCC*, 289). Section 2 of the poem addresses Pound directly, accusing him of hypocrisy in his use of the important image that begins the *Pisan Cantos*: "The enormous tragedy of the dream in the peasant's bent shoulders" (*C*, 425). Olson writes Corman that Pound's poem, rather than enacting any meaningful relationship with the experience of an Italian peasant during the Mussolini regime, reflects only "the social snobbery and fascism of the Poundian kinetic." Olson concludes that "the whole Italian stuff, and Dante, is of this social order: the American upper middle class seeking a social home!" (*COCC*, 289). Olson's poem comments further on the "method" of Modernists like Pound who, "with much less reason, from too much economics speak / of the dream / in a peasant's bent shoulders, as though it were true / they cared a damn / for his conversation" (*CPO*, 289). In the course of the poem, addressed primarily to the young German poet Rainer Maria Gerhardt but with

---

tant ways. Nevertheless, Olson remained more strongly attracted to Pound's vision, which offered a more directly political agenda (albeit one that in many respects Olson disagreed with) than that of Williams. According to Olson, Williams's depiction of the local in *Paterson* fails in two respects. It is a picture of "blueberry America" (*SW*, 84), essentially out of touch with what Olson saw as the more hard-edged reality of current society; and it is limited—because of its reliance on the local and its lack of a far-reaching political agenda—to the experience and expression of a single individual, Williams himself (*LO*, 129).

16. I interpret Olson's term *remonstrandum* as a coinage of redemonstrandum: a "reexplanation" or "pointing out again."

frequent asides directed at Pound and Eliot, Olson exhorts his European contemporary to seek meaning somewhere other than in the Europe he now inhabits—one constituted by the same sense of a "dead center at the top of time" Olson criticizes in the Eurocentric historicism of Curtius and Arnold Toynbee. Gerhardt, whom Olson will later celebrate as "the first of Europe / I could have words with" and the "last poet / of a civilization," is here said to be "shut in" like Curtius and Pound by his understanding of European history and culture.[17] Olson encourages Gerhardt to "come out" by discovering one of two things: a past as it existed prior to the current state of Western civilization ("the other side of time") or the new sense of "space" offered by America. Olson presents Gerhardt with a vision of the American continent untainted by either the Poundian notion of place as "civilization" or the "proper nominative" through which Pound defines his sense of culture:

> I offer you no proper names
> either from great cities
> on the other side of civilization
> which have only to be visited
> to be got the hell out of, by bus
> or motorcycle, simply because place
> as a force is a lie.
>   (*CPO*, 213–14)

Olson also chastises Gerhardt for supporting such a "lie" in the extent to which he has "lightly borrowed men, naming them as though, / like your litany of Europe's places, you could take up / their power." Gerhardt cannot assume the power or "magic" of his predecessors merely by invoking them, just as Pound cannot create a vital *paideuma* with his "back references," his "ruins," and the "old pieces" he has picked up in Europe and China:

> Admitting that among the ruins
>   with a like schmerz in every vessel of his throat
>   he repeated, "Among the ruins, among them
>   the finest memory in the Orient"

17. See "The Death of Europe," Olson's 1954 elegy for Gerhardt, in *CPO*.

one will go about picking up old pieces
  bric-a-brac, he snorted, who did not know whereof he
    spoke
he had so allowed himself to be removed, to back-trail
or put it immediately out of the mind, as some can,
stuff the construction hole quickly with a skyscraper
                              (*CPO*, 216)

This passage characterizes Pound's failure in several respects, culminating in an image of the Modernist (fascistic) architecture of *The Cantos* (a perversion of epic form suggested by the impersonal modern structure of a "skyscraper"), a construction that represses those layers of human history or experience lying underneath the foundations of Western civilization.[18] As Olson writes in the contemporaneous essay "Human Universe": "Value is perishing from the earth because no one cares to fight down to it beneath the glowing surfaces so attractive to all" (*SW*, 59). Later in this poem, Olson admits that he is "envious" of both Gerhardt and Pound for their ability to "handle . . . large counters" (and for Pound's ability to win "prizes"), but at the

---

18. The passage also contains among its general criticisms of Pound at least two specific references. One is to a note Pound sent Olson on February 12, 1948, that included the admonishment "Don't bother me with a lot of 2nd hand mass produced brickabrak out of the 3 cornered corner what-not." On his last visit to Pound at St. Elizabeth's (three days earlier) Olson had apparently approached his elder with some of his ideas and was stung enough by Pound's dismissive reply that he sent him two notes reminding Pound of his earlier request to "let the traffick between us be complete." (All of these are unpublished materials housed in the Olson archives at the University of Connecticut, Storrs.) Although the correspondence between the two poets continued in limited form until the spring of 1949, Pound's refusal to give Olson what he considered serious consideration must have been one of the factors contributing to the eventual breakdown of their relations. Olson's reference to "bric-a-brac" is an ironic comment on what he sees as Pound's practice of "picking up old pieces." Olson ends "To Gerhardt . . ." with a reference to his own poetry of "anti-cultural speech, made up / of particulars only, which we don't, somehow confuse with gossip." Olson likens the cultural "name-dropping" in which he feels Pound engages to a kind of intellectual "gossip."

The second reference is to a moment documented in the seventh of the "Cantos" Olson wrote after his visits to St. Elizabeth's. Pound's lament that he had once had "the finest memory in the Orient" is taken by Olson as a sign of his "megalomania" (*COEP*, 81). Olson's use of the quote in "To Gerhardt . . ." is an ironic commentary on Pound's preference for the culture of the "oriental" world—Europe, Africa, and Asia—to that of the occidental world of the Americas (see *COEP*, 131–32).

same time he rejects the sense of hierarchy he sees as implicit in their work: "There are no broken stones, no statues, no images, phrases, composition / otherwise than / what Creeley and I also have." Instead, Olson offers Gerhardt the alternative world of the Mayan Indians—"the predecessors who, though they are not our nouns, the verbs / are like!" Gerhardt is invited to leave behind "Europe's things" ("there") and to "come here,"

> where we will welcome you
> with nothing but what is, with
> no useful allusions, with no birds
> but those we stone, nothing to eat
> but ourselves, no end and no beginning, I assure you
> (*CPO,* 219)

Along with Pound's vision of history, Olson rejects the metaphysic of Eliot's *Four Quartets*—"In my beginning is my end" / "In my end is my beginning." Eliot's Christian vision represents another form of Western "idealism" that attempts to classify experience rather than allowing for the phenomenal and multifaceted experience of the Mayan world as Olson depicts it in "Human Universe." Unlike Pound and Eliot, Olson will "sing" to Gerhardt in "our anti-cultural speech, made up / of particulars only."

Olson's attempt at a redefinition of "history" continued to dominate his thoughts and work throughout the early 1950s and was bolstered by his discovery in 1953 of the Greek historian Herodotus.[19] In a brief article "It Was. But It Ain't," Olson contrasts the historical method of Herodotus with that of Thucydides. Herodotus accepts as an important aspect of history the spoken record of the people themselves, the oral history of their experience; Thucydides gives credence only to "evidence" that is visibly ascertainable and that conforms to a preconceived notion of history supporting the interests of the state. The writings of Herodotus, Olson argues, have been suppressed by Western historians in favor of the more "conventional" Thucydides.

19. It was in this year, at any rate, that Olson began to mention Herodotus in his writings.

Such "human" accounts of history as those of Herodotus are judged to be "dangerous" for Western society because they challenge the status quo on which our "knowledge" is built. The untrammeled "energy" in personal accounts is unpredictable and thus a threat to all our institutions. Herodotus' method of oral "mythology" (from the root "muthos," the mouth) refuses to privilege the "objectively true" history of what "did happen," of "politics . . . as usual [in] the pursuit of gain." He claims instead, in Olson's words, that "the voice is greater than the eye" and that "truth is what is said, not what is seen" (*HU*, 142–43).

Olson's understanding of Herodotus, one heavily indebted to J. A. K. Thomson's *The Art of the Logos,* rests primarily on Olson's own interpretation of two key concepts: that suggested by the Greek root *istorin,* "finding out for oneself," and that of history as "mutho-logos, the practice of life as story" (*SVH,* 21).[20] This discovery of Herodotus reconfirmed Olson's long-held belief that "history" should reflect individual exploration and personal experience rather than doctrine or state ideology and that it should contain as much of the oral element as possible. It should also contain an element that has been lost to "historical" understanding since Socrates: the understanding of the world and events that we now call "mythology." Herodotus was the "last historian," Olson claims, because he was the last one "to be taken seriously as . . . a mythologist, a 'poet' " (*SVH,* 21).

Olson's subject, like that of Herodotus, consists increasingly in the histories of those individuals who are left out of history books. Olson attempts to explore such a history through the persona of Maximus, the Herodotean historian of Gloucester in *The Maximus Poems.* In "Letter 23" of the first book he writes, "I would be an historian as Herodotus was, looking / for oneself for the evidence of / what is said." In *Maximus* and elsewhere, Olson takes an interest in those aspects of history that are

20. For a discussion of Thomson's ideas and their impact on Olson, see George Butterick, *A Guide to "The Maximus Poems" of Charles Olson,* 145–47. Olson elaborates his formulation of Herodotus' historical stance on several occasions; see, for example, *Muthologos,* 3–4; and *SVH,* passim.

"ingrained in our daily lives" and that reflect "what man does," rather than "only what he has done" (*SVH*, 14, 26).

To describe "what man does," Olson adopts as an alternative to conventional history the method of "morphology." It describes the forms, origins, and functions of people and objects without relying on the "proper nominatives" that block off a more immediate understanding of historical phenomena and without relying too much on the chronological sequence of dates and events.[21] Olson lists the works of Frobenius (cultural morphology), Carl Sauer (morphology of landscape), and Brooks Adams (economic morphology) as well as Lawrence's *Studies in Classic American Literature*, Williams's *In the American Grain*, and Pound's *Guide to Kulchur* as important models of "morphological" study, a kind of work he claims "[too] few good men will bother with."[22] The morphological method of history Olson proposes concentrates not on political events but on the "forms" of human life represented by cities, colonies, and settlements; population migrations and adaptations to new environments; and demographic and technological change. In Olson's view, it is precisely these things, not the lives of famous people or the progress of political states, that should form the basis of history and of historically based poetry. "I see history as the one way to restore the familiar to us," he says, "to stop treating us cheap" (*SVH*, 29). Olson defines history as "the *function* of any one of us"; it is concerned not with "events of the past" or with the "news" as conveyed by "radios newspapers magazines mouth" but with the "life value" of the individual, his or her own "morphology" (*SVH*, 17–18).

21. Morphology is defined in the *American Heritage Dictionary* (1969) as "the biological study of the form and structure of living organisms." The term also has uses in the fields of geology (geomorphology) and linguistics ("the study of word formation, including the origins and functions of inflections and derivations").

22. All these works were central to Olson's crucial years of development as a writer: Olson was introduced to Frobenius and Brooks Adams by Pound in 1946 and discovered Sauer's work on a visit to California in 1947. The works of Pound, Williams, and Lawrence, of course, laid an even earlier foundation for Olson's ideas.

As early as 1947, Olson had the idea for a poem to be called "Red, Black, and White," a "morphological study" of the role of different racial groups in the American West. Olson's interest in the "morphology" of the American continent was further evidenced in his plans and research for a long poem called "West," which, had it been written, would have been even more ambitious in scope than *The Maximus Poems*. The same preoccupation was exhibited in his "Bibliography on America for Ed Dorn," in *Call Me Ishmael;* in his essays on Mayan culture in *Human Universe;* and in the topoi of mapping, sea voyage, and geological landscape in *The Maximus Poems*. Olson continued to believe that a study of America had to be deeply connected with an awareness of the influence of environment on history.[23] It had to be geographical as well as temporal, taking "space (rather than time) to be the central fact to man born in America."[24]

Pound's work also contains elements of what can be called "geographic imagination": his use of "periplum" or sea voyage as a central trope and structural device and the exactitude of geographical detail in parts of *The Cantos*. After all, it was Pound who had first, in Olson's estimation, turned time "into what we now must have, space & its live air" (*CORC,* vol. 5, 49–50). Pound's use of geography provided an important basic model for later works, such as Williams's *Paterson* and Olson's *Maximus*. But those Cantos in which Pound addresses American history, rather than that of Europe or Asia, are devoted primarily to ideas of government and economics; they display a lack of geographic texture, and they evince little of Olson's interest in exploring the influences of geography on the American experience.

Olson, by contrast, engages in the earlier sections of *The Maximus Poems* in a sustained experiment in morphology. In his attempt to rediscover "history" as "a new localism, a polis to

23. Robert von Hallberg cites Olson's continuing belief in Frederick Jackson Turner's thesis of the influence of physical environment, especially that of the frontier, on American history (*Charles Olson,* 236).
24. Olson, *Call Me Ishmael,* 11.

replace the one which was lost . . . from 490 B.C. on" (*SVH*, 25),
Olson includes in the poem both spoken and written narratives,
thus foregrounding the communal life of the town and the local
organization of daily life. He also explores in some detail the
geographical and topographical contours of Gloucester and its
environs as well as other areas along the New England coast.
Thus, the poem reiterates Olson's historical method: his inclu-
sion of local documents, his use of oral history to "mythologize"
the life of a particular locale, and his awareness of human life
unfolding through social community and relationship to the
surrounding environment all contribute to the poem's sense of
immediacy.[25] As Don Byrd suggests, Olson's poetry differs from
that of Pound and other Modernists in not being determined by
the kind of historical information that serves as the basis for
Modernist works. Olson allows "the energy of the poem to arise
directly from its sources," thereby gaining "an immediacy of
mythic and historical material which is missing in modernist
poetry."[26]

Olson's poetics of immediacy, one he had cultivated since the
time of "Projective Verse," was further supported by the notion
of "process" he found in Alfred North Whitehead's *Process and
Reality*. According to Whitehead, the process of form making
that is at the basis of any artistic expression begins with a
"conflict" between the individual and perpetual chaos, the "mul-
tiples" that surround him or her. Such a conflict results initially
in the need for the individual artist to "impose his or her order
of order on the multiples." In the final stage of the creative act,
the poet must gather back into his or her own experience those
areas previously excluded in the desire to form a coherent per-
sonal order. It is at this stage that the poet must actualize the
potential for "acquiring real unity with other entities" so as to
move from the "private individual fact" into the "passing on" of
energy that defines artistic creativity.[27]

25. The documents to which Olson refers include town records, deeds and
wills, account books, family papers, maps, and local histories found in libraries
up and down the coast of New England.
26. Byrd, *Charles Olson's* Maximus, 25.
27. Whitehead, *Process and Reality*, 245.

For Olson, as for Whitehead, artistic creation is an organic process involving an "autoclytic multiplication," or "the chance success of a play of creative accidents" (*SVH*, 49). In contrast to Pound, for whom the poetic process involved a "yanking and hauling" of chaos into ordered form in an attempt to "make it cohere," Olson argues that within the "space-time continuum" he now takes history to be, "kosmos is history, and therefore alternatively chaos" (*SVH*, 49). The individual must continually create self and world out of this chaos, at each moment establishing a new order, a new beginning. "Coincidence" and "proximity" replace the static notion of the "aesthetic" that determined the possibility of "creative success" as defined by the old order—that of Pound as well as Socrates.

In conjunction with Olson's adaptation of the ideas and terminology of Whitehead came an increasing interest in the thought of Carl Jung. By the early 1950s Olson had begun reading and assimilating Jung's writings, which appear to have provided much of the impetus for Olson's notion of the projective in "Projective Verse" as well as important material for the later sections of *The Maximus Poems*.[28] Jung's essay "On Synchronicity" had particular relevance for Olson; in it Jung defines a relation between events that are not causally connected but that are linked by their simultaneous experience of a given archetype. This view, as Charles Stein notes in his book on Jung and Olson, has much in common with Olson's method of describing historical events outside of any causal or chronological sequence, as if revealing in their juxtaposition "inherent schemes of order" that can be grasped only within a space-time matrix independent of a diachronic understanding of experience.[29]

Olson's changing view of history and chronology and his changing conception of the poetic process contributed to equally

28. See the discussion in Charles Stein, *The Secret of the Black Chrysanthemum*, especially 25–32.
29. See ibid., 23. Olson's concomitant use of the scientific discoveries of early atomic physics, especially Werner Heisenberg's uncertainty principle, may be a related attempt to describe events in the physical world in such a way as to reflect a new epistemological orientation emphasizing contingency rather than causality.

dramatic changes in his stance toward literary influence and tradition. Although at the time of *Call Me Ishmael* he had stressed the influence of Shakespeare and Homer in his reading of Melville's work, Olson evinced in his later writings little or no interest in the notion of literary influence as such, a concept he came to see as reflecting an outmoded and unnecessarily dualistic understanding of experience. In fact, one of the aspects of Pound that Olson valued most was his stubborn rejection of a tradition composed of the established canon of writers. In a letter to Cid Corman dated October 8, 1950, Olson complained of the tendency of literary magazines to print only work reflecting a narrowly defined "literary inheritance." Citing Eliot's sense of "tradition and the individual talent" as the guiding mentality of the "little mags," he offered Pound's eclectic method as a better model for dealing with the past. The "drive" and "energy" of Pound's active engagement with history, Olson claimed, allowed him to "use" the past without falling into Eliot's "human positionalism"—a belief in the primacy of "tradition" or of the "past for its own sake" (*LO*, 6).

Olson's poetic mode of allusion by direct quotation places his texts in the same kind of dialogic relationship with his predecessors that Pound establishes vis-à-vis his sources. As in Pound's work, the inclusion of fragments of past discourse emphasizes the poem's relationship to space and time and thereby extends the poem beyond a purely intertextual realm in which other poems are its only referent. Furthermore, Olson's use of quotation contributes to what Robert von Hallberg calls the "scholar's art": a formulation of philosophical, historical, and methodological principles that can be conveyed to the reader and to a new generation of poets through the poetry itself as well as through classroom teaching and lectures, nonpoetic writings, and personal contact and example. The poet, in Olson's view, has a responsibility to help other members of society to interpret the world: "The poet is the only pedagogue left, to be trusted" (*HU*, 19).

Nonetheless, Pound's use of models and sources, radical as they are within a still more confined tradition of English and American literature, are so tied to a culture based on Western literary, artistic, and epistemological systems as to prove of little value to Olson. Although Olson's stance toward Pound does not represent a wholesale rejection of Western cultural artifacts, as some critics contend, it does cause Olson to be extremely selective in his choices of valid literary and historical material. Olson is not interested in those "donative" figures whom Pound judged "important" according to his criteria for intellectual or literary excellence; rather, Olson is drawn to those artists or thinkers he considers to be "of essential use" to the needs of the present and to the formulation of a "projective," "post-modern" stance. Pound's donative artists, by reflecting on their own period, represent for him a moment of cultural renaissance that will form, by comparison, an implicit critique of modern culture. Olson takes Pound to task for just such a use of the past as a means of criticizing or dismissing the present.

Instead, Olson conceives of an ideal creative process free from the weight of past discourse: "My shift is that I take it the present is prologue, not the past. Is its own interpretation, as a dream is, and any action—a poem, for example. Down with causation. . . . And yrself: you, as the only reader and mover of the instant. You, the cause. No drag allowed, on either. Get on with it."[30] If present experience can be liberated from reference to the past, then the poet can be liberated from reference to previous literary models, and the traditional distinction between poetic writing and the creative potential contained in everyday life will lose its validity:

> And it struck me . . . that poetry, as being written today, especially by or in our language, yields a future that is unknown, is so different from the assumptions that poetry has had, in our language, that the life one lives is practically the condition of the poetry, rather than the poetic life being a thing in itself. And one could almost say that these two words today [life and poetry] have practically flown together, *flowed* . . . together.[31]

Olson did not discover the writings of Whitehead until 1954, but long before he was to use Whitehead's theories to help explain his own process Olson had established a mode of writing

30. Olson, *Additional Prose*, 39.
31. Olson, *Poetry and Truth*, 12.

that clearly showed his dissatisfaction with a reliance on past models. Olson's characteristic style was from early on highly idiosyncratic, decentering, and confusing to readers expecting the structure of traditional logic. His use of incomplete sentences or fragments, his twisted or truncated syntax, his unusual and often disconcertingly personal method of punctuation, his colloquial and consciously unacademic diction, and his frequent capitalizations, abbreviations, and repetitions all contribute to the sense of a spontaneous, undigested, and destructured discourse. Olson's use of commas, for example, to separate the sentence into smaller units of thought or breath, rather than into larger syntactic units, gives the impression of raw thought or utterance as it comes to the mind unmediated by the strictures of past usage. In the same way, his unclosed parentheses represent visually and syntactically the unfinished thought, the lack of any final closure in a given pronouncement. Both Olson's prose and poetry are left syntactically open, naked to the eye of the reader. We must attempt to understand not only the work's meaning—that place it holds as argument within the context of other discourses—but also the way in which it represents the operations of the writer's mind and records his voice and breath visually on the page.

Olson, then, adopts not only a radically new social and epistemological orientation but an equally radical discourse within which to express his ideas. His idiosyncratic mode of writing allows him to adjust quickly to his topic, mood, or environment; it also allows him to react to ideas and events as they strike him, without acceding to the rules of scholarly or even socially acceptable discourse. For Olson, the "self" is not constituted primarily by reading previous texts and reacting in similar language to what is read. Instead, the self is a complex mechanism composed of biological, psychological, social, and historical factors. It is a mechanism that ideally is ready to respond to all stimuli, to "read" physical relationships in the world just as members of Western society read books. For Olson, the modern Western "self" has been too greatly derived from a belief in the centrality of society and "culture," of "history as such"; not enough attention has been paid to the individual's place in a cosmic or biological frame of reality.

Against Pound's singular vision of "kulchur," the highly personalized and idiosyncratic collection of "luminous details" from a European past that the focusing vortex of his ego seeks to unite, Olson places a vision of the communal, of the "human universe." Olson gains an appreciation for the importance of a unified communal vision as well as for the person's direct relation to the immediate environment from his study of the past and present cultures of the Yucatán. Among the present-day descendants of the Mayan culture, Olson finds a "harmony with the universe" made possible by a concrete and particularized notion of the physical world.

In his "Mayan Letters" Olson expresses his belief in the more accurate sense of the human being's place held by the ancient Mayans and maintained to some degree among the modern-day inhabitants of the Yucatán. Instead of depending, as Western societies do, on a narrow "humanism" defined by "a whole series of human references," Mayan civilization valued human participation as "object" in a "field of force" defined by the larger world of nature (*SW*, 112). In modern Western culture, the person's "miscentered" and hierarchical frame of reference distorts his or her relation to the object world. The Mayan culture offered Olson an alternative notion: that of a "self" in direct contact with the environment.

This same desire for an unmediated relation with the object world is reflected in the poetics Olson outlines in "Projective Verse." Just as with objects in nature, the "objects" in the poem must be treated without regard to "any ideas and preconceptions from outside the poem." Olson seeks to allow the "speech-force of language back" into poetry, so that "by speech, solidity, everything in it can now be treated as solids, objects, things . . . allowed to have the play of their separate energies." A mode of writing structured by the force of speech, rather than by imposed linguistic and stylistic conventions, represents a rupture with traditional forms of logos, a break "which brings us up, immediately, against tenses, in fact against syntax, in fact against grammar generally, that is, as we have inherited it." The act of "speech" enacts an involvement with nongrammatical factors such as the breath and the fractured nature of thought, which resist the structures of inherited convention and lead to a more fragmented and spontaneous syntactic field: "Do not tenses, must they not also be kicked around anew, in order that time, that other governing absolute, may be kept, as must the space-tensions of a poem, immediate, contemporary to the acting-on-you of the poem?" (*SW*, 20–21).

Olson's implicit questioning of grammar and convention in his own writing and his directed attack on them in his poetics are part of the larger question he attempts throughout his later life to answer: "how far a new poet can stretch the very conventions on which communication by language rests." Olson seeks a poetic language and style that achieve in their break with past discourse and tradition new and as yet untapped possibilities of expression: "It is my impression that *all* parts of speech, suddenly, in composition by field, are fresh for both sound and percussive use, spring up like unknown, unnamed vegetables in the patch, when you work it, come spring" (*SW*, 21).

Olson's vegetable metaphor for poetic language points toward his belief in an organic relationship between language and nature, one that allows for linguistic structures not dependent on "historical" measures of writing. Although Olson is capable in his own writing of intricate tonal effects, he disapproves of "a largeness of tone" at the expense of the personal rhythms generated by the poet's own breath and voice. Olson suggests that to find his or her "rhythmic" energy in nature, a person must replace the dominant Western tradition of "knowledge-without-respect-for-rhythm" with a notion of art as "act," originating in rhythmic impulse: "The point is, energy is only prime to nature. And nature is not man. Man is artist, or he does not live; his act (the act which makes him rival of nature) is ART. This is his special attribute, the distinguishing one: that he can make forms, using nature's energy, which are as prime & essential as nature's forms" (*CORC*, vol. 7, 240).

In the kinetic art Olson envisions, writing would not be based on inherited forms that engender a mechanical reproduction of art as "produce." Instead, writing would find its impulse in those means of expression that contain a sense of the immediate confrontation with the rhythmic and spatial world: dance, music, and the human voice. For Olson, the content and emotional impulse of the poem should never be subjugated to the necessity for a culturally or canonically determined tone, form, or music; as he writes to Cid Corman, the work should not have any largeness "beyond your own size—which again is a matter of YR RHYTHM" (*LO*, 84).

According to Olson, Pound is often guilty of such an all-encompassing "largeness" of poetic and historical vision that he fails to register his own impulses, moving instead into "that selection out of, that 'the light in the conversations of—the letters of—the intelligent ones,' or at least the literate ones" (*HU*, 112). Olson compares Pound to a "ping-pong ball" that bounces off the exteriors of people and things without examining their internal natures. Olson sees writers such as Herman Melville and D. H. Lawrence as exemplifying the opposite tendency, "the ability to go *inside* a thing, and from its motion and his [motion] to show and to know, not its essence alone . . . but its *dimension*, that part of the thing which ideality . . . tended to diminish" (*HU*, 112).

What Western philosophical traditions of ideality, logic, classification, and causality have replaced is the notion of a rhythmical interaction with nature that allows, in Olson's terms, for a physical engagement with the spatial dimension of the object world. A loss of respect for the world's rhythms has caused our "acts," and thus our writing, to go "askew" over the course of the past two millennia. We can restore ourselves and our literature only when we face the immense task, the post-modern imperative, of living and writing in the "instant" and thus of risking "havoc and wreck" (*HU*, 113). It is only by returning to the sense of relevance conferred by an "actual earth of value"—a meaningful relationship to an external, "objective" reality—that the poet can reestablish a place in the world and thereby engage "history" as a kinetic reenactment of life itself.

5 OLSON AS MENCIUS
AND HIS MASTER, POUND

A Study in Poetic Tradition

Most critical discussions of Olson touch in some way on his relationship to his Modernist predecessors Pound and Williams. Olson's relationship to both poets has been explored at some length, yet the issue of Olson's general attitude toward influence and tradition is still contested. Some critics consider Olson little more than an "imitator" of the work of such predecessors; others view him as a radically antitraditional poet who sought to create his own idiosyncratic poetic system through a wholesale rejection of past systems of discourse. In the last chapter, I argued that even though Olson learned a great deal from Pound's ideas and practices, his critique of Pound's historical method and awareness led him to question some of the fundamental assumptions behind the work of his Modernist forebear. In this chapter, my reading of Olson's 1954 poem "I, Mencius, Pupil of the Master ... " elaborates a paradigm for Olson's relation to predecessors and tradition and indicates that his navigation between complete rejection or acceptance of the Pound tradition informs poetic decisions in such areas as form, syntax, and diction.[1]

1. Several critics deal at least briefly with the question of Olson's relation to his predecessors and to tradition. In this chapter, I address in some detail discussions by Paul Bové and Marjorie Perloff. Also see von Hallberg, "Olson's Relation to Pound and Williams"; Riddel, "Decentering the Image"; Altieri, "Olson's Poetics and the Tradition"; Butterick, "Ezra Pound and the 'Truculent Ummugrunt' "; and Harper, "The Sins of the Fathers." Seelye, *Charles Olson and Ezra Pound*, remains a basic source of information on Olson and Pound. General studies of Olson, such as those of von Hallberg, Paul, Christensen, and

To arrive at a more just and accurate sense of Olson's relation to his tradition, I pay more careful attention than previous critics to the evidence provided by an early draft manuscript and later corrections of "I, Mencius . . ." as well as to other biographical material relating to the writing of the poem. In the second half of the chapter, I explore the valences of particular metaphors in the poem. I conclude that "I, Mencius, Pupil of the Master" not only foregrounds what were for Olson central issues of influence and tradition but also creates its own metaphors to describe the actual process of influence.

In Olson's important correspondence with Robert Creeley we find a continual and profound involvement with the work, the ideas, and at times the personalities of both Pound and Williams. But as Olson writes Creeley of his debt to Pound: "This whole question [of influence] is intricate" (*CORC*, vol. 7, 244). Olson goes on to explain in this letter of October 3, 1951, that he cannot accept being labeled an "imitator" of Pound, even given that he finds many of Pound's ideas useful or illuminating. In an August 4, 1951, letter two months earlier Creeley had written of a "tradition" that "preserves itself" without the "buttressing of imitation." In other words, for Creeley the work of the poets of the tradition of Whitman, Pound, and Williams is "in each case peculiar to the intelligence, the body, involved in the expression" (*CORC*, vol. 1, 53).

Olson's reply suggests an attitude similar to Creeley's but even more adamant about reserving a place for the individual poet within his or her tradition: "My sense is, that right here is *tradition,* that, the work we value, especially when the man is alive behind us, is to be gone by" (*CORC*, vol. 7, 244). Olson

---

Bernstein, take a middle road in characterizing Olson's relation to Pound as primarily positive but problematic. Byrd, in *Charles Olson's* Maximus, is perhaps too negative in his assessment of Olson's reaction to Pound, asserting that Olson's terms *projective* and *prospective,* for example, are intended to distinguish his practice from Pound's "fascist" and "retrospective" one. Riddel traces in Olson a development of Pound's own implicit critiques of logocentrism. Altieri discusses Olson's Objectivism as a reorientation of the "Romantic meditative mode," and Butterick and Harper address Olson's relation to Pound's Modernist poetic.

further explains his position in an October 12 letter to Creeley: he complains about "this easy business of" comparisons between him and Pound ("to beat me with that stick") but at the same time recognizes Pound's importance, along with D. H. Lawrence, as one of the "two men [who] stand forth out of the half century." He hopes that the critics, especially "those who still pipe for T. S. E[liot]," will "for christ sake, just give me my air, whatever it is—the issue, anyway, will only emerge in the issue" (*CORC*, vol. 8, 44–45).

On one of the few later public occasions in which he addresses the question of influence—his essay on Melville's *Billy Budd* entitled "David Young, David Old"—Olson presents the relationship between Hawthorne and Melville as one that eventually detracted from the younger Melville's gifts as a writer. Comparing the labored writing of *Billy Budd* with what Olson sees as the more naturally written *Moby-Dick,* Olson concludes that *Billy Budd* fails in being of "magnitude proper to the man [but] proffered in the style and process of another" (*HU*, 107–8). Olson implicitly lays the blame for this failure at Hawthorne's feet because between the original version of the tale as Melville first conceived it and his subsequent rewriting of it, "Hawthorne intervened, and stole a strength away." Olson's essay emphasizes his own predilection for Melville's more "spontaneous" art over the more self-consciously literary style of Hawthorne. The essay also indicates Olson's attitude toward influence in general: that to think too much about a predecessor, to "work over" those impulses that come spontaneously from inside oneself by using "the hand of" another, detracts from the strength and vitality of the writing and "thickens the blood around the heart."

Olson's description of the relationship between Hawthorne and Melville can apply equally to his own literary apprenticeship with Pound. Although the difference in age between Pound and Olson was substantially greater than between Hawthorne and Melville, and their personal interaction came early in the younger writer's career, rather than late, Pound was one of Olson's proclaimed "father figures," fulfilling much the same role as Hawthorne had for Melville. Indeed, it is tempting to read Olson's account of this relationship—and by analogy his relationship to his own predecessors—as a typical instance of Bloomian "anxiety." We may even propose the following twist to Bloom's paradigm: by misreading *Billy Budd* (Melville's "crisis poem") as a case of an ephebe's work destroyed by an older writer's influence, Olson may fail to realize that the writing of *Billy Budd* is made possible only by Melville's sublimation of the "stronger" Hawthorne. Melville is relatively passive in this process and unaware, it would seem, of the repressed hand of Hawthorne in his own work.

But we can take this analogy too far: if Melville is not cognizant of this process, Olson certainly is. As Robert von Hallberg remarks, Olson not only recognizes the impossibility of true originality in poetry but actually aims "at a language that deliberately and conspicuously denies itself originality."[2] Feelings of poetic "anxiety" and competition are not unknown to Olson, but he lessens the weight of such anxieties by the projection of his mental energies into vastly diverse areas of knowledge and speculation. His eclecticism, like Pound's, extends outside the boundaries of a single period, a single culture, or a single discipline to form a personal vortex of usable ideas.[3]

In *Destructive Poetics*, Paul Bové describes what he sees as Olson's "antitraditional" or "destructive" tendencies. Bové emphasizes Olson's subversion of the mainstream critical tradition represented by the New Criticism, a tradition whose "imposed, teleological, ironic, atemporal, distanced structures" and "traditional language of abstract concepts and ironic symbols" falls within "the continuous linearity of the Western onto-theological tradition."[4] Bové attempts to show how both Olson and Whitman resist the attempts of the New Critics, as well as those of

2. Von Hallberg, *Charles Olson,* 39.
3. A perusal of the checklist of Olson's reading compiled by George Butterick in *Olson: The Journal of the Charles Olson Archives* (1974–76) demonstrates the truth of this assertion. Also revealing is the bibliography to Butterick, *A Guide to* The Maximus Poems," in which he cites the range of works Olson used in writing his epic.
4. Bové, *Destructive Poetics,* xv.

neo-Romantic critics like Harold Bloom, to appropriate their work into a "tradition."

Bové's discussion raises important questions about the role of critical orthodoxies in canonizing poetic writing. Nevertheless, despite the polemical attractiveness of Bové's conception, it seems clear that Olson recognizes and belongs to a tradition, if not the one Bové identifies as *the* tradition. Indeed, Olson's work is deeply involved with the tradition of open-form poetry established by Whitman, Pound, Williams, Crane, Cummings, and the Objectivists.[5] For Olson, as for Pound, tradition is not simply an unchanging, idealized order needing to be "destroyed." On the contrary, the "tradition" to which Olson belongs is constituted by a dynamic and nonexclusive system of poets, poems, and institutions. It is true that Olson's stance resists certain aspects of tradition: those having to do with inherited literary and social forms and with the modes of experience that inform a poetics.[6] Olson's work, however, does exist and operate as part of a tradition — to deny this would be to deny the importance of "Projective Verse," which depends so heavily on its references to the earlier movement of Pound's Imagism, and to deny the importance of the institutionalization of Olson's poetics at Black Mountain and more generally among younger poets. Olson's link to tradition is expressed largely through his appreciation of the value of community (Black Mountain as a little "city," for example). Olson's notion of "tradition" is not so much that of a chronologically based "line" marked by shared influences as of a group of poets who share an environment and a sense of poetic process.

In light of this understanding, Bové's conclusions about Olson and tradition seem oversimplified:

> "Tradition" cannot be fixed as any canon of works or even any canon of interpretations. There are as many "traditions" as there are

5. As Ekbert Faas remarks, Olson was able to state "as early as 1953, at the height of Eliot's fame and influence," that the line of Pound, Williams, Crane, and Zukofsky would replace the school of Eliot as "the great and future school of American poetry" ("Charles Olson and D. H. Lawrence," 115).

6. Olson repeatedly rejects traditions of poetry that rely on "the interference of the lyric ego"; he instead prefers a poetics that encompasses various life experiences not tied to a Western cultural tradition.

authentic poets of destruction who look with their eyes at the world about them and who imitate Herodotus as historian and try to find out things for themselves. . . . It is precisely the "freedom" from any definitive "tradition" which prevents any feelings of anxiety in Olson about his relation to the past. . . . Indeed, Olson's liberty from the burden of the past comes from his insistence that the poet must stand in a destructive, not an imitative, relation to the past, with the result that the past is seen in all its uncertainties, ambiguities, and contradictions, and not in the formal certainty of an aesthetic fiction.[7]

Bové's analysis of Olson's debt to his predecessors disregards several important facts. First, even though Olson does not particularly favor a "canon of works or . . . interpretations," his use and discussion of other poets, especially Pound, demonstrate a recognition of a tradition of American avant-garde and Modernist writing that displays a greater degree of shared practices and ideas than Bové's comments suggest. Olson would not concur with the notion of a different tradition for every poet.

Second, Olson is no more interested in "destruction" as a poetic mode than in "imitation." His poetics seeks to use materials of the past to construct a new sense of reality for the present and future. Those aspects of Olson's project that Bové links with "deconstructing" a tradition—"taking a personal look at the facts" and destroying "the completed linguistic form"—are not so much antitraditional as representative of the poetic practice poets such as Pound and Williams made possible.

Finally, Olson's writings do reveal "feelings of anxiety about his relation to the past." Although these feelings seem more a result of the burden placed on him by critics ready to dismiss him as a "Pound imitator" than by the canon or by a Bloomian tradition of the Sublime, the feelings exist nonetheless, at times quite visibly. Olson realizes that no relationship of the artist to the past can be wholly "imitative" or wholly "destructive"; both elements must be present in the genesis of any significant work of art.

Marjorie Perloff's attempt to characterize Olson's relation to his poetic tradition takes the approach opposite to that of Bové.

7. Bové, *Destructive Poetics*, 270–71.

She suggests that Olson's relationship to Pound and Williams is purely imitative. Perloff discredits the originality of Olson's "Projective Verse" by placing quotations from Olson's text side by side with similar passages in Pound and Williams. She then proceeds to read "I, Mencius, Pupil of the Master" in light of the poetics outlined in "Projective Verse." In a somewhat cursory discussion of the poem, Perloff states that the poem is "flat," that it is "no more than a superficially clever poem," that it "basically restates the same theme over and over again," and that it is "not in any way remarkable in terms of its prosody" (*OIP*, 299).

Despite Perloff's important scholarship in the field of modern poetics and her valuable exegesis of Pound's work and the "experimental" poetic tradition, I differ with her undeservedly negative portrayal of Olson's writing vis-à-vis his derivation from Pound and Williams. Perloff's emphasis on Olson's lack of both originality and generosity misrepresents his literary achievement. As I read him, Olson is not only an enormously creative poet but also a writer well aware of his place within a tradition and highly respectful of the work of predecessors within that tradition.

Perloff claims that "Projective Verse" "is hardly the break-through in literary theory that it is reputed to be" and that it is "essentially a scissors-and-paste job, a clever but confused collage made up of bits and pieces of Pound, Fenollosa, Gaudier-Brzeska, Williams, and Creeley" (*COIP*, 295). Although Olson's manifesto is partially based on ideas previously articulated by other writers, this does not in itself constitute a substantive criticism of Olson's essay. Olson certainly makes no secret of the fact that he picks up where Pound and Williams left off. Nor does Olson share Perloff's idea of originality; for him, adopting and revising the terminology of other writers are ways of paying them homage while renewing a discourse that can be shared by a particular community and can serve as a common language of usable materials. Olson's use of the ideas of his predecessors and contemporaries is not fundamentally different from the way in which Pound himself constantly adapted his own ideas about poetry both from contemporary sources—Wyndham Lewis,

T. E. Hulme, Ford Madox Ford, Remy de Gourmont, Basil Bunting, C. H. Douglas, Gaudier-Brzeska, Fenollosa, and Frobenius—and from earlier "authorities" such as Confucius, Cavalcanti, and Erigena. In fact, the incorporation of ideas and quotes taken directly from other sources is characteristic of poets in the Pound tradition, and Pound's example no doubt gave later poets permission to exercise the same liberty.

Particularly troubling to Perloff is what she perceives as Olson's overly hostile attitude toward Pound and Williams. But a full examination of the facts reveals that Olson's relationship to these two poets is more complex than Perloff's analysis suggests. Olson does not *reject* influence, although some of his comments quoted out of context seem to indicate that he does. Nor does he reject Pound and Williams, who remain his two most important and honored influences. What Olson does reject are the attempts of critics, readers, and editors to place him in the role of "imitator," or "Poundling," and to evaluate his poetry within a hierarchy that places Pound and Williams above him.

In her article, Perloff quotes an ostensibly dismissive passage from a letter to editor Cid Corman in which Olson scolds Corman for comparing Olson's poems to those of Pound and Williams: "I know what's missing in the music. but it's olson which ain't there, not Williams and Pound. And you should know that's who is missing. Not these two inferior predecessors" (*COIP*, 298). Perloff does not include the rest of the quotation, which puts Olson's seemingly arrogant comment in perspective. Olson writes, "Not these two inferior predecessors—just as I am inferior, to myself! and predecessor, of myself!" In the context of the letter, Olson's meaning is clear: the poetry of Pound and of Williams is certainly great, perhaps greater than his own if measured by the criteria of their own time and artistic sensibility. Olson calls Pound "the man in this century" and "the leading poet alive in the world" and grants him special status as the "one / true / immediate / predecessor." But great as Pound and Williams are, their "music" is from the past, and it is no longer "the moving music of other men . . . [of] any of us who are now singing." Olson rejects the "establishing of relations" and the making of "value comparisons" that Corman's critique presupposes: "What they did is there. What we do, is. That's all" (*LO*, 130–32).

Pound and Williams, Olson writes, are "two holy cows / two wholly acceptable / measures." They are sacred and unattainable as measures from the past, but more importantly they should be seen as leading to the present and the future, just as Olson's past work is only a preparation for his present "live speech." Seen in this light, the latent possibilities contained in the self are greater than any inherited ones. Olson's anxiety is not over what has been done in the past but over the attempts of various historians and critics to represent the past as more important, more valuable than the present.

In her reading of Olson's poem, Perloff applies what are essentially New Critical strictures to Olson's style. The "inevitability of the verse line" that Perloff seeks as a governing principle of poetry is exactly what constitutes the formal, closed verse rejected by Olson and other practitioners of open-form poetry. It is precisely such an inevitability—that sense of an oppressive form and syntax "which print bred" in English poetry—that Olson seeks to avoid in writing a poetry that will be the direct transcription of the poet's experience onto the page and in using the typewriter as "the personal and instantaneous recorder of the poet's work." Olson speaks of a verse that will "have the reading its writing involved, as though not the eye but the ear was to be its measurer, as though the intervals of its composition could be so carefully put down as to be precisely the intervals of its registration" (*SW*, 23).

Olson's poetry, though not regulated by the same kinds of formal considerations governing most lyric verse, is by no means carelessly or haphazardly put together. The creative spontaneity Olson espouses for the "recording" of the poem is only a first step, and it must be followed by a process of careful composition and revision requiring the same sense of craft Olson values highly in Pound and Williams. An early typescript shows at least two sets of revisions to "I, Mencius . . . ," which include changes in diction, punctuation, capitalization, spelling, spacing, and line endings as well as substantial additions and deletions and organization into sections. In Olson's copy of *Black Mountain Review,* where the poem first appeared in published form, he makes further corrections—mostly in spacing, indentation, and the arrangement of sections.[8]

It is apparent from these corrections that one of Olson's principal concerns, perhaps *the* principal concern at this stage of his career, is with the organization of lines and line endings. The emphasis in Olson's poetic technique on the line as a visual, syntactic, aural, and mnemonic feature (as well as the physical unit of the breath) makes clear the possibility of a direct connection (though by no means an "inevitable" one) between form and content. The reasons for Olson's line endings—the validity of which Perloff questions—may not be apparent to every reader, but they are certainly apparent to the poet himself. They are formed by his particular feeling for the rhythms of his own breath and by the sequence of sounds his ear makes possible—in Pound's terms, "the musical phrase rather than the metronome." It is, in Olson's own words, the responsibility of the poet to "record the listening he has done to his own speech and by that one act indicate how he would want any reader, silently or otherwise, to voice his work" (*SW,* 22).

Thus, a reader who is aware of the possibilities of field composition should be able to understand the logic of the poet's choices, even if that reader would not write the poem in exactly the same way. Perloff's contention that Olson's version of a given stanza of the poem can just as easily be "transposed" into her own version is untenable—just as a similar claim about a poem of Pound or Williams would be. I first quote Olson's stanza:

8. These manuscripts are in the Olson archives at the University of Connecticut. The changes in Olson's typescript are too numerous to discuss in detail. Two of the most important are the ending, which was changed from "we do not see / bad verse" to the much stronger "We do not see / ballads / other than our own" and the addition of the crucial beginning lines of section III—"We'll to these woods." In his copy of *Black Mountain Review,* Olson changes the title to "I, Mencius, Dog of the Master."

> that what the eye sees,
> that in the East the sun entangles itself
> from among branches,
> should be made to sound as though there were still roads
> on which men hustled
> to get to paradise, to get to
> Bremerton
> shipyards!
>
>   (*CPO*, 319)

Here is Perloff's transposition:

> that what the eye
>   sees
> that in the East
>   the sun untangles itself
> from among branches should be made
>   to sound
> as though there were still roads
> on which men hustled
>   to get
>   to
>   paradise
>   (*COIP*, 300)

One of the basic principles of open-form poetry in the Pound tradition is that the way the poem appears visually on the page influences our apprehension of it in terms of sense, sound, and visual image (logopoeia, melopoeia, and phanopoeia).[9] Perloff's version divides Olson's lines so that the syntactic structure of thought or statement is broken down into imagistic fragments that are both seen and heard as smaller verbal units. But the composition of Olson's original lines forces the reader to return in a jarring way to the margin, strongly emphasizing the enjambed nature of the passage. The juxtaposition of longer lines (two and four) with shorter lines (three and five), followed by

9. Olson evokes Pound in relating Pound's logopoeia to the use of the syllable: "I am dogmatic, that the head shows in the syllable. The dance of the intellect is there, among them, prose or verse. Consider the best minds you know in this here business: where does the head show, is it not, precise, here, in the swift currents of the syllable? Can't you tell a brain when you see what it does, just there? . . . So, is it not the PLAY of a mind we are after, is not that what shows whether a mind is there at all?" (*SW*, 19).

still more fragmented lines at the end, creates an awkward and limping rhythm matching Olson's disgust at the scene he describes. Perloff's arrangement, especially of the lines "from among branches should be made / to sound / as though there were still roads," removes Olson's punctuation and creates a new and different enjambment that affects the physical and intellectual act of reading the lines and actually changes the meaning of the passage. Furthermore, by ending her transposed passage where she does, Perloff removes entirely the sense of ironic commentary in the lines "to get to paradise, to get to / Bremerton / shipyards."[10]

Although I am not entirely convinced by such schematic analyses of Olson's "projective" poetry as that offered by Paul Christensen, who seeks to plot the form of Olson's poems according to a theory of "semantic spacing," I do agree with Christensen's basic contention as well as that of Donald Davie that the positioning of words, lines, and strophes on the page reflects the poem's meaning, "and, quite possibly . . . the thinking process itself."[11] Davie gives Olson credit not only for successfully adopting Pound's technique of using the typewriter as a means of "scoring" the poem but also for providing a more specific explanation of the technique than Pound (or Williams or Cummings) does. The use of devices such as spacing, punctuation, quotation marks, and upper and lower case has not, according to Davie, been granted its full importance by many critics, who see such matters of visual presentation as "merely typographical." Davie comments:

> But why *merely?* Of course it is true that the ear will allow itself to be persuaded by the eye only up to a point; and when a poet tries by typography to persuade the ear of a rhythm that to the ear is nonexistent, then it must be allowed that his arrangement is "merely typographical," and for this he may be blamed. But not only may the reader's ear be assisted, simply by the look of verse on the page, to hear a rhythm it might otherwise have missed; but at times the look

10. Olson's intention seems even more pronounced when we see that he had changed the lines from the original "to get to Hell, to get to / Bremerton / shipyards."

11. Christensen, *Charles Olson,* 83.

on the page may actually *create* a rhythm that could not be conveyed to the reader's ear by any other means.[12]

On a visual level, Perloff's version of Olson's lines makes a pretty picture and even creates an ideogrammatic feeling of branches and entanglement, but this is clearly not the experience Olson is trying to produce. Most importantly, in terms of the sound of the poem, Perloff's transposition changes the rhythms significantly, slowing down the pace of the lines, altering their movement and their interaction with the breath. As is clear to those who have heard Olson read his work, he is extremely sensitive to the interplays of vocalic and consonantal sounds and to the emphasis given a certain line. Perloff's example, far from forming a critique of Olson's method, actually supports the claim he and other poets of the Pound tradition have made that the way a poem is written, its construction on the page, has a discernible effect on the way it is apprehended, read, heard, and understood. In composing an open-form work, the poet does not "simply break off where he happens to break off"; he or she creates a new form with each new poem, a task that can involve a more refined understanding of meter and line than does the use of more traditional forms.

"I, Mencius . . ." is not only an important example of open-form, or projectivist poetry; it is a central poetic statement of the stance Olson and his contemporaries adopt toward their "master," Pound. The poem makes direct reference to Pound's poem "A Pact" and thus places Olson in a direct line of derivation from Whitman and the more Whitmanic Pound of *The Cantos*, while at the same time distancing Olson from the practices into which he felt Pound's poetry, especially the Confucian "Odes," had recently fallen.[13] I quote Pound's poem first.

---

12. Davie, *Ezra Pound*, 112–13.

13. Pound published his version of three hundred Chinese "Odes" as *The Classic Anthology as Defined by Confucius* on September 10, 1954, with Harvard University Press. Olson's manuscript of the poem "I Mencius, Pupil of the Master," sent to Robert Creeley, is dated "october 1954."

> I make a pact with you, Walt Whitman—
> I have detested you long enough.
> I come to you as a grown child
> Who has had a pig-headed father;
> I am old enough now to make friends.
> It was you that broke the new wood,
> Now it is time for carving.
> We have one sap and one root—
> Let there be commerce between us.[14]

Here are passages from "I, Mencius. . . ." From section I:

> the dross of verse. Rhyme!
> when iron (steel)
> has expelled Confucius
> from China. Pittsburgh!
> beware: the Master
> bewrays his vertu.
> To clank like you do
> He brings coolie verse
> to teach you equity,
> who layed down such rails!
> (CPO, 318)

From section II:

> o Whitman,
> let us keep our trade with you when
> the Distributor
> who couldn't go beyond wood,
> apparently,
> has gone out of business
> (CPO, 319)

When seen as a poem about tradition and about the need to clean one's house continually of the influences and works that are no longer useful, "I, Mencius . . ." is not the peevish ranting of a disappointed epigone; it is an interesting and significant "disciple poem." In it the pupil Olson (Mencius) at once honors his master Pound (Confucius) for his earlier work, castigates and disowns him (though not permanently) for his recent work, and turns for solace and guidance to an even earlier model, that of

14. Pound, *Personae*, 89.

Whitman, the founder of the tradition to which Pound himself belongs. In the analogy Olson establishes in the second section of the poem, Pound is reduced to the role of "distributor" of Whitman's goods, and the "pact" he had made with his father is invalidated by his current state of poetic "bankruptcy."

Olson's poem is full of echoes of what Pound had written forty years earlier. In addition to the pact itself, involving either "commerce" or "trade" between a "grown child" and his father (and in the case of Olson and Whitman, grandfather), there is in both poems a play between "wood" as raw material for carving or carpentry and wood as a living sign of organically shared experience. But in each case, Olson changes the image slightly, emphasizing that while indebted to Pound, he also recognizes his independence from Pound. Even the word *trade,* as opposed to Pound's use of the Latinate and more formal *commerce,* is an intentional, though subtle, manifestation of Olson's desire to make clear the distinction between his generation and Pound.

Trade, as opposed to commerce, is the more basic and un-pretentious activity on which the American way of life—and Whitman's ideal—is founded. It suggests a totally egalitarian exchange, as opposed to the more explicitly financial sense suggested by commerce. Olson is no doubt thinking of another meaning of trade as well, that of an occupation or craft that he and Whitman share—"poetry is our trade." Given Olson's interest in etymology, he may also have in mind other, less current usages of the word, some of which resonate in the particular context of this poem.[15] *The Oxford English Dictionary* lists several different meanings of the noun *trade,* including a "course, way, trail . . . path or track" (related to the word *tread*) and a "course or way of life, of action." All these senses of trade are appropriate here, especially in light of the many images of linear movement and tracks or roads throughout the poem: "as

15. For an instance of Olson's belief in the importance of etymology for restoring the originary force of language, see his June 27, 1951, letter to Robert Creeley (*CORC,* vol. 6, 81–82). Olson owned a copy of H. L. Mencken's *The American Language,* and he expressed the need on more than one occasion for more complete etymologies in American dictionaries.

though there were still roads / on which men hustled"; "and our feet / we do not march"; "we'll to these woods / no more / where we were used to go"; "who layed down such rails"; "go still / now that your legs." In the line Olson addresses to Whitman, "let us keep our trade with you," we may also hear an echo of the maritime expression "to keep [a] trade," a steady course (following the trade winds). Olson's choice of a single word, then, works both as a calculated rejection of Pound's expression and as an homage to the Poundian concept of "language charged with meaning to the utmost degree" (*CPO*, 318–20).

Olson also reverses the idea of a son now ready to "make friends" with a "pig-headed father." On the contrary, the son is now rejecting the model of a father whom he had loved, whose "old clothes" he had worn, and who had taught him so much. Olson also addresses the extent to which Pound has disappointed an entire generation of poets, setting the poem in the first-person plural rather than the first-person singular. Here we see an example of a choric poetic voice through which one poet expresses the needs and emotions of his entire generation. The time for carving, for the individual poet as solitary craftsman, is past; now it is time for a "dance" in which the younger poets of the Whitman-Pound tradition become themselves the "process" of creation, while their former teacher Pound (Old Bones), now too old to learn the new steps, can only watch from the sidelines:

> We'll to these woods
> no more, where we were used
> to get so much, (Old Bones
> do not try to dance
>
>   go still
>   now that your legs
>
>   the Charleston
>   is still for us
>
>   You can watch
>
> It is too late
> to try to teach us
>
>   we are the process

                    and our feet
                              We do not march
        We still look
                    And see
                         what we see
                              We do not see
                              ballads
        other than our own.

                              (*CPO*, 320)

This evocative third section marks the need of Olson and his
contemporaries to move into a stage of maturity where they are
no longer merely sons or followers but the new guardians of past
wisdom. The "woods . . . where we were used to get so much"
represent the organic nature of their earlier apprenticeship,
which was similar to the one Pound shared with Whitman—
"one sap and one root." In other words, although the underlying
metaphors have remained constant in Olson's poem, the terms
under which they appear have changed—the allusions to
Pound's poem form a sad commentary on the present state of the
"master's" poetry.

The form of the foregoing passage is important as well. Here
the lines do break up, as do Perloff's "transposed" lines in the
earlier passage, but this time for a reason. The last section of the
poem embodies a movement away from the rest of the poem
(from Olson's bitter tirade against Pound) and from Pound
himself, especially his practice in the "Odes." The visual open-
ness of this section is in contrast to the tighter, tougher lines of
the earlier sections, with their enjambments, often awkward
phrasing, and harsh sounds. The final section reflects a calmer,
more introspective feeling and suggests the open possibilities of
a new aesthetic based on the free movement of "dance," rather
than on the "march" of Pound's new rhyming verse.[16]

The language and syntax of this final section also mark a
departure from earlier passages. Olson confines himself to ex-

16. The analogy of poetry to dance is made even more explicit in Olson's
original lines—"sound / is in our feet."

tremely simple, almost exclusively monosyllabic words and composes in brief sentences, almost fragments. (Compare this with the feeling of syntax stretched to its limits in the earlier passage—"that in the East the sun untangles itself / from among branches, / should be made to sound as though there were still roads / on which men hustled / to get to paradise, to get to / Bremerton / shipyards"). Olson is also using to full advantage the musical possibilities of his poetry: not only does the arrangement of the lines cause us to read more slowly and deliberately and to make the rhythmic juxtapositions between thoughts; the repetition of certain sounds, words, and syntactic structures also contributes to a lighter, more musical feeling that approximates the movement of dance. Notice in particular the softening effect created by the repeated use of the liquid "l" and "w"; "We'll . . . woods . . . where we were . . . what we saw . . . Old . . . still . . . legs . . . still . . . late . . . still look . . . ballads."

Finally, the passage marks a more personal allusion. One of Olson's memories from his visits to Pound at St. Elizabeth's, recorded in his journal entries entitled "Cantos," was that Pound had danced his "Yiddish Charleston" for psychiatrist Jerome Kavka—it was, as Olson writes, a "dance which Pound does, with gesture, movement and words" (*COEP*, 66). Perhaps Olson associates the dance with Pound as he first knew him—energetic and erudite, if also irascible and politically difficult. Now it is a sign, like so much else in the poem, of how much Pound has fallen from his former glory. That dance from Pound's generation, one he wrote for Louis Zukofsky that was included in *An "Objectivists" Anthology*, has become "still"—it is frozen in a dead past. Yet Olson gently rescues the passage from becoming a mere denunciation of his former master by repeating the word "still" in its other sense ("We still look"). In this context, the lines have new meaning: the Charleston is *still* for us; it remains always a constant source of poetic inspiration. Olson is not only admonishing Pound to "go still"—to stop writing—but he is also urging Pound to *continue,* to "be of use," as Pound would put it, even when the "great 'ear / can no longer 'hear." Olson's choice of diction incorporates both the idea of stasis and that of move-

ment; it indicates the two possible stances the poet may adopt in
relating to tradition and a poetic past; and it suggests the degree
of Olson's own ambivalence about his forebear. In revising this
section, Olson softened considerably the attack on Pound,
changing several key phrases. In the final version, "where we
expected / to get so much" becomes "where we were used / to get
so much"; "it is too late / to catch on" is changed to "It is too
late / to try to teach us"; and "we do not see / bad verse" is
happily revised to "We do not see / ballads / other than our
own."

The opening lines of "I, Mencius . . ." signal Olson's aversion
to Pound's new poetry, and his sense of betrayal by Pound, who
"brings coolie verse / to teach you equity." Pound's "Odes" are
a betrayal in several senses: they betray Pound himself, who
"bewrays" (reveals or gives away) the fallen nature of his
"vertu"; they betray Olson and other younger poets who had
believed in and learned from Pound; and they betray their orig-
inal author, Confucius, an exemplar for both Olson and Pound
of clean writing and thought. In Olson's view, Pound had aban-
doned the Confucian principles of sincerity and claritas, while
also forsaking the poetic principles he had established with
Imagism forty years earlier—"that no line must sleep / that as the
line goes so goes / the Nation"—and in doing so had been "em-
braced by the demon / he drove off!" (*CPO*, 319).

The poem demonstrates Olson's sense of Pound's decline,
even in the few years since the visits to "Grandpa Pound" at St.
Elizabeth's. At the time of Olson's visits in the mid- to late
1940s, Pound had in a sense played the role of Confucius to
Olson's Mencius—the elder master to an eager pupil. Despite
reservations about Pound's views, Olson had still maintained
high hopes for his master. In Olson's account of one of his visits
he writes of a translation of Confucius Pound was then begin-
ning; Olson even discusses the matter of Pound's trade:

> If I were laying out a plan, I should immediately put him in some less
> enclosed place, give him privacy and simple care, books and paper,
> and freedom to continue his literary work. This could be done within
> the framework of the Federal prison system, if it were recognized

that the rehabilitation of such a prisoner as Pound includes allowing him to work at his "trade." There is no need in his case to teach him basketweaving, machine tooling, or carpentry. His craft is there, and society can still use his gift for language if it wants to. A translation of Confucius could be a fruit of his imprisonment. Otherwise it is all waste.[17]   (*COEP*, 46)

The parallels between this passage and the poem of eight years later may be unintentional, but the identification of Pound with Confucius certainly is not. In the poem, Pound becomes Confucius—"that Confucius himself / should try to alter it"— though a noisy and misguided Confucius, a senile version of the great thinker and poet he had once been. If we look more closely, however, it is Whitman who is the real Confucius, the true progenitor, and Pound is only the "distributor" who wears the mask of Confucius. As Olson wrote in his 1948 essay "Grandpa, Goodbye":

> A long time ago (what, 25 years?) Pound took the role of Confucius, put on that mask, for good. I'm sure he would rest his claim not, as I have put it, on the past, but forward, as teacher of history to come, Culture-Bearer in the desert and shame of now. (I don't think it is possible to exaggerate the distance he goes with his notion of himself—at the end Gate of the last Canto Confucius is to be one of the two huge figures standing there, looking on.   (*COEP*, 101)

At another point during his visits, Olson remarks how "[Pound's] attraction to Confucius must be the old thing . . . [to] confuse our opposite with ourselves" (*COEP*, 71). Even if Olson is aware of a clear distinction between Pound and Confucius, he had at one time sought to make the connection himself. Pound was sixty when Olson first met him at the hospital, and Olson was struck then by the comment Pound attributed to Confucius—"that after a man is 60 he is no longer active, but influences the action of younger men" (*COEP*, 86). By the

17. Pound did work on translations of much of the prose writing of Confucius during the period of Olson's visits. James Laughlin published Pound's English versions of *The Unwobbling Pivot* and *The Great Digest* in the 1946–47 issue of *Pharos*; Pound's version of four chapters from Mencius appeared in *The New Iconograph* in 1947; and his translation of Confucius' *Analects* came out in the Spring and Summer 1950 issues of *The Hudson Review*.

writing of "I, Mencius . . . ," with Pound turning sixty-nine, even that influence is sadly in jeopardy.

Olson's desire to keep trade with Whitman, just like Pound's earlier decision to allow himself commerce with his father, is a metaphor for the conscious use of one poet by another or, rather, for an ongoing relationship between them that must be mutually beneficial. Even the activities associated in the poem with influence—going (or not going) to "these woods . . . where we used to get so much" and deciding not to wear "shoddy mashed out of the Master's old clothes"—point to an active decision on the part of the younger poet concerning the role of his predecessor in his own education and development and a willingness to take responsibility for his own choices.

The "shoddy" Olson evokes is a revealing metaphor for the process of influence. As a raw material made from the broken-up fibers of previously worn clothes, it is a manifestation of what happens when one poet makes direct use of parts of an earlier poet's work, recombining them in new ways in his own poem. But at the same time, the later meaning of "shoddy," as connoting something inferior in quality, cheap, or derivative, is clearly also intended. Olson at once suggests the nature of Pound's influence on him and his contemporaries and the debasement of that influence. This influence declines in value, as does "shoddy merchandise" and as has the original value of the word *shoddy,* once meaning a kind of wool cloth and now a term of insult. Olson depicts the shoddiness of Pound's art in the Confucian "Odes," the falsifying attempt to pass them off as something other than what they really are. Olson objects vehemently to the other forms of artistic and spiritual degradation he sees in American society, analogues to the decline of Pound's work from the beauty and *vertu* of *The Cantos* to the "coolie verse" perpetrated in his translations of the "Odes." Olson mentions specifically the "open galleries" that "sell Chinese prints, at the opening," instead of displaying Whistler's art; the change from Pound's beatific vision in the *Pisan Cantos* ("le paradis n'est pas artificiel") to the present state of men hustling "to get to paradise . . .

to / Bremerton / shipyards"; and the expulsion of Chinese wisdom and beauty by the mechanized and clanking "steel" of "Pittsburgh." Nevertheless, Olson's admonition to "bite off Father's where the wool's got too long" implies not a complete rejection of Pound's influence but a detaching of the undesirable part of Pound's practice from that larger body of influential work that can remain intact.

Clearly, this shoddy is not a metaphor for a Bloomian poetic strength that must be challenged by the later poet or for some burden of the past. On the contrary, Olson implies that a positive reaction to a forebear is the only one that can lead to any creative union, any valuable art: Olson cannot continue to use Pound's poetry when he no longer finds it of worth. Olson does not "wrestle with" his predecessor Pound and ultimately attempt to "overthrow" him; he simply decides to leave Pound, as Creeley puts it, "sitting in the dust . . . where he should be left" (*CORC*, vol. 3, 74–75). Olson and Creeley realize that it is not enough simply to "react" against Pound ("to throw [oneself] back to the Georgians") or to "renounce" him or his "method"; it is a question, as the ending of Olson's poem makes clear, of moving ahead, "beyond Ez." "To shift the load," Creeley cautions, "take it away from him, but NOT lose particulars . . . of METHOD."

Perloff views Olson's statements about Pound and Williams as brash and unacceptable rejections of his all-important predecessors. Yet in an age in which the notions of anxiety of influence and burden of the past have become so widely accepted, it is hardly surprising that the tremendous pressure placed on Olson as the "heir apparent" to the legacy of Pound and Williams should cause some kind of defensive reaction on his part. Not only did Olson have in Pound and Williams two substantial "predecessors" with whom to negotiate; he had the added problem that they were both *living* predecessors. Both were still active poets throughout most of Olson's lifetime (Williams in particular was quite productive until his death in 1963), and Pound actually outlived Olson by two years. Even in Bloom's Oedipal scheme, later poets generally have only the "daemon" of a dead poet to confront; Olson was never permitted even to come out from under the literal shadow of his forebears, who continued to grow in critical esteem and to have new work published alongside (and at times in preference to) his own. Even after the publication of "I, Mencius . . . ," Olson continued to feel resentment about the place of his forebear and about his own earlier slavish imitations of Pound. Olson's correction in the revised draft of the word *couldn't* to *wouldn't* in the line "who wouldn't go beyond wood" indicates his sense that Pound was not performing up to his full capacities (and, perhaps, that he was giving "Poundians" like Olson a bad name). Olson's feeling that he had become the "dog" rather than the "pupil" of the master was a sign of his continued worry that he was living and writing under Pound's shadow.

Such a feeling on Olson's part may lead us to wonder if "I, Mencius . . ." is a Bloomian "crisis poem," one in which Olson must either break with or fall under the spell of his predecessor. As I have already made clear, the very notion of the poem as a psychic battleground in a struggle with a predecessor is a problematic one, especially for a poet who openly declares his sources and debts. Olson had extensively explored his relationship to Pound in both poetic and nonpoetic writings well before the time of "I, Mencius . . . ," and he had made clear his debt to his forebear on numerous occasions in his contacts with other poets and students. Furthermore, Olson's poetic practice and concerns in the mid-1950s had already moved quite markedly away from those of both Pound and Williams, and it was now to Olson, rather than to Pound, that younger poets such as Duncan, Creeley, and Ginsberg looked for their principal source of guidance and "inspiration." Finally, Olson's poem cannot be considered a "crisis poem" in the true sense because Olson continued throughout the 1950s and early 1960s to place a high value on Pound's central output, that of *The Cantos*. The "Rock-Drill" sections of *The Cantos*, which did not appear until 1956 (and which Olson had presumably not yet read at the time of "I, Mencius . . ."), became an important source for Olson's "The

Song of Ulikummi," a tribute to Pound that Olson read at the 1965 Spoleto Festival.[18] Another sign of Olson's continuing respect for Pound is a 1958 letter to Robert Duncan in which Olson proposes an anthology containing the work of both Pound and Williams, alongside that of his generation, including himself, Duncan, Creeley, Ginsberg, Levertov, John Wieners, and Philip Whalen.[19]

Rather than as a "crisis poem," I read "I, Mencius . . ." as the last of a series of writings commemorating breaks with Pound, all of them painful for Olson but none of them final. The most significant of these breaks, and the one that may have ultimately allowed Olson to differentiate himself more clearly from Pound, was his decision to terminate his visits to St. Elizabeth's, a decision marked by his essay "Grandpa, Goodbye." Notes that Olson wrote to Pound at around the same time indicate that the relationship between the two poets was never an untroubled one. Still earlier, in thinking about an epic to be called "West," Olson first had an inkling of the importance Pound was to have for him. In a notebook entry from 1945 Olson writes:

> Maybe Pound discloses to you a method you spontaneously reached for in all this talking and writing. What about doing on a smaller scale—the West? But he has already taken the same frame, as you will note from your notes on the poem to be called "West" you wrote 4 yrs. ago. But should you not best him? Is his form inevitable enough to be used as your own? *Let yourself be derivative for a bit. This is a good and natural act. Write as the father to be the father* [my emphasis].[20]

18. Olson's poem is dedicated to Pound, who "freed the languages of the world." In Olson's marginal notes to his copy of *The Fifth Decad of Cantos,* apparently made after the appearance of "Rock-Drill" and before the composition of "The Song of Ulikummi," Olson suggests a connection between the notion of the Rock-Drill and certain lines in Canto 47 some twenty years earlier: "gnawed through the mountain" and "By prong have I entered these hills." These lines, and the image of the "rock drill" itself, are certainly related in Olson's mind to his own translation from the Hittite in "The Song of Ulikummi": "fucked the mountain / fucked her but good his mind / sprang forward . . . went right through it and came out / the other side."

19. From an unpublished letter of April 7, 1958, in the Olson archives of the University of Connecticut.

20. Olson, *Olson* 5 (1976): 11.

Olson was not always to hold this view of things, but it is startling to see how deliberately he had planned from the first, even as early as the 1941 note to which he refers, to use Pound as a central model for his work. Even though Olson's term *the father* to describe his predecessor may remind us of the neo-Freudian vocabulary adopted by Bloom, Olson's acknowledgment of the deliberate act of derivation is antithetical to the emphasis on repression in Bloom's theory. Indeed, Olson openly expresses his "anxiety" about Pound as well as a sense of his growing independence from Pound's influence: "You have some pretty notion the moment verse crosses yr path: it is fear and anxiety you are not a poet. Which is very much beside the point. If you trust yr vocal roundness as a consequence of yr. objectivism, you need not worry one day. In this roundness you outdo Pound, whatever his scholastic powers."[21]

By the time of "I, Mencius . . ." Olson's poetry had indeed achieved a "vocal roundness" that differentiated it from the work of Pound and Williams. Olson's poetic technique, and its central notion of "composition by field," was neither a radical break with his tradition nor a totally imitative practice. It was an extension of the possibilities Olson found in those American poets of the previous generation who he felt had something to offer his generation.

Pound and Williams are more than simply "presences" (or, in a Bloomian sense, "absences") in Olson's text; they are important "guides" to his work and life. Olson's collected library at his death, which contained far more books by Pound and Williams than by any other poet, is the concrete manifestation of his continuing use of both writers.[22] Olson and his contemporaries in the Pound tradition served as the "container" for Pound's ideas, though these poets spoke for Pound in a way he could

21. Ibid.
22. See, in continuous issues of the journal *Olson*, the reports on Olson's library. Olson had in his collection thirty-one books by Pound and twenty-two by Williams. Only Melville is better represented in the library, as can easily be explained by the formal research Olson did on Melville for his thesis and for *Call Me Ishmael*.

never have envisioned. The relationship between Pound and Olson is neither the case of a frustrated poet unable to achieve the greatness of his masters nor that of a revolutionary "poet of destruction"; it is an important example of a writer responding to his own time and place in a manner that would have been impossible without the model of another.

6 OBJECTIVIST ROMANTIC

Ezra Pound and the Poetic Constellations of Robert Duncan

> In the constellation of Poetry there are thousands of distant stars and more immediate planets, lighting the night sky of those who delite in that art with a plenitude of brilliancies, and in time each new poet in his vocation comes to realize that he has a kind of horoscope or constellation of his own in which particular poets of the past appear as influencing spirits in his shaping of his poetic destiny.
>
> Robert Duncan, *Fictive Certainties*

> [Duncan] has created the most exciting poetic world since that of Ezra Pound.
>
> James Laughlin, *Sagetrieb*

Even more than Charles Olson, Robert Duncan is the postmodern poet who has provided the most compelling and comprehensive study of Pound's poetry and Pound's contributions to poetic language and form. Building on Olson's "Projective Verse," Duncan has enriched our understanding of the derivation of a radical postmodern poetics from the work of Modernist precursors, and he has analyzed more deeply the psychic and artistic factors that affected Pound and his generation.

As Charles Altieri remarks, Duncan's work is based on "a tension between 'the actual real and the real of the imagination'" that leads "to a rich descriptive engagement with the oppositions that plague modern sensibilities as they struggle with models of the real that exclude and repress energies still present in the imaginative traditions." For Altieri, Duncan is an Objectivist poet who "preserves the immediacies called for in the doctrine of sincerity" and exemplifies "how objectivity is ultimately not simply agreement about external conditions but about the possibility of locating what imaginative acts can share."[1] In this chapter I elaborate the dialectic of Duncan's

---

1. Altieri, "The Objectivist Tradition," 17–18.

engagement with the Objectivist and the imaginative poetic modes and thereby situate Duncan's struggle in his reading of the work of Pound. Duncan's use of Pound's work as a consciously applied corrective to his own natural tendencies as a writer exemplifies an unusually synthetic pattern of influence. Like other poets in the Pound tradition, for whom influence appears as a largely conscious and voluntary process, Duncan maintains an openly derivative stance. At the same time, however, Duncan's need to maintain a fruitful poetic relationship with a forebear so different from himself has led him to use Pound's model in a manner distinct from that of other poets of the Pound tradition. Duncan's readings of Pound in *The H. D. Book*,[2] as well as in his own poetry and poetics, often involve attempts to explicate aspects of Pound's work that respond to Duncan's own Romantic sensibility. Duncan privileges in particular those parts of Pound that reflect an openness either to a mystical or spiritual consciousness or to sensual and erotic impulses generally figured by representations of the feminine.

Thomas Kinsella, another poet for whom Pound is an important model, identifies in Duncan "the basic joint devotion to freedom and rigor" and "the ability—at a crucial stage—to learn openly from the forms of Pound's *Cantos* and find the necessary personal revolution."[3] Kinsella's comment perfectly sums up the art of derivation for Duncan: an "open" use of his predecessors but always with an eye to the "personal revolution" implicit in going beyond the work of those same poets. In Duncan's derivation of Pound's conceptions and poetic stance we find an influence that is not so much a direct transfer of ideas as a matter of artistic and intellectual inspiration. Duncan does not merely restate Pound's meaning; neither does he distort it. Instead, he enters into a "field of possibility" provided by Pound's work.

Like Pound, Duncan is never satisfied with received notions of what constitutes acceptable poetic sources. Seeking to distance

2. A series of essays published in various journals. Although Duncan clearly thought of it as evolving into a complete whole, it has never been printed as a book.

3. Kinsella, in *Sagetrieb* 4 nos. 2–3 (1985): 315.

himself from any rigid orthodoxy of poetic practice, Duncan constantly makes clear his commitment to models that challenge us to widen our definition of open-form poetry. Certainly Duncan's interest in such poets as Dante, Whitman, Williams, H. D., Moore, Zukofsky, Olson, Levertov, and Creeley is consistent with his position in the Pound tradition,but as Michael Bernstein comments, Duncan "is [also] able to supplement the paternity of Ezra Pound by placing alongside his mentor's 'instigation' writers like Shelley, Rilke . . . Gertrude Stein, and Sigmund Freud, all of whom, but for the inescapable evidence of Duncan's own works, one would have presumed unassimilable into such a tradition."[4] In addition, Duncan claims in his Romantic heritage Spenser, Shakespeare, Keats, Blake, Coleridge, Goethe, Emerson, Poe, Baudelaire, Rimbaud, Mallarmé, the Surrealists, and Wallace Stevens as well as the most "unassimilable" poet of all, Milton. The inclusion of Milton in Duncan's canon is part of a self-conscious polemic against what he sees as the restricted lists of acceptable writers maintained by Pound and Olson. This inclusion is also an attempt to bring Milton's poetry into a camp that Pound would accept—poetry as "news that stays news":

> I come in heavy over and over again on Milton because Milton was disallowed by Ezra Pound from the main track of poetry, so in general I'm making it impossible for us to read Duncan without both Ezra Pound and Milton. Now, that forces Ezra Pound into a different court and it forces Milton into a different court, but it also forces a whole track of poetry into a different one. It was one Charles Olson would not accept; and Williams attacked Eliot for coming back to put a memorial on top of him. That's not the way I think of my Milton; my Milton is news, not memorial.[5]

Duncan does not feel confined by any particular tradition, even the relatively "open" tradition set forth by Pound's criteria for "good writing." Duncan suffers little from the "anxiety of influence"; his own notion of poetic history puts him at odds with Harold Bloom. Instead of the strictly canonical and agonistic tradition Bloom identifies in poets of the Romantic Sub-

---

4. M. A. Bernstein, "Bringing It All Back Home," 185.
5. Interview with Jack Cohn and Thomas O'Donnell, 543–44.

lime, Duncan emphasizes the role played by active choice in the application of appropriate models: "Blake recognized that he was in the tradition of Milton. That wasn't laid on him; nobody came along and said, 'Blake, you is in the tradition of Milton.' He could have been in the tradition of a million other cats. True tradition is entirely voluntary; it's entirely in your own hands" (Quoted in *AV*, 121). Bloom may read even such instances as Duncan's use of Pound as cases of "misreading," finding in Duncan's language and poetic stance an agonistic reaction to the ideas and language of his predecessor. I maintain, however, that Duncan's derivations of Pound and other predecessors demonstrate the multiplicity of potential responses by a younger poet, without undermining the previous poet's stated intention.

Duncan resembles Pound in his deliberate assimilation of earlier writers into his own poetry and in his production of critical statements that rationalize this process. Like Pound, Duncan believes that literary influence is not merely a process of revising past works or elements of these, but rather a much broader interaction between earlier and later writers, one involving cultural attitudes and epistemological assumptions as well as literary forms and language.

In the first poem of *The Opening of the Field*, "Often I Am Permitted to Return to a Meadow," Duncan illustrates his idea of influence as an enriching process of (self)-discovery, evoking the "folded field" from the *Zohar* where Abraham discovered the cave of his ancestors. This narrative serves as an allegory for the relationship Duncan proposes to establish with his own poetic predecessors. For Duncan, there are four primary ancestors, father figures who inhabit this "hall": Pound, Williams, Lawrence, and Olson, the last of whom is at once father figure and contemporary. Duncan speaks of a poetic "fathering" of the self (there is also a "mothering" of the self in his poems to H. D.) that does not involve an Oedipal child / father relationship—a "repression" of the self or of the father—but rather an opening of the psyche to additional sources through the re-creation of new fathers. Duncan provides here an alternative metaphor to that of "misreading": poetic growth as "re-creation," which implies that new readings are found in a textual realm *and* in an interaction with the physical space inhabited by historically (or actually) present forebears. Such an interaction makes possible a greater involvement with matters not included in the psychopoetic framework Bloom's model provides; Duncan seeks to discover the emotional, spiritual, and intellectual centers informing all aspects of a previous poet's life, work, and ideas.

The tradition with which Duncan identifies is not exclusively his own; it is formed by a process of copossession that he shares with such poets as Olson, Levertov, and Creeley. For Duncan, tradition is neither a fixed nor a canonical entity; nor is it the wholly idiosyncratic creation of a single writer. Duncan's sense of tradition, like that of Olson, Ginsberg, and other poets of the countercultural movement of the 1950s and 1960s, is a largely communal sense of continuity always (re)established by the poets who come after and who form it as an active process in their own poetics. Duncan "creates" a tradition, or helps to create it, only as part of this ongoing process and in conjunction with other poets who share his understanding of what models are to be most valued. This is a live tradition defined by what is felt to be of vital importance at the particular historical and cultural moment. Thus, Michael Bernstein is not entirely correct when he suggests that "the tradition whose pupil he [Duncan] proclaims himself is, in the first instance, his own imaginative construct,"[6] although Bernstein is correct in his assumption that Lawrence, Williams, and Pound would not have seen themselves as a tradition or as ancestors of any given poet.

Duncan's tradition, far from being as arbitrary as Bernstein suggests, is made coherent by his insights about the direction of modern poetry, a feeling for the necessary form his own work will take. Bernstein's assertion that Duncan's concern with his predecessors "increasingly begins to seem like the central poem of his imagination" is overstating the case somewhat and sounds markedly similar to Bloom's idea that the central subject of poetry is the poet's relationship to past poets. Duncan, like

6. M. A. Bernstein, "Robert Duncan," 180.

Pound and Olson, is primarily interested in representing states of physical, mental, and emotional experience in his poems, and the additional layer of meaning given by the reference to past works is only of secondary importance. Further, as in poems such as Pound's "A Pact" and Olson's "I, Mencius, Pupil of the Master," Duncan's relationship to his poetic predecessors remains personal as well as purely imaginative or linguistic.

Duncan differs from Pound and Olson, however, in his respect, even humility, before the acknowledged "greatness" of his ancestor poets. If Duncan is a more forgiving reader of his predecessors than Olson, he is also more syncretic in his use of poetic sources. Rather than viewing ancestors as alternatives between which he must choose (which Olson does), Duncan sees them as sources of differences that can be combined and recombined in productive endeavors. Sometimes, as in the case of Pound and Milton, Duncan's effort involves a reconciliation of what are normally considered opposites in an attempt to disturb existing canonical boundaries. More often, as in the case of Dante and Whitman, on whom Duncan wrote companion essays, his readings of two poets create a fabric of interconnections that contributes to our appreciation of both. Duncan's own art often involves a forced resolution of such contraries, as in his use of Zukofsky and Olson, two poets "who could be posed as polarities of what poetic consciousness might be" (*FC*, 213). Unlike Pound, whose ideogrammatic linkages in *The Cantos* generally establish an order of relations between concepts, Duncan uses a method of grand collage that seeks to allow new and unintended relations to enter the poem, never excluding such relations through what he considers Pound's "totalitarian" discriminations. (For further discussion of Duncan's collage method, see chapter 7.)

Duncan's early exposure to Pound and the other experimental Modernists was part of a poetic formation that from an early age involved the construction of a programmatically derivative poetic voice:

> By my eighteenth year, I recognized in poetry my sole and ruling vocation. . . . But I could find no ready voice. I was, after all, to be a poet of many derivations. Putting it all together, poem by poem

and even with individual poems line by line, I have had to go by the initial faith in the process of poetry itself, for I do not know, outside of the integrity of this working feeling, what may constitute the integrity of the whole.   (*YC*, i)

Like Pound and Olson, Duncan is selective and deliberate in his use of poetic sources, but he differs from both of them in the way he incorporates those sources into his own work. Duncan's choice of models is not based on rigorous standards of technique, as is Pound's, nor is it guided by a sociohistorical stance toward reality like Olson's. Instead, Duncan's use of models is determined, or rather guided, by the "movement" and "association" of his readings of poetic and nonpoetic texts, readings that cannot always be rationally explained but that enter his work as formal and spiritual "presences."

At the same time that Duncan enters into a historical dialogue with past writers, his aesthetic emphasizes a fluid use of sources that is not found in Pound's or Olson's work. The various "texts" that form Duncan's "true book" are ordered primarily by his personal reading experience; they are not part of a system, not defined or catalogued as in Pound's "ABC's," "guides," or "model curricula" or Olson's "bibliographies." Even though Duncan is interested in what his poems can teach each reader, he generally does not take on the role of poet-pedagogue, as Pound and Olson do; his is the quiet lesson of the mystic or sage. Furthermore, Duncan's use of other writers and texts becomes part of his stated aesthetic in a way that it is not for Pound or Olson. Where they both use the work of others primarily as a means to the end of supporting their own arguments or convictions, Duncan makes explicit that he is a "derivative" poet: that to derive as well as "to emulate, imitate, reconstrue, approximate, duplicate" is itself an important part of his art.[7] As Don Byrd remarks, "He has made the gathering of diverse influences into a poetic."[8]

•   •   •

7. See Duncan's introduction in Donald Allen, ed., *The New American Poetry*, 406.

8. Byrd, "The Question of Wisdom as Such," 39.

Duncan's desire to be inclusive does not prevent him from privileging certain traditions in his own work and in his reading of the work of others. He expresses throughout his writing a concern for a "tradition of [spiritual] sensibility," which he also delineates in Pound's writing:

> As important for me is Pound's role as the carrier of a tradition or lore in poetry, that flowered in the Renaissance after Gemisthos Plethon, the Provence of the twelfth century that gave rise to the Albigensian gnosis, the *trobar clus,* and the Kabbalah, in the Hellenic world that furnished the ground for orientalizing greek mystery cults, Christianity, and neo-Platonism. . . . *The Cantos* returns again and again to speak with sublime and ecstatic voice. In his affinity for Plotinus, Proclus, Iamblichus, or the 9th century Erigena, in his poetic cult of the sublime Aphrodite ("crystal body of air") and of Helios, not without Hellenistic hermetic overtones, in his fascination with form in nature ("germinal") having signature, Pound, as does H. D. in her later work, revives in poetry a tradition or kabbalah that would unite Eleusis and the Spirit of Romance, Gassire's lute and the vision of the Spirit Euterpe which came out of the Rosicrucian John Heydon on Bulverton Hill. This tradition of the spirit.[9]

Duncan's writing, both in style and content, reflects his interest in the Pound of *The Spirit of Romance* and sections of *The Cantos,* the same Pound who continues throughout his life to search for beauty and meaning in the work of the troubadours, Cavalcanti and Dante, Sappho and Pindar, and the mystical tradition—the luminous "tradition of the spirit." Olson, however, regards all such matters as Pound's "gentilities," and in the religious "sectaries" courted by Pound and Duncan, Olson finds only false wisdom, an attempt to create symbols that are not constituted by the immediate reality of the poet's "one self, the man or woman he is" (*HU,* 69).[10]

---

9. Duncan, "The Lasting Contribution of Ezra Pound," 23–26.
10. As Olson makes clear in a letter to Robert Creeley, he is dissatisfied with those very sections of *The Cantos* in which Duncan finds so much meaning: "Is it not true, that Ez. is more fine than strong, that it is such gentilities as rain, grass, birds on a wire, 5, now 3, Metechevsky or whatever, tents, the trilling, rather than the thrusting, that are where he scores? He goes literary with lynxes, Dioces, and fuckings, and can only stalk through the heart-lands by the wit of attack, attack" (*CORC,* vol. 2, 92).

The differing uses Olson and Duncan make of Pound's work demonstrate that there is no single "Pound" whose influence can be easily delineated. Instead, each poet in the tradition draws on Pound. Don Byrd summarizes the major differences between Olson's and Duncan's uses of Pound in this way:

> Characteristically, they were attracted to different aspects of his work. . . . In Pound's *The Spirit of Romance,* Duncan found the statement of a literary tradition of which he was a part, and much of his prose work, including "The H. D. Book" and the essay on Dante, is an attempt to clarify that tradition and define his own place in it. Unlike Pound, Duncan finds the tradition usefully carried on by Shakespeare and the poets of the nineteenth century. Many of his poems . . . are conscious definitions of a continuing romantic tradition. From the beginning, however, the romantic Pound was of little interest to Olson. . . . Olson was attracted to Pound the historian and the instigator of poetic methodology.[11]

Not only do Olson and Duncan appreciate and find valuable very distinct parts of Pound's work—different sections of *The Cantos,* for instance—and see his importance as a writer and model as lying in different areas; they also read his work within markedly different contexts, different traditions. As we have already seen, Pound is most immediately valuable to Olson as a guide to certain sources in, for example, history, economics, and anthropology and as a guide in the use of extraliterary sources, discourses, and attitudes as valid material for poetic composition. Duncan, too, finds Pound an important mentor or guide but in the more Dantean sense of a spiritual guide into the depths of poetic experience. In a literary essay from his book *Derivations,* Duncan describes Pound in *The Cantos* not in terms of a stance toward reality but in terms of a more imaginative, quasi-Romantic quest:

> In the *Cantos* of Ezra Pound, the voices of the guide are distorted by shifts in the making. The poetry, the making, opens gaps in the correspondence with the City of God. A poetry is possible which will introduce the peril of beauty to all the cells of history. . . . I with Ezra Pound sought the orders of history and heard the great bell-notes

11. Byrd, "The Question of Wisdom as Such," 42–44.

ring between the work and the self that gave intimations of the creation, the continuum in chaos.[12]

Duncan sees himself as neither a postmodernist nor a Modernist but as a post-Romantic poet: "Well, I'm not a Modernist. . . . I read Modernism as Romanticism; and I finally begin to feel myself pretty much a 19th century mind. . . . I don't feel out of my century, I like this century immensely. But my ties to Pound, Stein, Surrealism and so forth all seem to me entirely consequent to their unbroken continuity from the Romantic period."[13] As can be seen from Duncan's passionate involvement with the major figures of the Modernist movement, his embrace of Romanticism is not a rejection of Modernist tendencies but rather a defense against a Modernist orthodoxy that precludes any Romantic elements. Duncan sees Pound's poetry as paradigmatic of the possibilities of a twentieth-century art that involves the Romantic imagination focused through a modern awareness and technique:

> "Make it new" was the call to order of the day for one who took Pound as his mentor as I did, and, for Pound too, one got the idea that what was involved was not only a spiritual commandment from Confucius but also a technical revolution. I was to be a Romantic, but it was to be no simple Romanticism, such as courses in college portrayed and despised in the portrayal, for in the Romantic too there was to be now no element that was not seen as the function at once of the poem and of the mind; and no element of poem or mind that was not to be seen as a function of a social and historical consciousness. In the Imagist revolution, there had been the announcement that "a new cadence means a new idea"—how a thing was made and what a thing were inextricably one.[14]

Michael Bernstein discusses Duncan's place in the Poundian tradition in terms of just these contexts:

> Rather than stepping back from the titanism of *The Cantos* to the security of a more modest enterprise, Duncan's work continues— and thus renews—the modernist tradition at its most ambitious by

12. Duncan, *Derivations Selected From 1950–1956,* 91.
13. Quoted in Ekbert Faas, *Towards a New American Poetics,* 82.
14. Duncan, "Reading Zukofsky," 422.

undertaking a synthesis of heterogeneous "origins" as potentially
disruptive to one another as those in Pound's own work. . . . One
can, however, by now clearly recognize that Duncan has taken his
primary imagination from the history of imagination and conscious-
ness rather than, as did Pound and Olson, from "ideas" put "into
action" in the realm of concrete *praxis*.[15]

The heterogeneous elements in Duncan's poetry derive from a
general tendency toward inclusiveness and integration, which
are made possible, in part, by his use of fragmentation and
collage techniques. He rejects what he sees as a restrictive for-
mulation in Olson's "Projective Verse," the idea that open-form
poetry is to constitute a rejection or correction of the closed
form: "But I find that [correction of closed form] superfluous.
Would you want to go back and correct, let's say, Housman?
What do you think you would arrive at? Actually the open thing
is really to contain any closed form. Any passage or anything else
can be contained as part of a large open form."[16] Duncan's
challenge to Olson's notion of projective or open-form writing
constitutes a central aspect of his poetics, one in which he differs
from many other followers of Pound and Williams. Duncan's
idea that traditional, closed poetic forms can exist within a larger
open structure allows him to use in his poetry almost any form
of writing, including those of poetic models that were off limits
to a more doctrinaire projectivist such as Olson.

Despite their differences, however, the poetics of both Olson
and Duncan are inspired by Pound's manifestos and especially
by *The Cantos*. The idea of open-form poetry is as central to
Duncan's thought and work as to Olson's and mandates a stance
open to the world, to nonlinguistic experience. Likewise, the
formulation "composition by field" and the whole notion of
"field poetics," which had passed from Pound through Williams
to Olson and Duncan, suggest that a poem should be conceived
and formed within a larger field of objects and energies that the
poem can communicate but never completely contain. As Olson
observes, the "process" by which the projective poem reaches

15. M. A. Bernstein, "Robert Duncan," 187–88.
16. Quoted in Faas, *Towards a New American Poetics*, 82–83.

completion is never confined within the intramural structure of the poem itself; rather, through this process the poet brings the energy of objects or experiences in the world directly to the reader: "A poem is energy transferred from where the poet got it (he will have some several causations), by way of the poem itself to, all the way over to, the reader. Okay. Then the poem itself must, at all points, be a high-energy construct and, at all points, an energy-discharge" (*SW*, 16).

The title of Duncan's 1960 book, *The Opening of the Field*, indicates the importance these notions have for his poetry. Like Olson, Duncan sees Pound and Williams as central to the liberation of verse from closed form—that is, to the creation of a new openness in poetry comprising formal experimentation and the capacity to move in areas of discourse not sanctioned by the New Critical poets and critics of the 1940s and 1950s. In "Projective Verse" and elsewhere, Olson's rejection of closed form, of the nonprojective, is part of a larger rejection of Western cultural norms. Duncan, however, had to find a middle ground incorporating a Romantic or Sublime tradition within the framework Olson and his Modernist predecessors had established. Even though Duncan finds parts of Olson's project compelling and a necessary antidote to the prevailing poetry of the time, his concern with a language that can define a relationship between human and object and locate a more subjective or subconscious experience of reality makes it impossible for him to reject the Romantic Sublime tradition.

Pound, both as the instigator of a new poetics in the Imagist movement and as a poet who allows a formal openness in *The Cantos,* is a model for Duncan of the poet's potential to explore hitherto uncharted or even prohibited areas of artistic form and expression in an "adventure of poetics." Duncan quotes from Pound's Imagist credo of 1912, where he writes of "an intellectual and emotional complex in an instant of time" that brings "that sense of sudden liberation; that sense of freedom from time limits and space limits; that sense of sudden growth, which we experience in the greatest works of art." For Duncan, the discovery of Pound, along with other Modernist writers such as

Stein and Joyce, means "that in an art everything was possible, nothing circumscribed the flowering of being into particular forms" (*FC*, 66–67).

Duncan's continual search for artistic "openness" is largely a reaction to the dominant poetic mode of the postwar era in which, according to Duncan, the poem was seen "as a discipline and a form into which the poet put ideas and feelings, confining them to a literary propriety, giving them the bounds of sound and sense, rime and reason, and the values of a literary—or social—sensibility." The Romantic and mystical sensibility Duncan seeks, as well as the constant drive toward liberation of sources, forms, and ideas, is a refuge from a critical and poetic school "which thought of form not as a mystery, but as a manner of containing ideas and feelings; of content not as the meaning of form, but as a commodity packaged in form." Duncan's fear of poetry becoming a "commodity," a "Container Design," a "product on the market," forms a link with Olson's poetic and critical practice, which are largely based on a rejection of received Western values, the "pejorocracy" of modern American civilization. For both poets, Pound is the definitive model of a poet and critic who, as Olson puts it, "stayed clean." Pound refuses, at least in *The Cantos,* to enter the "business" of poetry, to mold his work to the taste of an audience or to the demands of convention. Instead, Pound in *The Cantos* "remains involved . . . in the agony of the contemporary," showing in the turbulent passages of his poem "the troubled spirit of our times": "A profound creative urge, like So-shu, churns in the sea of Pound's spirit everywhere, as it churns in the seas of our own history; so that we see it most just where contention will not allow our reason to be undisturbed" (*FC*, 79).

In other words, as Duncan writes in *The H. D. Book,* Pound's poetry in *The Cantos* is unlike the work of Eliot and Stevens, with their "melodious poetic respectability"; Pound's work disturbs us, forces us to examine things more closely. Duncan praises Pound for the rigor of poetic discipline that makes possible this examination of truth and value in economics and politics as well as in language and literature:

Pound has sought a cure of tongues by the discipline of the eye, some restraint that would keep words grounded in meaning. The pomp of Milton or the luxury of Swinburne had led men to value effect and enthusiasms in themselves as "poetic," towards an inflation of language. Protesting against the "prolix" and the "verbose," against words "shoveled in" to fill a metric pattern or to complete the noise of a rhyme-sound or "decorative vocabulary," Pound insisted that there be "absolutely no word that does not contribute to the presentation." If we think of his later concern for a monetary credit that is grounded in an actual productive order, "the growing grass that can nourish the living sheep," and his cause against the great swindling of confidences in usury, commodity speculation, money changing and inflation, we find a basic concern for the good credit of things; both words and moneys are currencies that must be grounded in the substance of a real worth if they be virtuous.[17]

While recognizing the value of Pound's "sanctions," his concern for "the equities," Duncan is not satisfied with an aesthetic that emphasizes only rigor and clarity and thereby sacrifices Romantic Sublime impulses, the part of creativity that lies in the realm of the spirit or the subconscious. Olson attacks Duncan in "Against Wisdom As Such" for seeking a false wisdom, one lying outside his own direct experience. But Duncan defends what he calls his "pretentious fictions": "I like rigor and even clarity as a quality of a work—that is, as I like muddle and floaty vagaries. It is the intensity of the conception that moves me. This intensity may be that it is all of a fervent marshmallow dandy lion fluff" (*FC*, 65).

Duncan's diverse sources fulfill needs that are not only "poetic" but are part of a search for a larger social and sexual identity as well. He found early in his development as a poet that only a poetry of trial and error, of experimentation with very different models, could satisfy his many disparate urges: "The structure of my life like the structure of my work was to emerge in a series of trials, a problematic identity. A magpie's nest or a collage, a construct of disparate elements drawn into the play they have excited, a syncretic religion" (*YC*, ii).

17. Duncan, "The H. D. Book," I, 3, 18–19.

Duncan tried from his earliest work onward to establish a ground between the two traditions of poetry he loved and admired: a Poundian poetry of "controlld [*sic*] strength . . . having the power of exactitudes and discriminations of tone" and the more "rhetorical," Romantic mode of Milton, Hopkins, Dylan Thomas, and Duncan's favorite model as a fledgling poet, George Barker. In "Persephone," an early poem of 1939, Duncan was already trying to infuse some of the "magic of the poetry of Ezra Pound" into his own verse. Although at this stage Duncan could not yet make his way through the more documentary or political sections of *The Cantos,* he was deeply moved by "Pound's autohypnotic evocation of a world in which gods and elemental beings moved" (*YC,* iii–iv). This same world of *The Cantos* continued to serve as a source of inspiration for Duncan during the decades to come. Without it, the first of Duncan's "mature" volumes, *The Opening of the Field,* could not have existed. Although many of the poems in *The Opening of the Field* are not ostensibly Poundian, moving toward a mystical evocation of desire and spirituality, the most successful poems are those that achieve a sense of Romantic fervor while fulfilling Poundian standards of craft, concision, clarity, and musicality and employing techniques of ellipsis, juxtaposition, and allusion adapted from *The Cantos.*

To understand fully Duncan's use of Pound's poetry in forming his own poetic practice in *The Opening of the Field,* let us examine his reading of Canto 91, from the "Rock-Drill" section, a Canto that exemplifies for Duncan the transcendent quality in Pound's later work "of the poem's moving, as the poet holds in his mind a sacred and divine universe, of a sacramental and divining dance of Mind in syllables, words, and articulations of line" (*FC,* 211). Duncan was moved to write about this Canto, perhaps the most lyrically beautiful part of the "Rock-Drill" section, on two separate occasions, ten years apart. In 1979, he finds Canto 91 to be a prime example of this "unconditional beauty" in Pound's art, an order of poetry "where Beauty is a sense of universal relations, of being brought into the intensities of even painful feeling." Pound is at times embarrassed, accord-

ing to Duncan, by a "womanly" beauty in his poetry that shows
"a hint of vulnerability," and Pound prefers instead to break into
a rough and realist "man-talk," "a subliminal voice from some
barracks or locker-room." Yet despite his professed disdain for
the lyric or Romantic subjects that had already been "spieled on
endlessly" by himself and "9,000,000 other poets," Pound in-
creasingly returns to practice "the *trobar clus*," where such
things as "Spring, Trees, Love, Wind have enduring and hidden
meaning." Canto 91 plays on images of eyes, light, and crystal
and represents for Duncan the powers of the imagination to
reveal hidden meanings through visionary experience. Duncan
quotes from the beginning of Pound's poem, then comments:

> that the body of light come forth
>   from the body of fire
> And that your eyes come to the surface
>   from the deep wherein they were sunken,
> Reina—for 300 years,
>   and now sunken
> That your eyes come forth from their caves
>   & light then
>   as the holly-leaf
>   qui laborat, orat.

> We recognize an image in the process of the poem not because of
> some device of speech, not as a descriptive arrangement of words or
> a striking word, but because we see as we write. In the memory of the
> first poem and the picture, the poem, moving the imagination, was
> remembered as an actual experience of a frog leaping and the plash
> of the pond; the picture actually seen by my eyes was remembered as
> a picture seen.[18]

Also reappearing in Canto 91 is one of the central ideograms
of the "Rock-Drill" section, that of *hsien,* which takes on new
radiance in one of Pound's most memorable images as the "ten-
sile" light of the silk cocoons that "the peasant wives hide . . .
now / under their aprons / for Tamuz / That the sun's silk / hsien
[picture of ideogram] tensile / be clear" (C, 612). We feel here
what Duncan describes as a "painful" beauty, as the sun and the
earth, the godhead and the "peasant's bent shoulders" are com-

18. Duncan, "The H. D. Book," II, 9, 72–80.

bined in a vision that enacts, to use one of Duncan's favorite phrases from Pound, "our kinship with the vital universe." Finally, the poem enacts Pound's historical sweep, his "universalizing Mind": side by side are the voyagers Apollonius, Odysseus, and Sir Francis Drake, the poets Bernart de Ventadorn, Cavalcanti, and Dante, and in a negative portrayal the philosophers Marx and Freud. Canto 91 is above all the poem of magnificent women, what James Wilhelm calls the "Queen's Canto." It opens with the evocation of "Reina" of the sunken eyes and proceeds to evoke Undine, Helen of Tyre, Princess Ra-Set, Eleanor, Artemis / Diana, Empress Theodora, "Merlin's moder," Joan of Ark, and Queen Cytherea (with whom the poem ends), not to mention peasant women and water nymphs. Even a kind of chaste, mystical marriage between Merlin's parents is described, for which Pound brings in the language of Celtic myth that is so important to Duncan's own poetry: "By the white dragon, under a stone / Merlin's fader is known to none" (*C*, 613).

It is likely that Duncan finds valuable and inspirational many aspects of Pound's Canto, and indeed of Pound's poetry in general, at the time of *The Opening of the Field.* Along with Pound's imagery of light and the notion of a higher order it suggests to Duncan, the feminine presence in Pound's later poetry is for Duncan a redeeming element in Pound's work, an indication of a newfound spirituality. At the same time, Pound's later portrayal of the feminine as essentially representative of a state of ordered beauty amid the chaos of (male) political and economic life—Pound's "rant"—implies for a reader such as Duncan a "threatened chastity of mind," a repression of the necessary sexual dimension. For Duncan, female presence and beauty can never be wholly separate from sexuality, from Eros, from the desire between men and women that represents to him, along with the homoerotic impulse, an essential component of the human psyche.

In an earlier installment of *The H. D. Book* Duncan writes extensively of Pound's incapacity to admit the darker side of life, his refusal to allow "that the sublime is complicit, involved in a total structure, with the obscene—what goes on backstage":

> For Ezra Pound, the operation of the work outside the spirit of its art, the excess in which what might have been aesthetic, beautiful, or later, in Vorticism, energetic, becomes psychological—sensually, sexually, or religiously sentimentalized—the psychic chiaroscuro of and in any thing—is distasteful, even abhorrent. . . . Spirit in the *Cantos* will move as a crystal, clean and clear of the muddle, even the filth, of the world and its tasks thru which Psyche works in suffering towards Eros. . . . Healthy mindedness is an important virtue for Pound's art—the clean line. . . . Pound insists upon the "well-balanced," the "mens sane in corpore sano" base. . . . To think at all, to imagine or to be concerned with, that state of the human psyche whose light is Luciferian and whose adversity is Satanic—much less to admit that in our common humanity we are ourselves somehow involved in that state—is, for Pound, to go wrong, to darken reason, a morbidity of mind.[19]

For Duncan, a vision of life that contains Eleusis must also include "the eroticism of D. H. Lawrence," the unconscious world opened up by Freud, and "the mire where Christ was born"; similarly, in an aesthetic realm (always mirroring the spiritual) an appreciation of the craft of Venetian stonemakers should not exclude the fleshly drama conjured up by a painting of Rubens.

It is Whitman, rather than Pound, who provides a poetic model for including this side of human nature. Despite the historical link Pound represents "in the succession from Whitman to us," Pound and his Modernist legacy mandate against a Whitmanic "longing" for sexual, spiritual, even linguistic freedom:

> The generation of poets who were contemporary with psychoanalysis also had a bias against abstraction; Pound, Williams, and we as their progeny have sought to test language, as if many of its functions were unreal or unsavory, against a control taken, in mimesis of the empiricism presumed in the scientific method, from the observable "objective" world. But I would see the process at work in Dante's

19. Duncan, "The H. D. Book," II, 3, 132–37.

and Whitman's falling-in-love in light of another reading out of
Freud, in which Eros and Thanatos are primary, at work in the body
of the poem even as they work in the body of man, awakening in
language apprehensions of what we call sexuality and spirituality.
Parts of language, like parts of the physical body, will be inspired;
syllables and words, like cells and organs, will be excited, awakened
to the larger identity they belong to.   (FC, 162)

In the "Rock-Drill" section, in addition to those women
present in Canto 91, we find Queen Elizabeth and Cleopatra
(important thinkers as well as great rulers), Empress Maria
Theresa, Isis and Kuanon, St. Ursula, Isolt, Piccarda Donati,
Fortuna and Luna, and Helen of Troy. As in Dante's *Paradiso,*
we find here the noble equivalents of the "dangerous women"
who inhabit Pound's hell in the early Cantos. In Duncan's own
poetry, particularly in *The Opening of the Field,* he continually
returns to an evocation of women: as a personal and sexual
presence, as an embodiment of desire, and as a representation of
an aesthetic order—"the Muse." In "Often I Am Permitted to
Return to a Meadow," for example, Pound's queens are united
with the "Lady" from his adaptation of Cavalcanti's "Donna mi
priegha," who becomes Duncan's guide:

Wherefrom fall all architectures I am
I say are likenesses of the First Beloved
whose flowers are flames lit to the Lady.

She it is Queen Under The Hill
whose hosts are a disturbance of words within words
that is a field folded.

                                                    (OF, 7)

Duncan's poem "The Maiden" from the same collection is a
tribute to famous women of myth and literature and to women
poets. Here Pound's vision of woman as embodying a crystalline
purity is "tainted" with an always nascent sexuality:

Because we thirst for clarity,
the crystal clear brook Undine wakes
unquenchable longing, in which
jewels innocent show in lovely depths.

    Her persistence makes

Freud's teaching that a child has sexual fantasies
terrible.

(OF, 27)

Duncan recalls the water spirit Undine from Canto 91 — "Thus
Undine came to the rock / by Circeo / and the stone eyes again
looking seaward" (*C*, 610). He also remembers Persephone
(Proserpine, Kore), who is a central figure throughout *The Can-
tos*, one of the "Poundian trinity" of "three goddesses in one."
She is especially memorable in the "Lynx" passage of Canto 79
(in a line Duncan quotes from in "The Truth and Life of Myth"):
"Kore, Kore, for the six seeds of an error" (*C*, 490). Duncan's
nod to Pound is only in passing here, for he prefers to return
instead to Dante's vision of evocative physical beauty, rather
than Pound's more reserved and statuesque mythology:

> *Lovely to look at,*   modesty
> imparts to her nakedness willowy
> grace. Bright with spring,   *vestita*
> *di nobilissimo colore umile ed onesto sanguigno*
> Dante saw her   *so that the heart trembled.*
> In Hell   Persephone showd
> brightness of death her face, spring
> slumbering.

The grace and stateliness of the "maidens" Duncan evokes in the
poem — Ophelia, Rachel, Cora, Dante's Beatrice — suggest his
appreciation of Pound's conception of the feminine. But Dun-
can's use of women is more reminiscent of the Dante / Whitman
tradition he often invokes. Freud and Lawrence appear, along
with Hamlet of "dark earth," and remind us that the state of
girlhood is a precursor to puberty and the onset of sexuality.
Like Whitman's, Duncan's sexual honesty will not allow us to
forget our true nature: "Men have mothers. They are of woman
born / and from this womanly knowledge / womanly" (*OF*, 28).

Duncan sees in Pound's early writing on Imagism and on the
troubadours the possibility of an almost Whitmanian aesthetic,
but one that is too firmly entrenched in the past. Pound's thought
"does not go forward with contemporary scientific imagination

to a poetic vision of the Life Process and the Universe but goes back to Ficino and the Renaissance ideas" (*FC*, 190). In Duncan's "opening" poem, "Often I Am Permitted to Return to a Meadow," he creates an ideogram that can include both of his predecessors and that has indications of both past and future.

> It is only a dream of the grass blowing
> east against the source of the sun
> in an hour before the sun's going down
>
> whose secret we see in a children's game
> of ring a round of roses told.
>
> (*OF*, 7)

The "dream" and the "secret" are words from the realm of mystery, a level of language Duncan feels Pound tries to exclude from his poetic world. These are words "pregnant" with meaning, and they bring "children" into the field of knowledge and experience that make up the poem and the book, this particular manifestation of future life is, like the female sexuality that produced it, absent from Pound's vision.

But the image works on two other levels as well: the "grass blowing / east against the source of the sun" is a metamorphosis of a Poundian ideogram, that of east as the sun caught in branches, and a powerful evocation of the Pound of the *Pisan Cantos* and after—"a man on whom the sun has gone down" (*C*, 430). These same three lines also allude to Whitman, to the grass of *Leaves of Grass* blowing in the winds of time and to the "mysterious" and "prophetic" message of *Democratic Vistas* and that dream vision, "Song of Myself."[20]

There is also a Duncanesque pun here: "the source of the sun" is also the source of the *son*, Whitman as father to Pound in the last "hour" of his life and subsequently Pound as the father to Duncan himself. Duncan is now a child seeking "permission" to

---

20. I am also reminded throughout the poem of a whole complex of images from the *Pisan Cantos*: grass; various kinds of fields; meadows, orchards, furrows, and the insects, birds, and animals that inhabit them; and the wind— "part of the process." Pound, like Duncan, views the life of these fields as of sacred importance—*aram vult nemus*.

enter his phase of "mature" poetry, ready to take responsibility for the field as "a given property of the mind / that certain bounds hold against chaos." "We see" (vision as phanopoeia and as apotheosis) the clear and defined image (though through a dream) as we experience the explicitly musical (melopoeic) properties of language in the nursery-rhyme line "of ring a round of roses told." We also encounter the logopoeia of a "dance of the mind" at the end of the poem, a dance that involves the juxtaposition of two central images. The last line of the poem, "everlasting omen of what is," reconciles past, present, and future, bringing together in the poetic process a childlike openness to new experience, the work of the present poet, and the inspiration provided by predecessors such as Whitman and Pound.

As Norman Finkelstein has observed, "Often I Am Permitted . . ." is a "seminal post-modern lyric"; it is an embodiment of the Poundian virtues of precision and workmanship but at the same time allows the freer play of "rhetoric" that is a legacy of Whitman and of the Romantic tradition.[21] It is a poem intended to be read in the tradition of Whitman, Pound, and Williams as an "open" and "inclusive" work, less interested in its own autonomous "intramural" relations than in its multivalent relationship to sources in the natural world (spatial), in poetic models (temporal), and in the realm of an informing spiritual experience (eternal and virtually unbounded) that allows a larger field of poetry to be "folded" into the poem.[22] The poem also serves more locally as an introduction to the poems that follow it in the book and, indeed, through the open-ended "Structure of Rime" sequence, to poems that are to come after the end of the book. Most of the poem's resonances are not apparent without

21. Finkelstein, "Robert Duncan: Poet of the Law," 81.
22. See Murray Krieger's discussion of "contextualist" poetry in *The Play and Place of Criticism*. In an extreme manifestation of New Critical ideas, Krieger measures the success of a poem in terms of "whether or not it builds intramural relations among its elements strong enough to transform its language into new meanings that create a system that can stand on its own," while leaving the less important "clouds of referential meaning . . . trailing behind" (158–9).

a knowledge of the other poems in *The Opening of the Field* and, indeed, without some previous knowledge of Duncan's work and derivations.

Duncan's vision of the field, "meadow," or "pasture" as a communal place consisting of various interacting living communities, yet also open to the human community, establishes the poem and the book to follow in the choric tradition of Duncan's predecessors. It moves from the personal statement of the title to the shared vision of a secret *"we see* in a children's game." Like Duncan's poem, the secret can be appreciated only in the context of a larger community of concerns. Duncan's poetry in *The Opening of the Field* demonstrates the desire he shares with Pound and his other primary models to reach outside the concerns of a contained, isolated, solipsistic, or hermetic "lyric self" to the needs of a poetic or artistic community, to the needs of a "world community" of common ecological and spiritual concerns, and to the sense of community as nation exemplified by Whitman's *Democratic Vistas* and Pound's "American Cantos."

In his four volumes since *The Opening of the Field,* Duncan has illustrated, through his derivations from a wide range of diverse sources, his continuing artistic struggle with the same dual forces whose interaction shaped his earlier work. In *Roots and Branches* (1964), Duncan turns for his title to Pound as well as to H. D. and Williams, who move him "in their passion, in their ripeness, the fullness in process of what they are."[23] But despite the derivation of its title, *Roots and Branches* moves conspicuously away from Pound's influence in the direction of sources more in line with a Romantic mode of expression. In *Bending the Bow,* particularly in the *Passages* sequence, Duncan finds his most convincing poetic voice. While the poems in *Passages* owe a great deal to sequences such as *Paterson, The Maximus Poems,* and *The Cantos,* they also represent Duncan's most important work so far.

23. Duncan, "The H. D. Book," II, 4, 41.

As we see in the next chapter, Duncan's poetry in *Passages* is replete with allusions not only to Pound and his poetry but to an entire world of poetic possibilities suggested by Pound's work, by the discoveries he had made a generation earlier, and by the derivative poetics he had in a sense invented. We must not be put off, however, by the knowledge that Duncan's sources are often taken at second or third hand, derived from an earlier derivation, for as he himself suggests in the title of one of his poems, these are "transmissions" from the world to the inner cosmos, the "field" of his work. Because Duncan believes in the "requiredness" of his appropriation of certain sources, a reading of his poems must attempt to come to terms with such appropriations. Rather than seeing the derivation as diminishing the originality and freshness of his work, the reader must try to appreciate the richness that his use of sources brings to the texture of the poetry.

Sometimes such reading is difficult, and the "many energies" that "shape the field" of his poem come to resemble, in Duncan's own words, "a compost" rather than "a vortex." It is unclear at times what Duncan's aesthetic intention is, let alone whether he succeeds in accomplishing it. Yet we must feel that he has touched, through his use of Pound in particular, some of the central questions of poetry in our time. Duncan is constantly seeking the answer to the question of what is "modern" in modern poetry, and in *Ground Work: Before the War* (1983) he deliberately foregrounds the issue, asking, "Whatever after Ezra Pound would I do with that?" (*GW*, 86). Is poetic rhetoric still appropriate or even possible in the latter half of the twentieth century, or does "that injunction from Pound / to direct into specifying energies" preclude "such childish things" as the ornate beauty of a poem by Ben Jonson? It is precisely this struggle between two modes of poetic discourse—which affect not only language but every level of experience—that is central to Duncan's thought and his poetry and that informs the very substance and argument of much of his work.

In *Passages* 36, included in "A Seventeenth Century Suite in Homage to the Metaphysical Genius in English Poetry," Duncan

contrasts in thought and form his visceral feeling for the beauty
and carnal presence of the lady Truth in Ben Jonson's masque
with the strict rules of Pound's poetics. Duncan outlines these
rules in tight stanzas and controlled language reminiscent of
"Hugh Selwyn Mauberly":

> The river of her being is in flood.   It fills her eyes.
> Then what's invention or novelty   when *she*
> surprises us? We'd hide our being overcome?
> strive for the essential,   or   make it new?
>   She makes her grandstand and revives
> emotional enormities,   old ways, grand ways, in me.
>   Her left hand
> holds a curious ring of keys in which   rooms
>   —heavens and hells—
> beyond our hopes and fears   are lockt.

>   I'd like to clear the air,
>   take on a "modern" stance, Poetics 1924,
>   a language without ornament
>   a measure   functional thruout,
>   nothing fancy,   all
>   without excess,   expressive,
>   recalling in archaic mask,
>   the gesture stylized,   to speak
>   from energy alone.

>   The essential, nothing more!
>   The temper, fire and ice.
>   Line, hard cut,   without device.
>   Eyes, hierarchical, straight forward.
>   Having that rigor
>   testimony before the court demands.

> But there she stands!   as she is, insistent,
> in court dress,   elaborately personified,
> decorate with *impresae* and her symbolic fuss.
> And everywhere,   the language is too much.
>   (*GW*, 87–88)

The language is "too much," yet Duncan feels that it is
impossible to give it up entirely. Throughout *Ground Work:
Before the War* Duncan vacillates between these two modes of
poetry, continuing to celebrate both Pound's *techne*—the "art-

fulness, steady and careful / (wary) study of the work at hand"
(*GW*, 97)—and the Romantic impulse, the overflowing abun-
dancies in other traditions of English poetry. Robert Duncan is,
perhaps more than any poet of the twentieth century, acutely
aware of the insufficiency of any single poetic style or method-
ology to capture the "polyphrastic relations" in a period of
rapidly increasing complexity and disconnectedness. Like his
master Pound, Duncan is a poet determined to take the risks
that will expand our awareness of both language and experience.

7 IN HARMONY WITH THE MASTER
Formal and Political Structures in Duncan's Poetry

I can't imagine the failure of certain models. Ezra
Pound has never failed me as a model; I mean he still
is my master.
  Robert Duncan, *Allen Verbatim*

Pound never theoretically could face what he was ac-
tually doing in the "Cantos"; they didn't have what
he understood to be form. I mean, he wanted to man-
age the "Cantos" as a totalitarian poem; they didn't
prove to be totalitarian so he was as distressed by
them as by the democracy from which he came. We
couldn't have a more extreme example of democratic
composition than we had out of that man who kept
hoping he'd rescue himself by having totalitarian or-
der.
  Robert Duncan, to Howard Mesch

During the period from World War II until his death in 1988,
Duncan was the most persistent and ardent advocate among the
poets of his generation for a continuing experimentation in
poetic form that was in keeping with the seminal advances made
by Pound and his Modernist contemporaries. As early as 1938,
when Duncan was nineteen, he became aware of the innovative
formal qualities that characterized High Modernism in all the
arts. Among his principle discoveries of this period was Pound;
Duncan was chiefly struck by Pound's experimentation with
"changes in energy, movement and tone, so exactly made." In
works by Modernists such as Pound, Joyce, and the sculptor
Constantin Brancusi, it was, Duncan realized, "the composition,
not the exposition, of content that counts."[1] Pound's "compo-
sition" in *The Cantos* was responsible for an art that aimed for
"the dissociation of ideas."

  1. Duncan, "The H. D. Book," II, 3, 137.

Duncan's initial interest in reading Pound was motivated by the important position Pound held in the first decades of the century within a group of Modernist writers and artists who for Duncan constituted the basis of a "new poetics" and an entirely new way of approaching art and literature. Displaying little of the ambivalence Olson sometimes felt toward his Modernist predecessors, Duncan praised them for their advances and sought to understand, rather than judge, their deficiencies. In a section of *The H. D. Book* written in the mid-1960s, Duncan explained the sense in which Pound and his contemporaries provided models that continued to be relevant a half century later:

> Pound, writing in 1914, felt that a break was necessary with the preceding generation in poetry: "Surely there was never a time when the English 'elder generation as a whole' mattered less or had less claim to be taken seriously by 'those on the threshold.' " For my own generation, our elders—for me, specifically Pound, H. D., Williams, and Lawrence—remain primary generative forces. Their threshold remains ours. The time of war and exploitation, the infamy and lies of the new capitalist war-state, continue. And the answering intensity of the imagination to hold its own values must continue. The work of our elders in poetry was to make "a Dream greater than Reality"—a time-space continuum in which their concern for quality and spirit, for romance and beauty, could survive. Estranged from all but a few among them, they made a new dimension in which eternal companions appeared.[2]

Anticipating the concerns that would dominate the *Passages* sequence beginning in *Bending the Bow* the following year, he expressed in this 1967 essay his appreciation for the vital connection the Modernist movement had established between literary form and political engagement. For Duncan, the preceding generation of writers represented a historical era that called forth a revolution in poetic technique and in psychopolitical stance. Like his Modernist predecessors, Duncan and his postmodern contemporaries lived in a time of crucial sociopolitical activity; like Pound and others of his generation, they had to find within their poetics an "answering intensity of the imagination" as well

2. Duncan, "The H. D. Book," I, 7, 134.

as a "time-space continuum" adequate to contain a powerfully new statement of social, political, and spiritual values and concerns. Like Pound in particular, they had to accomplish this monumental task apart from mainstream cultural and artistic movements, substituting "eternal companions" for the "estranged" culture of a largely alien society. In a March 9, 1963 letter to Olson, Duncan had suggested the essential change in cultural orientation that took place for the generation of High Modernists who reached their adulthood and artistic maturity just before World War I. The cultural turmoil of the period around World War I had impelled writers toward an idea of poetic form that could incorporate history, "a syncretic world-poem where locality and field are crucial."[3] Duncan valued as a model for his own generation the imaginative act of a work like *The Cantos,* which could contain within it personae of many times and places, thus providing a poetic analogue to "the flux of cinematographic art" and exemplifying a sense of "virtu moving through time."

In the last chapter I discussed the important role derivation plays in Duncan's work. For Duncan, this "gathering of diverse influences" also constitutes a formal principle in his poems, a means of textually incorporating parts of what he calls "the conglomerate," the poetic "information" that provides a continually developing source of inspiration. Duncan's favorite conceptual model for the poem is that of the "cell," an entity that is never completely self-sufficient—it is separated from the outer world only by a thin semipermeable membrane—but that contains within it inner surfaces whose "aggregate amounts to something large." Duncan views *The Cantos* as a primary model of the poem as "cell": "Pound's inspiration in his Cantos, ultimately distressing to him, is in such an increase in the internal surface of the poem. It does not homogenize; for its operations are not archetypal or simple. Its organization is not totalitarian

3. The correspondence of Olson and Duncan is among Olson's papers at the Homer Babbidge Library at the University of Connecticut. This particular letter is also reprinted in *Maps* 6 (1974): 65–67.

but co-operative. . . . Every intense realization for me goes to inform anew the field of the poem."[4]

With the idea of the poem as cell, Duncan evokes the organic notion of the poem as physical and living form. The cell is an ideal model for Duncan, suggesting at once physical growth and process, inherent complexity, and a dynamic interrelation between the poem and the exterior world. Duncan views Olson's "Projective Verse" as a further exemplification of this same physical conception; in Olson's projective poetry the syllable—"the immediate minim, the immediate sounding event of our speech"—takes on the energy of a single "molecular particle" within the larger cell of the poem as a whole.[5]

The idea of developing the internal complexity of poetic form is of central importance to Duncan, who sees himself as carrying further or redefining unresolved aspects of *The Cantos,* that great American work of "polyglot assemblage."[6] The work that Pound ultimately saw as a failure ("a mess") because of its lack of "coherence" is attractive to Olson, Duncan, and Ginsberg for precisely that reason—they see in it a statement of the impossibility of total coherence or total closure. For Duncan in particular, the uncompletedness of this large form, this cosmic form as "a creation in process," is a liberating factor. It underlies his thesis that the poem is "an organically incremental process," a "cell" in constant movement and mutation that overflows not only the permeable boundaries established between forms and genres but also those imposed between the works of one poet or poetic work and another. In this sense, the operation of a single lyric within the tradition of a long poem or poetic sequence such as "Song of Myself," *The Cantos,* or Duncan's own *Passages*

4. Duncan, "Notes 1973," 51.

5. Duncan, "The H. D. Book," II, 4, 44. Duncan also shares with Olson an interest in Whitehead, and Duncan's poetics is informed by Whitehead's notion of "process" as much as by Pound's. For a discussion of Duncan's use of Whitehead, see Mark Johnson, "Robert Duncan's 'Momentous Inconclusions.' " The central idea Duncan develops from Whitehead's philosophy is that poetry, like nature, is in a continual state of process, never completed and always in "passage" to another level of experience.

6. Duncan, Interview with Howard Mesch, 83.

and "The Structure of Rime" represents an intertextuality not only of language or semiotic systems but of forms themselves.

Duncan, following Pound, seeks a craft that allows him to explore "the form of the total process," rather than one that imposes a fixed form on the natural "force" of poetic expression:

> THE CRAFT: art or skill of rendering a medium (in poetry, the sound and sense of the language) as a force fit for the complex of impression, perception, information, emotion, apprehension, in which the impetus and intent of the work arises. Pound gave us to "compose in the sequence of the musical phrase," thus opening up wider and more complex articulations of feeling and thought, and in rhythmic structure to preserve "the shape of your words, or their natural sound, or their meaning," thus directing our concern to what is happening—shape, sound, and meaning in movement.[7]

Whereas for the Objectivists craft is primarily a vehicle for exercising greater control over the poetic medium, Duncan prefers a less rigorously technical use of the term. He chooses to experience his craft not as an artisan forming his material but as an artist allowing the natural energies of language to enter into a poetic composition. The term that Duncan uses to describe his own poetry—*collage*—indicates his belief that the poem is open to just such a process of experiencing "what is happening," of assembling a form based on a cosmic "poetry of poetries." Although *The Cantos* gave him the model for the form of collage, Duncan's own use of the form, particularly in the poetic sequence *Passages,* attempts to go beyond Pound's understanding of the collage form as a vehicle for the "reincarnation" of various themes and personae throughout the poem. Duncan's collage is a means of exploring correspondences in the universe that defy rational understanding.[8]

By the time Duncan visited Pound at St. Elizabeth's in 1947, he had been reading Pound diligently for ten years, using the discipline of Pound's poetics as a corrective to the excesses of his own exuberantly Romantic nature, while also attempting to

---

7. Duncan, "The Lasting Contribution of Ezra Pound," 24.
8. See Duncan's interview with Michael Bernstein and Burton Hatlen, 89.

write a few poems in a Poundian style.[9] Duncan went to Pound with the purpose of meeting and paying homage to a poet who was "an absolute master," but Duncan appears to have had little of Olson's desire to "help" Pound or serve as his advocate. Duncan had made it clear from the beginning of his correspondence with Pound that they had strong ideological differences, and thus he had achieved a distance from the older poet that Olson never had.[10] The visits were also much less prolonged than Olson's, consisting of a few afternoons during a single week, and they certainly did not have the same impact on Duncan that they had on Olson. Although younger than Olson, Duncan was by this time a more established poet who had been forming his own poetic voice and convictions since the late 1930s. Duncan was also less concerned than Olson about the direct relevance of Pound's political message. Like Olson, Duncan saw ways in which the form and content of *The Cantos* reflected Pound's politics. However, when Duncan adopted formal elements from Pound's work, he hoped to divorce them from Pound's political system by combining Pound's form and voice with those of other contradictory sources. Thus, what chiefly interested Duncan in Pound's work was the creation of a radically new poetic form and the way that form reflected a changing social and psychological reality.

Emphatically, Duncan was going to deal with Pound as a poet or not at all and would not humor him by listening to the "political rant" to which Olson was subjected. Nevertheless, Duncan found the sessions trying, particularly because Pound seemed to have no interest in developments in the arts, such as most recent work of Matisse or Stravinsky, for whom Duncan

9. See Duncan's poem "Persephone" (1939) in *The Years as Catches* (and my discussion in chapter 5). See also in the same volume his early poems "Spring Memorandum: At Fort Knox" (1941) and "Homage and Lament for Ezra Pound in Captivity, May 12, 1944."

10. Ekbert Faas quotes Duncan's summary of the contents of one of the letters: "Here you are a totalitarian, and I'm an anarchist; and here you are with my parents' anti-Semitism which I threw out the window with miles of other junk; and still you happen to be an absolute master for me in poetry, so poetry must be something different from what we assume it actually is" (*Young Robert Duncan*, 237).

professed a high regard. Pound was also not impressed by Duncan's poetry in *Heavenly City, Earthly City,* questioning why Duncan found it necessary to write the same kind of Romantic poem he felt Modernist poets had already gone beyond.

Nonetheless, Duncan's artistic engagement with Pound gained renewed importance as a result of their meetings. Duncan's "Variations upon Pound's essay *Cavalcanti,*" his translations of "Donna mi priegha," and his *Venice Poem* demonstrated a continuing effort to come to terms with Pound's art and influence. Duncan was also beginning to take a greater interest in the question of form as it applied to all the arts. In his essay "The Poetics of Music: Stravinsky," Duncan showed a new desire to address the more formal qualities of music and the visual arts as well as those of literature.

The Venice Poem, written in the spring and summer of 1948, was the early poem that owed the greatest debt to *The Cantos.* Duncan was preoccupied at the time of *The Venice Poem* with at least two of the same problems Pound and the other Modernists faced: how to incorporate larger forms in his poetry and how to understand the poetic medium in relation to the other arts. In the poem Duncan explored Pound's "tone leading of vowels" and "fugal" form as musical structures and also tried to derive poetic motifs from visual works of art. In *The Venice Poem,* unlike Duncan's earlier work, Pound's influence could be seen not only on the level of language and tone but also in terms of overall structure, technique, and conception.

At the same time, Duncan was increasing his own "erudition," taking courses in medieval history and Renaissance architecture and studying Greek with the hope of progressing to Sanskrit and Chinese. In Poundian terms, Duncan was gathering the "materials" on which to base a longer poem and with which to form his own "ideogrammatic configurations."[11] Just as Olson was beginning to adapt Pound's use of historical sources to his own project in what was to become *The Maximus Poems,*

11. For a fuller biographical account of the writing of *The Venice Poem,* see Faas, *Young Robert Duncan,* 245–64.

Duncan was finding Pound's brand of "culture," at least as a base, increasingly stimulating and fruitful.

Composing *The Venice Poem* forced Duncan to come to terms with the structure of *The Cantos* as "an assertion of relationships," which "grasped as a picture or ideogram is the *meaning.*"[12] Unlike traditional forms such as the sonnet, sestina, or quatrain, in which Duncan was no longer interested, the type of form represented by *The Cantos* had become by this time "very much my own." Even the words he used to describe poetic composition were suggestive not of literary discourse but of other artistic disciplines such as dance, painting, and architecture:

> How to increase the complexity of interpenetration of parts; how to make the poem go on as long as possible—that is to contain the maximum quantity of moving parts so that the final performance of choreography and design will keep me intrigued intellectually and emotionally: all this posed against the endurance of the ideal audience—the ideal audience being one that can take precisely as much as I could take myself.[13]

Strangely enough, despite Duncan's obvious concern with the formal relations in *The Venice Poem,* Pound thought the poem did not have enough of "a plan." For Duncan, who read *The Cantos* as a "stream of consciousness," a "time flow" with no particular unifying structure, Pound's comment must have been surprising. This second piece of negative criticism from Pound was disheartening to Duncan, who saw Pound's statement as a sign of dissatisfaction with the final form of his own *Cantos* and his failure to understand, or admit, the radically free form they took. Indeed, Duncan felt that in *The Cantos* Pound relied too heavily on a "preplan" to guide the structure of the poem.[14]

Duncan's response to Pound's criticism notwithstanding, it is true that *The Venice Poem* suffers from a lack of cohesion, due

---

12. Quoted in Faas, *Young Robert Duncan,* 257.
13. Duncan, in "The Poet and Poetry—A Symposium," *Occident* (Fall 1949): 39–40.
14. See "The Poetry of Unevenness," 92–94.

either to Duncan's inexperience with a poem of this length (we recall the dubious merits of Pound's first drafts of early "Cantos") or to the lack of any programmatic and unifying philosophical framework. If anything, the poem is based on a system of personal and aesthetic concerns that only occasionally bear the weight placed on them by so ambitious a project. The Poundian imperatives quoted in the poem—"We must understand what is happening," "Watch the duration of syllables, the melodic coherence, the tone leading of vowels," and "The function of poetry is to debunk by lucidity"—do not seem to guide the reader in any meaningful way. Although *The Venice Poem* represents Duncan's first understanding of "the full structural imperative of a form seeking to come into existence in the process of a poem," his description of that process indicates a different notion of plan from the notion Pound professed for *The Cantos*: "It was like dreaming and in the dream working out the dream and knowing coordinations of its form and content as a language, coming to know the meaning of what was happening."[15]

Unlike Pound, who wants so badly to "make it cohere," Duncan prefers to work in a state of dream or trance, relinquishing the controlling presence of the poetic ego to experience the "natural" forces at play in the language and form. *The Venice Poem* enacts such a liminal state between art and music and "upon the edge of poetry," and accordingly it has "no coherence / other than the melodic vein / suffusing in pearl luster / over all surfaces."[16] The resemblance of Duncan's poem to *The Cantos* remains one of surface; words and phrasing taken almost verbatim from Pound's work ring hollow here. In *The Cantos*, the more lyrical passages gain their power through contrast with the pages of historical documentation and political and economic commentary that surround them, thereby assuming a special status as states of experience alternative to the world of everyday events. Duncan's poem provides no such sense of a

15. Quoted in Faas, *Young Robert Duncan*, 261.
16. Duncan, *The First Decade*, 99.

sustained historical context, and the value Pound confers on his moments of lyrical intensity is correspondingly diminished.

Twelve years separated *The Venice Poem* from the publication of *The Opening of the Field,* but they were twelve years of intense activity. During this time Duncan participated in many of the most significant developments in American poetry. He was a leading member of the San Francisco Renaissance, a central force in what came to be known as the Black Mountain movement, and a friend and supporter of the Beat poets. Duncan sees his experiences in 1952 as the crucial turning point for his own work. It was in that year, reading Olson's *Maximus* and discovering the work of Levertov, that he first understood the importance of Olson's "Projective Verse," a "call to order" for postmodern poets that "landed in our world and made a proposition that you have to start doing something."[17] Soon afterward, Duncan's discoveries of Creeley and Ginsberg occurred, and with them came a new understanding of the possibilities contained in the work of earlier poets such as Whitman and Williams and of open-form poetry in general. He also read from the strikingly new forms of poetry that appeared in these years and constituted a revolution in poetic practice as abrupt as that brought about by Pound's Imagism early in the century. The most prominent of these were the first four books of Williams's *Paterson* (1951) and his *Desert Music* (1954); Olson's *Maximus Poems 1–22* (1953) and *In Cold Hell, In Thicket* (1953); Ginsberg's *Howl* (1956); continuing sections of Zukofsky's *"A"*; and Pound's "Rock-Drill" Cantos (1955).

In a letter to Olson on June 17, 1954, Duncan vowed to "rouse my mind and fix my attention."[18] He remarked the "drive toward a maximum energy" in "Projective Verse" and the "current" of new writing in the work of himself, Olson, Ginsberg, and Creeley, a current that "runs underground," not appearing "upon the surfaces of this literary world of not-critical

17. Interview with Jack Cohn and Thomas O'Donnell, 545.
18. This unpublished letter is in the Olson archives at the University of Connecticut, Storrs.

criticism." Duncan then complained about the critical reception of Pound's *Cantos* as well as of groups such as the Dadaists, Surrealists, and Objectivists, whose works were largely "indigestible to the professional readers." Duncan likened the current critical climate to a "Pandora's box of stagnant pre-occupations to be cleared away" that had to be replaced by the "clear in-sight hear-say testimony in act" of a "projective" stance. Duncan's wordplay here encapsulated the poetics that he, Olson, and Creeley, among others, were trying to advance. For Duncan, poets and critics must respond directly to the original somatic impulses behind poetic composition (in-sight hear-say) and pay closer attention to a poetic "process" (a testimony in act) unmediated by conventional attitudes and assumptions.

Duncan also defined his present relation to Pound in this letter, written only four months prior to Olson's announced dissatisfaction with Pound in "I, Mencius . . . ." Duncan claimed that Pound's economic standard in *Social Credit* should be expanded to include all areas of language and poetry. In Pound's work, "the language [itself] is a social fund, an air, water, earth or fire, an elemental wealth in which we, any, all have a social credit: unbounded, to claim. Inspiration (in-breathing), currents, roots and light/heat." Following Pound's example, Duncan argued, poets in the tradition had to continue the "critical task" to which "Projective Verse" pointed. "If it is we is [*sic*] a literary movement with our fortunes to win I gladly default," he wrote. "But if it is there might be, even if only in—as if accident— academe, a spark from that flinty task to arouse us, get a move on, it's to be done."

Duncan moved part of the way toward the world of academe two years later, joining Olson to teach at Black Mountain. At the same time, he began writing the poems included in *The Opening of the Field*. In the four years Duncan spent on this book, the Pound tradition continued to develop its new poetics, as the fifth book of *Paterson*, Zukofsky's *"A" 1–12*, Pound's *Thrones,* and Olson's *The Distances* all appeared. These texts, along with Whitman's *Leaves of Grass* (now Duncan's "bedside book"), served as background for Duncan's new poetry, the "field" into which he was now "permitted"—"a made place, / that is mine, it is so near to the heart, / an eternal pasture folded in all thought" (*OF*, 7).[19]

It was during this time that Pound's notion of the ideogram became a central formal principle in Duncan's work. In a letter to Olson from the summer before he began *The Opening of the Field*, Duncan wrote that he was "reading again Cantos 85, 86, and 87 and realizing that some of these ideograms are coming into my language."[20] Exactly which ideograms he had in mind we can only guess because his use of them in his own poetry was more metaphoric than literal. Nonetheless, his experimentation with the ideogram as a structure of language was a significant stage in the development in his work. The ideogram, at least as interpreted by Fenollosa and Pound, is an active, verb-oriented structure that always moves the writer or reader toward a new or at least a more developed understanding or sensibility; thus, for someone of Duncan's poetic temperament the ideogram remains semantically open. Duncan found the ideogrammatic form to be a liberating conception; an ideogrammatic experience of the cosmos as "a creation in process" would differ from what he saw as a traditionally paradigmatic notion of the universe. According to Duncan, Pound's notion of "design" as "intent in an open possibility" was inspired by his discovery of Fenollosa's essay "The Chinese Written Character as a Medium for Poetry." Pound's discovery of a "moving syntax" came from Fenollosa's claim that "the true noun does not exist in nature": "Things are only the terminal points, or rather the meeting points of actions, cross-sections cut through actions, snap-shots. . . . The eye sees noun and verb as one: things in motion, motion in things, and so the Chinese conception tends to represent them."[21]

19. At the same time, Duncan continued to be interested in literary Modernism. He applied for a Guggenheim in 1957 to "undertake the study of the poetics of Stein, Pound, Eliot, H. D., Marianne Moore, William Carlos Williams, and Wallace Stevens."

20. This letter of August 28, 1955, is published in *Maps* 6 (1974): 58–60. In this letter Duncan writes, "And we've, both of us, got Grandpa [Pound] to thank for the way station of the ideogram (which allows for movement . . . the individual discovery)."

21. Duncan, "The H. D. Book," II, 1, 106.

Duncan's relation to Pound's use of the ideogram remains a problematic one. Although we see in Duncan's poetry examples of his adaptation of Pound's ideogrammatic method, I take issue with Laszlo Géfin's contention that Duncan's primary method of collage is essentially ideogrammatic simply because it involves the "incorporation of foreign matter."[22] To call Duncan's poems "collage ideograms," as Géfin does, is to confuse two distinct concepts and to promote a reductive understanding of both Pound and Duncan. The primary purposes behind Pound's method of ideogram, or "pictographic script," are condensation and scientific accuracy. Pound views the ideogrammatic method as "the method of science" and understands it to be based on a perfectly reliable and simple conception of language and referentiality. The method of the Chinese writer, according to Pound, "when he wishes to define red," is "very much the kind of thing a biologist does." There is no need in Pound's understanding for the kind of process Duncan envisions in the "grand collage" because according to Pound the ideogram "is based on something everyone KNOWS" (*ABC*, 22). Duncan's collage, however, is a method based on "faith," which can lead him into uncharted and irrational areas of personal experience. Pound explicitly contrasts the ideogrammatic mode with the metaphysical mode of Western thought that predominates in Duncan's thought and work.[23]

Nonetheless, in "The Truth and Life of Myth," Duncan discusses two of Pound's ideograms and refers to their impact on his own thinking. The first of these is the ideogram for the Confucian concept of sincerity, which Pound describes as "the sun's lance coming to rest on the precise spot . . . to perfect, bring to focus." For Duncan, this ideogram sums up the process of poetic composition, in which "the work of art is itself the field we would render the truth of" and in which we "focus in on the process itself as the field of the poem." Duncan differs from

22. See Géfin, *Ideogram*, 100–108.
23. "Fenollosa accented the Western need of ideogrammatic thinking. Get your 'red' down to rose, rust, cherry if you want to know what you are talking about. We have too much of this talk about vibrations and infinites" (*SP*, 78).

Pound, however, in his interpretation of the implications of sincerity for poetic composition, emphasizing the way in which a recognition of process allows "discord" to enter the form of the poem.

The second ideogram is "fidelity to the given word" or "the man standing by his word." Once again, Duncan revises Pound's use of the Confucian term for his own purposes: "This faithfulness, this truth to the word, I take to mean not that the writer deny the possibility of error and defend his statement, but that he face the possibility of error and seek the truth of his statement" (*FC*, 48–49).

More important to Duncan than the explicit use of these ideograms in his poetic technique is the way in which the ideogrammatic unit functions as a symbol for a more general principle of order in Pound's work. Although Pound's belief in "the Confucian myth of the state" troubles Duncan, he cannot help admiring the "heroic" gesture Pound makes in his "commitment to order," to "the Law." In his essay "The Lasting Contribution of Ezra Pound," Duncan cites as one of Pound's central legacies the introduction of Confucian thought and order (and the ideogram as emblematic of that order) into modern poetry. Duncan writes of his "concern with the nature of the Law," which is "inspired by the poet of *The Cantos*."

The law is a term that encompasses a broad range of meanings and resonances in Duncan's usage. It connotes everything from a universal or cosmic law of nature (like Pound's germinal consciousness, *directio voluntatis*, or *omnia quae sunt, lumina sunt*) to a principle of human behavior that has "its root in a man's inner order, the law of a lawful anarchism . . . opposed to the politics of coercion." The term also operates on a more formal level in the poem—as a law of creative order, of language and syntax.[24]

Duncan's questioning of the notion of the law in its range of manifestations anticipates the examination of political systems

24. Duncan, "The Lasting Contribution," 23–26.

found in his later work. It is in responding to the explicitly
political level of his nation in crisis that Duncan finally achieves
his strongest and most Poundian poetic voice as well as his most
complete synthesis of form and content. This political register
comes to the forefront in the poems of *Bending the Bow,* but it
begins to appear in *The Opening of the Field.* Duncan's longest
and most important poem in the latter book, "A Poem Beginning
with a Line by Pindar," suggests a new voice in Duncan's poetry
based on a Poundian certainty in the poetic validity of political
conviction. In contrast to *The Venice Poem,* the power of polit-
ical statement in this poem gives force to Duncan's rhetoric and
allows his lyricism a larger sweep. If Duncan's poetry had always
contained a prophetic strain, here his prophecy involves areas of
the psyche that operate outside the context of merely personal
relevance and that suggest a shared human consciousness of
social existence.

In "A Poem Beginning with a Line by Pindar," the poet
becomes a healer who through his activity can return "bright-
ness" to a world whose beauty is threatened by the stupidity and
avarice of political leaders. Duncan, like Pound and Whitman
before him, identifies personally with the deterioration of his
country:

> I too
> that am a nation sustain the damage
> where smokes of continual ravage
> obscure the flame.
> It is across great scars of wrong
> I reach toward the song of kindred men
> and strike again the naked string
> old Whitman sang from.
>
> (*OF,* 64)

Again he combines the visions of Whitman and Pound, this time
in a condemnation of the presidents throughout the previous
century of American history:

> Harding, Wilson, Taft, Roosevelt,
> idiots fumbling at the bride's door,
> hear the cries of men in meaningless debt and war.

Where among these did the spirit reside
that restores the land to productive order?
McKinley, Cleveland, Harrison, Arthur,
Garfield, Hayes, Grant, Johnson,
dwell in the roots of the heart's rancor.

　　　　　　　　　　　　　　　　(*OF*, 64)

The image of the "idiots fumbling at the bride's door" and the expression of hope for "restor[ing] the land to productive order" are reminiscent of Pound's denunciation of infertility as a reversal and desecration of the natural process in the "Usura Cantos" and elsewhere.

Whitman and Pound are central to Duncan as the prophetic American poets who in their old age were able to achieve an "unaltering wrongness that has style / their variable truth," a poetry made of "words that shed like tears from a plenitude of powers time stores" (*OF*, 63). From his opening invocation of Pindar's ode—"The light foot hears you and the brightness remains"—and with it a world of youthful beauty and exuberance exemplified by Cupid and Psyche, Duncan moves to an appreciation of the tragic loss of youthful radiance in the work of "the old poets." In the third section of the poem, he turns his full attention to "the old man at Pisa," the suffering Pound of the *Pisan Cantos,* a heroic figure "who must struggle alone towards the pyres of day":

　　　　　　　　　　　Psyche's tasks—the sorting of seeds
　　wheat　barley　oats　poppy　coriander
　　anise　beans　lentils　peas　　—every grain
　　　　　　　　　　in its right place
　　　　　　　　　　　　　　before nightfall
　　gathering the gold wool from the cannibal sheep
　　(for the soul must weep
　　　　and come near upon death);
　　harrowing Hell for a casket Proserpina keeps
　　　　　　　　　　　　　　　that must not
　　　　be opend . . . containing beauty?
　　no!　Melancholy coild like a serpent
　　　　　　　　　　　　that is deadly asleep
　　we are not permitted
　　　　　　　　to succumb to.

These are the old tasks.
You've heard them before.
They must be impossible. Psyche
must despair, be brought to her
                                    insect instructor;
must obey the counsels of the green reed;
saved from suicide by a tower speaking,
    must follow to the letter
    freakish instructions.

In the story the ants help. The old man at Pisa
    mixd in whose mind
(to draw the sorts) are all seeds
        as a lone ant from a broken ant-hill
had part restored by an insect, was
    upheld by a lizard

                (to draw the sorts)
the wind is part of the process
                        defines a nation of the wind—
    father of many notions,

                        Who?
let light into the dark?   began
the many movements of the passion?
                                    West
from east   men push.
                    The islands are blessd
(cursed)   that swim below the sun,

    man on whom the sun has gone down!
                    (*OF*, 65–66)

I quote this third section at length not simply for the allusions
to Pound himself but for the example of Duncan's writing in a
projective mode where the form, loosely based on that of the
Pisan Cantos, reflects its content. In the beginning of this section
we find a "sorting of seeds" as Duncan, through the workings of
Psyche, distributes them in evenly spaced rows in the line. The
careful listing of the types of seeds shows an awareness of their
uniqueness and functions as a celebration of the degree of atten-
tion that Pound brings to every "task," every act of writing. The
seeds become "charged with meaning," just as they are charged

with the possibility of fruitful production. Our return to the "field" here is the culmination of the Poundian metaphor Duncan repeats again and again in the book: of the seed as "generative imagination," as "ancestral grain," as "Corn that at Eleusis Kore brought" (*OF*, 43), as potentiality and desire, as tradition, as "fathering force / a temenos, / bounded by grandparents, that founds / one field" (*OF*, 56).

The story of Psyche becomes that of Pound, who, like her, experienced hell in his months at Pisa and who was saved from insanity by the "insect instructor," by the "green reed," by the lizard and the wind—all "part of the process." Pound's tasks, like those of Psyche, "must be impossible"; he cannot make *The Cantos,* his epic, cohere on either a personal or a sociopolitical level. Just as he cannot put his own thoughts and works "in order," he cannot save the world from destruction. In coming to terms with Pound's experience, which devastated him but at the same time allowed him to achieve the brilliant poetry of the *Pisan Cantos,* Duncan finds a moving story of suffering and redemption:

> As at Pisa, uprooted from his study and his *idées fixes,* "a lone ant from a broken ant-hill," Ezra Pound was to come . . . to a turning point, exposed, at the heart of the matter. Mussolini had been torn to pieces, like Cola di Rienzi, his Renaissance counterpart. "Manes was tanned and stuffed," Pound remembers in the first Pisan canto. The poet had hitchhiked his way to Pisa and surrendered, given himself up to the army. Had he expected death? His fellow prisoners were led off to the firing squad each day. And for the first time in the Cantos, in these Pisan cantos, some attitude of authority, some self is surrendered, so that a pose seems to have fallen apart, exposing the genuine, confused, passionate mind. "A lizard upheld me," he testifies. He is in the condition of first things.[25]

Duncan emphasizes the timeless quality of such a story in the lines "These are the old tasks. / You've heard them before." Just as the line of Pindar that begins Duncan's poem joins the work of Whitman, Pound, and Olson in Duncan's poetic experience,

25. Duncan, "The H. D. Book," II, 1, 109.

such archetypal stories as that of Psyche can be reintegrated into the modern experience of a prisoner in war. Duncan pays tribute to Pound's own art in *The Cantos,* whose landscape "is a multiple image, in which the historical and the personal past, with the divine world, the world of theosophical and poetic imagination, may participate in the immediate scene."[26]

Pound is "restored" in the passage, as he was restored to his own country after the war; he "defines a nation of the wind," becoming the "father of many notions." Continuing the metaphor of the germinating seed, Duncan views Pound as an agent of the new fertility in American poetry, spreading his ideas, both right and wrong, as if in the wind. The pun on "nation / notions" reflects Pound's own preoccupation with America as an "idea," an eternal possibility.

Pound's influence on Duncan operates on an intensely personal level as well. Duncan's question "Who?" and the hesitant revelation of "let the light into the dark? began / the many movements of the passion?" returns us to the level of Duncan's own experience, reflecting a tentative, yet almost mystical, union between the speaker (Duncan) and the older poet (Pound). But in the final lines of the passage, Pound once again takes on an archetypal role as the Odyssean voyager of his own *Cantos,* searching in vain for a country, for a place to rest. At the time of Duncan's writing, Pound was still without a home, living out what would be the end of his term at St. Elizabeth's.[27] In a section from *The H. D. Book* written three years later (1961), Duncan makes explicit the connection between Pound and Odysseus: "Like Odysseus's, Pound's exile can be read as the initiation of the heroic soul (the hero of Poetry) descending deep into hubris, offending and disobeying orders of the imagination and returning at last after trials 'home.' Odysseus offended Poseidon

26. Duncan, "The H. D. Book," II, 4, 33. Duncan continues: "In literature, Pound had written, 'the real time is independent of the apparent.' So Henry James mingles with lynxes and with the divine powers Manitou and Kuthera attending, and Mt. Taishan appears in the Pisan atmosphere."

27. Pound was released in May 1958 and returned to Italy. Duncan's poem is also from 1958, and though I do not know the exact dates of composition, I am assuming that he at least began it before Pound's release.

and is shipwrecked; Pound offends the Elohim and comes at last, like Job, to trials of old age and despair."[28]

Like Odysseus, too, Pound saved his greatest task for last. It was "the crucible of the war," the depth of his experience during his imprisonment, that made possible what was for Duncan one of the greatest works of twentieth-century poetry, the *Pisan Cantos*. Pound's imprisonment and "exposure to the elements," writes Duncan, "touched a spring of passionate feeling in the poet that was not the war but was his age, his ripeness in life." The "prophetic mode of high poetry" Pound achieved after the war was "a challenge" to young writers of the 1950s, unlike the works of Stevens, Moore, and Eliot, which remained "within the rational imagination" and did not "suffer from the creative disorders of primitive mind, the shamanistic ecstacies and the going 'after strange gods.' " Pound, along with Williams, H. D., and Lawrence, was a poet who "saw literature as a text for the soul in its search for fulfillment in life and took the imagination as a primary instinctual authority." He was, as Duncan puts it in one of his favorite phrases, on a continual "adventure in po-etry," charting new territory, taking risks in "seeking to fulfill [his] vision of the poet as seer and creator."[29]

It is in the *Passages* sequence begun in *Bending the Bow* and continued until Duncan's death twenty years later that his poetry bears the greatest stylistic, formal, and thematic resemblance to *The Cantos*. *Passages* is, like Pound's *Cantos,* a "work in progress," never to be completed, or as Duncan says in his introduction to *Bending the Bow,* "passages of a poem larger than the book in which they appear" (*BB,* v). Although Pound's original intention in *The Cantos* may have been to achieve a set form of one hundred "Cantos," following Dante, it was clear by the time Duncan began *Passages* that *The Cantos* would never reach a final state of completion. Duncan remarks in his intro-duction to *Bending the Bow* that Pound "sought coherence in *The Cantos* and comes in Canto 116 to lament 'and I cannot

28. Duncan, "The H. D. Book," II, 4, 36.
29. Duncan, "The H. D. Book," II, 1, 111.

make it cohere' " (*BB*, iv). In *The H. D. Book*, Pound's inability to "unite" *The Cantos*, to make them adhere to a predetermined form, to establish closure, is seen not as a failure but rather as a sign of Pound's unique vision of art as "dynamic form." Unlike Yeats, who chose to see *The Cantos* as "prescribed composition, or an architectural plan, having sets, archetypal events . . . imposing a diagrammatic order of such archetypes on history," Pound saw the important structure as the form the poem took "on the page." Duncan compares Pound's feeling for structure in *The Cantos* to his analysis of Clément Janequin's music, which is a "music of representative outline" rather than a "music of structure." For Pound, the ideal form is that of natural process, "the *forma,* the immortal *concetto,* the concept, the dynamic form which is like the rose pattern driven into the dead iron-filings by the magnet."[30]

Duncan calls Pound's final Cantos "the Cantos of Contrition" and reads them as the apotheosis of this poetry that "takes shape in the air," a work not ordered and arranged but always marked by "the defects inherent in a record of struggle." Duncan remarks how Pound sought in Mozart a symbol of musical coherence against the "chaos" of Beethoven and Bartók, but could not escape the fact that his own "struggle to form" was ultimately Heraclitean. Duncan quotes Heraclitus in support of his claim that all music, and by extension poetry, is by nature in conflict with itself, capable of discordance within its own structure. "[In] being at variance it agrees with itself," says Heraclitus of the (Orphic) lyre. "There is a connection working in both directions." Duncan's poetic sequence, like Pound's *Cantos,* will be "polysemous"; it will be connected "as in a mobile" not only by "what comes one after another as we read, but by the resonances in the time of the whole in the reader's mind" (*BB*, iv). *Passages,* like *The Cantos,* will be outside the realm of chronological time, the event of each line contributing to the "emerging articulations of time" in the work as a whole.

30. Duncan, "The H. D. Book," II, 4, 34–35.

Unlike *The Cantos, Passages* is not presented as a single, epic work; the fifty poems that make up Duncan's sequence appear alongside other poems in three different books.[31] Thus, the poems cannot be read as closed off from Duncan's other poetry, as constituting in any sense a unified, epic structure. Duncan's individual Passages are also shorter on the whole than a single Canto and can be read more easily as self-contained poems that relate to one another in oblique ways, rather than as part of a narrative continuity or as "building blocks" of an overarching structure. All but three of the *Passages* sequence also have their own titles, suggesting a greater degree of self-sufficiency. Their design is flexible, neither totally conforming to the pattern of such "long poems" as *The Cantos, Paterson,* and *The Maximus Poems* nor completely following in the tradition of lyrics or lyric sequences. As Duncan himself says, they are "not part of a great poem at all": "They're part of a tapestry . . . a weaving that would be at the same time loose enough; indeed, I'm dissatisfied with how little I am able to break up my close weave."[32]

Even if Duncan's poem/sequence is less a monument carved in stone (Pound's "Rock-Drill") than a "weave," the debt of *Passages* to *The Cantos* is unquestionable. Allusions to techniques and forms as well as to individual words, phrases, and ideas of *The Cantos* can be found throughout. The inaugural poem, for example, is entitled "Tribal Memories," which informs the reader immediately that on at least one level Duncan's series takes its cue from Pound's definition of *The Cantos* as "the tale of the tribe." Duncan's work also focuses, like Pound's poem, on memory—both the memory of the individual poet/persona and the mythic memory of the human race, the tribe, or the nation. Duncan makes clear the mythic stature he intends, vowing to send out his poems "among tribes setting each a City / where we Her people are / at the end of a day's reaches" (*BB,* 9). His "City [which] will go out in time, will go out / into time, hiding even its embers" (*BB,* 10) echoes the sacred city of Wagadu from *The*

---

31. *Bending the Bow* (1968), *Ground Work: Before the War* (1983), and *Ground Work II: In the Dark* (1987).
32. Interview with Howard Mesch, 85.

Cantos ("4 times was the city remade, / now in the heart inde-
structible" [C, 465]) as well as Pound's sacred cities of Dioce and
Ecbatan.[33]

In the second poem, "At the Loom," *The Cantos* makes its
physical entrance into Duncan's sequence:

> A cat's purr
> in the hwirr thkk   *"thgk, thkk"*
> of Kirke's loom on Pound's Cantos
>   *"I heard a song of that kind . . ."*
>
> my mind a shuttle among
>   set strings of the music
> lets a weft of dream grow in the day time,
>   an increment of associations
>   luminous soft threads,
> the thrown glamour, crossing and recrossing,
>   the twisted sinews underlying the work.
>
> Back of the images, the few cords that bind
>   meaning in the word-flow,
>   the rivering web
>   rises among wits and senses
> gathering the wool into its full cloth.
>
>   (*BB*, 11)

Duncan's poetic allusion to the beginning of Canto 39, also
picking up the back-and-forth dance of Canto 4—"beat, whirr,
thud, in the soft turf"—provides him with the visual and aural
imagery he needs to describe his own poetic process. "At the
Loom" not only contains some of Duncan's best poetry; it also
demonstrates the incorporation in his own work of parts of *The
Cantos*. Here his use of Pound is not merely for echoes, allusions,
or stylistic or thematic parallels; it involves a tangible process by

---

33. Duncan's essay "The Truth and Life of Myth," published in the same
year (1968) as *Bending the Bow*, makes clear the debt he feels to Pound's
mythopoeic vision in forming his own sense of "form as mythopoeia." Duncan
attributes much of his poetic development to "the mythopoeic weavings of
Pound's *Cantos* in which 'all ages are contemporaneous' " as well as to the work
of "twentieth-century mythologists" Cassirer and Freud and classicist Jane
Harrison: "My sense of the involution of a universe of contributing contingen-
cies, is such that my sentences knot themselves to bear the import of associa-
tions" (*FC*, 6).

which Pound's "material" enters into Duncan's "loom" and is reworked by virtue of his "craft." Duncan extends Olson's notion in "I, Mencius, Pupil of the Master" of making new clothes out of the master's "shoddy"; in the passage just quoted Duncan not only describes the process in his poem but physically reenacts it in the resulting language, form, and texture.

By formally acknowledging that *The Cantos* will be his primary poetic source in *Passages*, Duncan prepares the way for a series of poems that pay tribute to the various currents of Pound's opus. *Passages* 3 and 7, for instance, reflect the form of Pound's "fragments" in the final Cantos. (*Passages* 7 is also called "Envoy," recalling Pound's "Envoi" in *Hugh Selwyn Mauberly*—"go, dumb-born book.") These poems convey an eerie sense of affiliation with the final "fragments" of *The Cantos*, which were appearing at the time Duncan was writing and which marked Pound's gradual descent into silence as he neared the end of his life. Still more clearly, the designation of *Passages* 31 through 35 as "Tribunals" mirrors the title of Pound's *Thrones*. Like Pound's later Cantos, these poems express Duncan's continuing concern with the law, with the necessity for some unified spiritual and political order to be placed against the deterioration of the modern world.

On a more local level Duncan's poems adopt several of the devices of *The Cantos*, such as pictures (pictographs) in the text, Poundian fragmentation and juxtaposition, quotation from several sources including John Adams (Duncan provides notes at the end of *Bending the Bow*), and different adaptations of what can loosely be called the ideogrammatic method. In "At the Loom" Duncan applies Pound's technique of presenting and then defining or explaining a Chinese ideogram to the English language: he provides definitions for the words *warp* and *shuttle* from *The Oxford English Dictionary*, along with examples of the words' uses. Duncan derives a series of poetic images from the words' various gradations of meaning:

> warp, *wearp, varp:* *"cast of a net, a laying of eggs"*
>   from **warp-* *"to throw"*

> the threads twisted for strength
>   that can be a warp for the will.
>
> *"O weaver, weaver, work no more,"*
>   Gascoyne is quoted:
>   *"thy warp hath done me wrong."*
>
> And the shuttle carrying the woof I find
>   was *skutill*   *"harpoon"* —a dart, an arrow,
>   or a little ship,
>
>   *navicula*   *webershiff,*
>
> crossing and recrossing from shore to shore—
>
>   prehistoric **skutil*   **skut-*
>   *"a bolt, a bar, as of a door"*
>   *"a flood-gate"*
>
>   (*BB,* 12)

In both this poem and "Spelling" (*Passages* 15) Duncan most explicitly takes on the Poundian role of poet as teacher or pedagogue. "Spelling" not only reflects the influence of Pound's didactic poetry but also refers to Olson's dictionary-inspired writings and to Olson's belief in the revelatory potential of etymological roots. Duncan goes so far as to instruct the reader ("performer") of the poem to write the italicized words on the blackboard as he reads, in "earnest mimesis of a classroom exposition." Like Pound and Olson, Duncan takes the poem to be a lesson in language; he seeks a perfected use of language that will be accurate and sincere and at the same time charged with meaning through etymology, sound, and poetic expression. In "Spelling," instead of merely tracing words to their Anglo-Saxon roots as in "At the Loom," he establishes correlations of sound and etymology among words by examining their derivations from Greek and Old English.

"The Fire" (*Passages* 13) contains another adaptation of the ideogram, as Duncan places thirty-six words in a square on the page at the beginning of the poem and then reverses their positions at the end. Here the words can be read in any direction within their arrangement (either horizontally, as in English, vertically, as in Chinese, or even backward or diagonally). Thus, the words themselves, removed from any fixed syntactic or sequential relation to each other, can serve as visual images as well as units of language. Like Chinese ideograms, they exist as objects outside of syntax. In reading the poem, the semantic and imagistic connections between words occur in various patterns of meaning. The words take shape in the reader's mind both as individual mental images, as parts of a more complex picture made up by the whole square, and as a complex ideogrammatic configuration.

Duncan reinforces the sense of the visual in the poem by juxtaposing these two "word paintings" with descriptions of two paintings by Piero di Cosima and Hieronymus Bosch. Through the Bosch painting, Satan enters the poem in the form of a catastrophic vision of modern life that is redeemed only by the presence of the repeated but reversed grouping of words that ends the poem. As in *The Cantos,* the "political rant" that breaks out of the poet's tortured psyche ultimately falls away to reveal a transcendent vision of the natural world, an original world of light and shadow, earth and water, now and forever, "the condition of first things":

faces of Princes, Popes, Prime Usurers, Presidents,
    Gang Leaders of whatever Clubs, Nations, Legions   meet
       to conspire, to coerce, to cut down

    Now, the city, impoverisht, swollen, dreams again
    the great plagues—typhus, syphilis, the black buboes
          epidemics,   manias.

My name is Legion   and in every nation   I multiply.
    Over those who would be Great Nations   Great Evils.

They are burning the woods, the brushlands, the
    grassy fields razed;   their
       profitable suburbs spread.
   Pan's land, the pagan countryside, they'd
       lay waste.

cool	green	waver	circle	fish	sun
hold	wet	wall	harbor	downstream	shadow
warm	close	dark	boat	light	leaf
foot	purl	bronze	under	coin	hand
rise	smell	earth	loosen	plash	stone
now	new	old	first	day	jump

                      (*BB,* 44–45)

Duncan's strikingly innovative arrangement is perhaps as close an approximation as is possible in the English language of Fenollosa's description of ideograms as "the meeting-points of actions, cross-section cut through actions, snap-shots . . . things in motion, motion in things." This arrangement also exemplifies what Duncan finds valuable in Pound's Imagism — the image that charges language with meaning, thereby "giv[ing] value to an otherwise valueless language and world." Duncan writes of Pound's Imagist practice: "To evoke an image is to receive a sign, to bring into human language a word or a phrase . . . of the great language in which the universe itself is written." Duncan contrasts the practice of Pound and H. D., poets who infuse their language with "origins in a more than personal phantasy," with that of a poet such as Eliot, whose "images are often theatrical devices." What Duncan finds in Pound's poetry, and what he tries to instill in his own writing, is a meaningful myth of everyday language in which "our daily words [are] a language of poetry, having the power of themselves to mean, and our role in speaking [is] to evoke not to impose meaning."[34] Duncan's explanation in *The H. D. Book* of the poet's task as one involving a Jungian collective unconscious certainly applies to a poem like "The Fire," where "the things of the poem," the "powers of stones, waters, winds," become a ritual enactment of the search for shared meanings, for the mysterious and the sacred.[35]

Duncan is a poet so highly aware of his own use of poetic models that in his work the poem, book, or entire corpus can be viewed as an open field for the interplay of poetic sources. Duncan is not confused by this complex relationship to past writers and texts; instead, he speaks forthrightly about the natural process of derivation, which is a central aspect of all poetry. Duncan's metaphors for textual influence — the poem as a

34. Duncan, "The H. D. Book," II, 4, 28–29.
35. Duncan's visual block of text can also be seen as a forerunner of some of the formal experimentation carried out by the Language poets, although Duncan is not interested here in the ideological valences of the words he places together in the way that Language writers generally are.

"folded field," a weave of fabric, a "grand collage," or a cell permeable by a variety of materials—certainly imply an intertextuality that is not altogether different from Kristeva's textual cross-junction. But the concrete nature of Duncan's allusions to other poets and the self-conscious gesture he makes in adopting them as models—the "love" he expresses for their work and the "permission" he asks of them to write—suggest a different intertextuality from that described by Bloom, Barthes, or Foucault. In Duncan's work, the identification of the previous author as source remains an important, even necessary component of the poem's meaning; yet the personal and historical dimension of that reference is not subjugated to the purely textual relation of the two poems. The poetic form Duncan chooses supports his view that just as the individual poet is not subsumed by the tradition, neither are the predecessors in the tradition repressed by the developing poetic ego. Instead, there is a constantly balanced and respectful interaction between past and present, individual poet and larger tradition.

8 POUND'S WORDS IN THEIR POCKETS
Denise Levertov and Gary Snyder

Pound . . . stirs me into a sharper realization of my
own sensibility. I learn to desire not to know what he
knows but to know what I know; to emulate, not to
imitate.
    Denise Levertov, *The Poet in the World*

Pound [is] a teacher of poetic technology.
    Gary Snyder, quoted by Lee Bartlett

In the last four chapters I have explored the way in which
Pound's work served as a model for his two most central post-
modern descendants: Charles Olson and Robert Duncan. As
should now be apparent, these two poets represent radically
different and often conflicting conceptions of Pound's legacy and
of his value to younger writers. Although Olson's and Duncan's
works form the borders within which the postwar Pound tra-
dition operates, they by no means exhaust the creative possibil-
ities contained in Pound's writing. In this chapter I examine in
more condensed fashion the place of two younger poets in the
tradition: Denise Levertov and Gary Snyder.

    For different reasons, both of these writers were relative
latecomers to the postwar American scene: Levertov (b. 1923) is
British by birth and education and regards her move to America
in 1948 and her concurrent discovery of Modernist and post-
modernist American poetry as the turning point in her poetic
career. Through Creeley, whom her husband, Mitch Goodman,
had known at Harvard, she was introduced to the poets con-
nected with Black Mountain—especially Duncan, with whom
she established a long-lasting friendship and correspondence—
and she began an intensive reading of Williams and Pound. She
was soon publishing her poetry in *Origin, Black Mountain
Review,* and the annual anthologies published by New Direc-
tions. Her contact with "new rhythms of life and speech" and
her discovery of Olson's "Projective Verse" both helped her to

develop in a relatively short time from "a British Romantic with almost Victorian background" into an important figure in the Pound / Williams tradition of the 1950s and 1960s.

Snyder, seven years younger than Levertov, has spent most of his life on the West Coast. When he began his poetic career in the mid- to late 1950s he had ties with both the San Francisco Renaissance and the Beats, but he has remained relatively independent of direct affiliation with either group. Snyder was firmly defined within the Pound / Williams tradition by his appearance in *Black Mountain Review* no. 7 (1957)—alongside works by Zukofsky, Creeley, Ginsberg, Levertov, Dorn, Jack Kerouac, Jonathan Williams, Joel Oppenheimer, Michael McClure, and Philip Whalen. And, like many of these poets, he was also included in Donald Allen's *The New American Poetry*.

As poets, Levertov and Snyder are different in almost every respect; stylistically, thematically, temperamentally, and institutionally they appear to have little in common. What they do share, however, is a profound sense of affiliation with the poetic tradition I have been defining. Although neither Levertov nor Snyder experienced a personal and direct relationship to Pound, they both regard Pound and his poetic legacy as central to the development of their own practices. It is this sense of tradition and the way in which it informs their poetry that I explore in this chapter—first in terms of their work as a whole and then more specifically in readings of representative poems by each writer.

Levertov views herself not as a "woman poet" but as a writer attempting to develop an "androgynous sensibility" that will allow for a more "human" poetry transcending gender definitions.[1] While she values the work of certain female poets, most importantly H. D. and Muriel Rukeyser, most of Levertov's models and influences have been male: among the most significant are Pound, Williams, Stevens, Yeats, Shakespeare, Goethe, Rilke, Chekhov, and Neruda. Levertov's position as the only woman in this book raises the question of the overall status of

---

1. Levertov, *In Her Own Province*, 100.

women poets within the Pound tradition. If we keep in mind the status of women in modern and American poetry generally, the Pound tradition does not appear exclusively or even unusually male centered relative to other traditions of poetic writing, most of which are, at least numerically, dominated by male authors.

The theoretical question of whether the nature of Pound's writing or his sense of tradition in some way excludes women is a more complex one. Recent feminist criticism has explored the relationship between gender and ideology and has suggested the possibility of a gender-based poetics.[2] My readings, however, do not indicate in Pound an exclusively "male" poetics or the exclusion of women from his poetic tradition, which originates in part with Sappho. Pound's espousal of the sexual theories of Remy de Gourmont in the early 1920s does indicate a tendency to view women as passive, rather than active, participants in cultural tradition, and his portrayal of women in *The Cantos* is open to criticism on a number of grounds. But Pound's continued association with H. D., his assistance in publishing the poems of Marianne Moore, and his later correspondence with the poet Iris Barry indicate an openness and a lack of bias in dealing with women poets.

In a poem entitled "September 1961" Levertov pays homage to the three American poets of the previous generation who were a source of inspiration for her and her peers: Pound, Williams, and H. D. It is significant that, like Duncan, Levertov celebrates her female precursor H. D. not within the context of a tradition of women's writing but within the context of American poetic Modernism, thereby also placing herself within the immediate context of postmodern contemporaries such as Duncan, Olson, and Creeley, rather than in a line of female poets. The personal occasion for Levertov's poem was a distressed note she had received from Williams, saying, "I can't describe to you what has been happening to me." Williams had been experiencing an extremely difficult period in his life and work, his illness and loss

---

2. For one of the most influential discussions of poetics and gender, see Sandra Gilbert and Susan Gubar, *The Madwoman in the Attic*, 3–106. For a related discussion, see Alicia Ostriker, "The Thieves of Language."

of memory preventing him from writing or lecturing.[3] Levertov's poem stresses the interconnected life and poetry of the three forebears, all of whom had in some way withdrawn "into a painful privacy / learning to live without words" (*P*, 81). For her, the retreat of these "old great ones" from the poetic scene leaves the younger generation of writers alone in an alienating (urban) environment, far from the mystical union with the sea of inspiration their elders sought:

> They have told us
> the road leads to the sea,
> and given
>
> the language into our hands.
> We hear
> our footsteps each time a truck
>
> has dazzled past us and gone
> leaving us new silence.
>
> > (*P*, 81)

She tries to imagine what it will be like to write "without the light of their presence," with only "the words in our pockets, / obscure directions":

> But for us the road
> unfurls itself, we count the
> words in our pockets, we wonder
>
> how it will be without them, we don't
> stop walking, we know
> there is far to go, sometimes
>
> we think the night wind carries
> a smell of the sea . . .
>
> > (*P*, 82–83)

Williams was the first of the three "great ones" to have an importance for Levertov; with the aid of Creeley's insights into the nuances of American speech patterns, Levertov was able to unlock Williams's "measure" in the late 1940s and early 1950s. An appreciation for the work of Pound and H. D. took longer to

---

3. See the account of this period in Williams's life and of his note to Levertov in Paul Mariani, *William Carlos Williams: A New World Naked*, 764.

develop. When Levertov first arrived in the United States, she had read only "a minimal amount of Pound (anthologized in a Faber anthology)" and was much more familiar with *ABC of Reading* than with *The Cantos*.[4] Her knowledge of H. D.'s work was similarly limited to "a handful of early poems," until the 1957 publication of the poem "Sagesse" (see *PW*, 244–48). From Creeley and later Duncan, Levertov received her education about Pound and H. D. as well as Olson and the new poetry being generated in America. Pound in particular represented to Levertov a valuable alternative to the more "homespun" persona somewhat unfairly applied to Williams ("Buffalo Bill"), especially prior to *Paterson*. The crude imitations of Williams's work, poems full of precise and raw detail and written in a faintly "local" idiom, amounted to what Levertov later called the "Midwestern Common Style." Levertov found reinforced in Pound, as in H. D. and Duncan, her own rejection of merely "descriptive" or "self-expressive" poetry; in its exploration of unknown, sacred, or mythic aspects of experience the work of these poets signified an alternative not only to imitations of Williams but also to the prevailing "confessional" mode (see *PW*, 87–106).

Levertov's search for previously unknown sources for her poetry led her to adopt the characteristic method of poets in the Pound tradition: a synthetic use of poetic models that could be used in the juxtaposition or confrontation of apparently unreconcilable poetic traditions. It was a method that would ultimately allow her to incorporate a sense of social and political engagement into an often romantic or mystical idiom—a form of "pure poetry."

Like Duncan, Ginsberg, and Pound, Levertov increasingly frames her poetry as a reconciliation of divergent traditions: experimental Modernism, Romanticism, and religious mysticism. A list of influences on Levertov includes such diverse figures as Dante, Shakespeare, Donne, George Herbert, Hölder-

4. Quoted in Bertholf, Byrd, and Reid, *Scales of the Marvellous*, 85.

lin, Goethe, Wordsworth, Coleridge, Keats, Swinburne, Hopkins, Rilke, Yeats, Stevens, Lawrence, Lorca, and Neruda, not to mention Pound, Williams, Olson, Creeley, Duncan, and Ginsberg. The related question for Levertov, as for Duncan, is how to reconcile in a single poetic voice different literary traditions and the attitudes they represent—how to accommodate social, political, and historical concerns within a basically Romantic and mystical conception of the poetic project. Predecessors such as Williams and H. D., with whom Levertov has been more commonly associated, provide important models of poetry's "engagement" with the world, but it is in poets such as Pound (and Duncan and Ginsberg) that Levertov finds the possibilities of directly political expression and of a "revolutionary" stance.

Snyder's sources differ as much from Levertov's as Olson's from Duncan's or Pound's from Williams's; nonetheless, the importance Snyder places on the poet's embrace of a usable tradition allies him with the fundamentally inclusive poetics of Levertov. In an interview with Ekbert Faas in the late 1970s, Snyder defines literary tradition in terms that revise the famous Modernist formula—Eliot's "tradition and the individual talent"—while at the same time providing an alternative to a Bloomian view of influence in post-Romantic poetry. Snyder embraces a Buddhist notion of tradition according to which an understanding of one's own nature is not seen "in purely individualistic Romantic terms":

> The Romantic split between tradition and individual talent is no problem for the Buddhist. It's understood that you go to the tradition and study the lore handed down by men who have gone through the same process of meditation and study as yourself, and you respect and appreciate the accumulation of wisdom that they have brought forward. You tune that back into your study of yourself, you turn the soil over, and you actually work back and forth between absolutely naked self-examination and reference to a tradition that you respect.[5]

5. Quoted in Faas, *Towards a New American Poetics*, 116.

Snyder acknowledges the value of poetic tradition, both as a source of "useful" poetic models and as an important record of the history of ideas. But rather than support either Eliot's distinction between the needs of the individual and those of the tradition or Bloom's even more pointedly antagonistic relationship between the poet and his or her "repressed" ancestry, Snyder celebrates an openly declared and respectful relationship to the works of past authors. In his introduction to the Snyder interview, Faas rightly calls attention to the way in which Snyder resembles Olson in his relationship to literary tradition. Although I agree with Faas, I locate the model for Snyder's use of tradition and sources less in Olson than in Pound.

Snyder discovered Pound while a student at Reed College (before he was exposed to the work and ideas of Olson), and by at least one account Pound was his favorite poet at that time. It was chiefly from Pound that Snyder learned how to incorporate noncanonical and often nonpoetic sources into his work and how to blend or reconcile different traditions while forming his personal canon. Snyder's notion of poetry as the "soil we go back to" in our Western (and non-Western) heritage and his sense of the "usefulness" of certain works or authors as "tools" to be used in developing "the potentialities of Western consciousness" certainly owe a great deal to Olson's poetic stance, but they are no less reformulations of Pound's seminal ideas of vortex, of *krino* (to choose or select the particular source from among the many available), and of the donative author. Although Pound would not have subscribed to the explicitly Buddhist terms of Snyder's understanding of influence and tradition, he would have fully concurred with the substance of Snyder's assertions. Snyder clearly recapitulates Pound's gesture (also that of Duncan and to some extent that of Olson) of using hand-selected authors and texts as "materials" out of which to construct a new *paideuma*.

Snyder's notion of tradition also shares with that of Pound a sense of the delicate balance that must be maintained between poetry's social function and its craft. On the one hand, Snyder, like Creeley and Ginsberg before him, is attracted to Pound's conception that poets are "the antennae of the race." Snyder interprets Pound's phrase to mean that poets function as "an early warning system" that can stand far enough outside the "cause-and-effect network of a society in time" to identify potential problems that society may face. Yet equally important to Snyder's sense of the Poundian legacy is the idea of craft or *techne*. Snyder acknowledges the importance of Pound to his own technique of composition, calling him an important "teacher of poetic technology." This Poundian sense of craft manifests itself in Snyder's translations of the Chinese poet Han-Shan, in his technique of using words and images as exact markers of a "trail" of experience (riprapping), and in the idea of the poem as a highly energized "knot of turbulence."[6]

Following Olson, Creeley, and Ginsberg, Snyder reads Pound within an American lineage that includes Walt Whitman, Robinson Jeffers, and Kenneth Rexroth. Like Olson, too, Snyder rejects the European models he sees as constituting the canonical "Christian" tradition. To Whitman, Pound, Jeffers, Rexroth, Olson, and Ginsberg, among others, Snyder adds alternative sources such as "the Greek anthology, the Romans, the Medieval Chinese."[7] Although he later revises his absolute stand on European models in listing Hopkins, Yeats, and Blake as central to his reading, Snyder makes less active use of them than he does of American and Eastern sources. He claims to regard two of the central poets of Western culture—Dante and Milton—not as literary precursors but as "exercise[s] in cultural history."[8] If in this respect he sides more with Olson's sense of cultural relativism than with Pound's embrace of a Western literary and stylistic tradition, Snyder's poetry resembles Pound's in drawing on a fusion of "the Anglo-Saxon or Germanic derived aspects of the English language" and on techniques adapted from an "understanding and ear for Chinese poetry."[9] Like Pound's ideogram-

6. Snyder, *The Real Work*, 71.
7. Snyder, "From Anthropologist to Informant," 112.
8. In Faas, *Towards a New American Poetics*, 117.
9. Ibid., 104.

matic method and Duncan's grand collage, Snyder's technique foregrounds an eclecticism of sources. But Snyder's web of intertextual connections is less literary than the similarly adopted intertexts of Pound, Duncan, or even Ginsberg; a typical Snyder poem may juxtapose discourses even more various than those of *The Cantos*. Snyder mixes in his poems historical and literary texts of both Western and non-Western origin; political, social, and mythic structures; and discussions of biology and ecology.

Levertov and Snyder vary widely in their incorporation of Pound's practice into their poetic texts: Levertov looks to Pound's understanding of the musical qualities of poetic language, his involvement with the mythic, and his historicism, whereas Snyder is drawn to Pound's ideogrammatic method and social and economic critiques. Nevertheless, the two share a common inheritance from Pound. They attend closely to the visual and aural properties of language and to the deeply rooted areas of somatic and mythic energy that poetry contains. They both establish their poetics firmly within the Imagist / Objectivist legacy of the postmodern Pound tradition. At the same time, each revises the postmodern gestures of Olson and Duncan by developing alternative versions of Pound's historical poetics.

Pound's prose writings serve as a guide to poetic technique for Levertov, particularly in their emphasis on the importance of sound and musical structure. In a 1964 interview, Levertov identifies the role of Pound's influence in her movement away from a conception of the poem as purely visual image and toward the idea that sound, or melopoiea, can best convey the poem's meaning and emotion:

> I think the visual image is terribly important, but it must be accompanied by the melopoeia, and melopoeia of a distinctly expressive kind, not just the musical over and aboveness that Pound speaks of in his definition in *How to Read*. Something closer to onomatopoeia, actually . . . the way the form arises from the sound of the words. It's not a matter of purely connotative precision. . . . It's that thing Pound speaks of, quoting Dante, about words being buttery or shaggy. If one is speaking about something fine, thin, and sharp, one

has to choose the words that have the finest, thinnest, lightest, sharpest sound, and not the words that have round, dark, warm, thick sounds.[10]

Pound's directives in *ABC of Reading* and elsewhere ("The way to learn the music of verse is to listen to it," or "Poetry atrophies when it gets too far from music") bring Levertov back, as she puts it, to "an examination of my own poetic conscience" and reinforce "the hope or intention of discovering the innate form of an experience, what Gerard Manley Hopkins called the *inscape* of it" (*PW*, 250).

Much of the terminology Levertov evokes in her discussion of sound in poetry is drawn directly from Pound's critical vocabulary and from the tradition of poetics that descended from him to the postmodern generation. In "The Origins of a Poem" (1968), Levertov invokes Duncan's phraseology to discuss the musical potential of poetry, but it is really to a more generalized conception of the Pound tradition that she refers:

> The poet's task is to hold in trust the knowledge that language, as Robert Duncan has declared, is not a set of counters to be manipulated, but a Power. And only in this knowledge does he arrive at music, at that quality of song within which speech is not the result of manipulations of euphonious parts but of an attention, at once to the organic relationships of experienced phenomena, and to the latent harmony and counterpoint of language itself as it is identified with those phenomena. Writing poetry is a process of discovery, revealing inherent music, the music of correspondence, the music of inscape.   (*PW*, 54)

The phrases "song within speech," "latent harmony and counterpoint of language," and "inherent music" are all based on Poundian concepts, as are the poetic tenets of "attention," "process," and "discovery." In a later essay about the importance of the line break in poetry, Levertov again evokes Pound's notion of "melos" in the poem: more specifically that found in its "pitch-patterns" and "significant, expressive melody."[11]

10. Levertov, Interview with Walter Sutton, 328–29.
11. Levertov, *In Her Own Province*, 73–75.

The second phase of Levertov's engagement with Pound's writing was her reading of *The Cantos*. Initially, Levertov distrusts the form of Pound's epic, whose "chaotic" structure seems "at variance with Pound the critic's emphasis on clarity, on communication, and at the same time on music" (*PW*, 252). While she can appreciate the "lyric sections" of *The Cantos,* the rest seems to be only "connectives" or "dross." Levertov is first impressed by the mythic, mystical, and visionary moments in Pound's poem. In "A Vision," one of her own poems from the 1967 volume *The Sorrow Dance,* Levertov celebrates Pound's visionary sensibility. The poem begins with an epigraph of Pound from Spinoza: "The intellectual love of a thing is the understanding of its perfections." Levertov herself identifies this poem as an instance in which the mythic "arises from within the poet and poem rather than being deliberately sought" (*PW*, 82). Pound, like Duncan, Olson, and David Jones, is an example for Levertov of a poet who does not merely write "academic set-pieces on mythological themes" but "in whom [mythological] scholarship is an extension of intuitive knowledge" (*PW*, 82). Levertov's "vision" in the poem, that of two angels each over-whelmed by the iridescent beauty of the other, is at once a highly personal dream and a testament to Pound's belief in the force of "intellectual love" and "right reason." Although the overall feeling evoked by the poem is not particularly Poundian, its registers of both visual and aural imagery are reminiscent of the language of *The Cantos*: lines like "Blue and green glowed the wingfeathers" and "leapt up among blues and greens strong-shafted" clearly illustrate Levertov's desire to synthesize melopoeic and phanopoeic elements to achieve a total effect of sensory and spiritual attention. In lines such as "flame petallings, cream-gold grainfeather glitterings," Levertov goes beyond a controlled Poundian diction toward a mode of Hopkinsian exuberance (*P*, 223–24). Even the form of the poem, with its frequent enjambments and its overtures to a kind of "sprung rhythm" within an essentially free-verse form, expresses her attempt at a reconciliation of an Imagist / Objectivist mode with a Romantic and mystical legacy.

In moving toward a more political poetry, and the more inclusive form that such a poetry entails, Levertov enters her third, and final, phase of engagement with Pound, which involves a greater understanding of the overall structure of *The Cantos*. Along with other poets of the 1960s who are drawn to the balance of lyric and didactic moments in Pound's epic—the "interpenetration" of private and public worlds it represents—Levertov begins to see the virtue of Pound's mosaic method: "I begin to apprehend the poetry of history, that flickers both in the olive leaves and in the voices speaking of trade; in the ant and the lynx, the sensuous imagination and the dry implications of document, in legislation and song and all the fabric of news that stays news" (*PW*, 253).

This commentary on Pound's *Cantos* can also be read as a key to Levertov's own work. The sense of a "poetry of history" she discovers in Pound allows her to capture the movements of the "sensuous imagination" while remaining, as the title of Levertov's first collection of essays indicates, "in the world."

The only book in which Levertov sustains her political voice throughout—*To Stay Alive* (1971)—is also her most striking example of work in a Poundian vein. The long poetic sequence "Staying Alive" that makes up most of the volume is strikingly different in both typographical form and overall conception from the shorter "lyric" poems constituting the bulk of her earlier work. As Lorrie Smith comments, "Recurring themes and words reverberate like Poundian subject rhymes to give the poems structure and coherence. . . . Like *Leaves of Grass*, *Paterson* and *The Cantos*, Levertov's is a 'poem including history' as well as a poem included and inscribed in history: Levertov's personal case history is inseparable from and representative of the public events in which she is immersed."[12]

Smith argues that most of Levertov's writing prior to *To Stay Alive* was based on a late-Romantic poetics amalgamating notions of Keats's "negative capability," Emerson's sense of "organic form," and "Williams' mediation between the 'spirit of

12. Smith, "Song of Experience," 222.

here-and-now' and a 'supernatural' realm of values.' "[13] Smith
traces in the development of Levertov's work a fusion of "poetry
and revolution" that she attributes primarily to Levertov's in-
volvement in the 1960s with left-wing politics. I concur with
much of Smith's argument, but I would place greater emphasis
on the role played by Pound and the Pound tradition in the
development of Levertov's political poetics. I also argue that
Pound's influence allows Levertov to negotiate the opposing and
often contradictory claims made by the desire for aesthetic
beauty and the need for political expression.

In her essay "On the Edge of Darkness: What Is Political
Poetry?" (1973) Levertov includes Pound's famous definition of
epic as "a poem including history."[14] Like Olson and Duncan,
Levertov is at pains to reconcile her respect for Pound's inclusion
of historical and political material in *The Cantos* with her dis-
taste for the actual manifestation of his political ideas. In another
essay she identifies Pound more clearly as a "political" poet,
comparing his support of Mussolini with Neruda's admiration
for Stalin. Though she later was "considerably less forbearing"
toward Pound's advocacy of fascist thought, Levertov is still
willing in the early 1970s "to forgive [Pound] . . . a man of such
brilliant intelligence in certain areas, for what can only seem like
stupidity in continuing to cling to that belief in the face of so
much contrary evidence."[15]

Levertov's leniency toward Pound's politics may stem from
her belief in the fundamental sincerity and integrity of his poetic
thought and writing. She values Pound's ideogrammatic notion

13. Ibid., 214.
14. Levertov, *Light Up the Cave*, 115.
15. Ibid., 132. In an essay of 1972 she writes, "Racist and rightist views are
abhorrent to me — but I look on these when they occur in Pound as an aberration;
and who among us does not have some kind of aberration? And all the evidence
points to Ezra Pound's personal dealings with whoever came into contact with
him as being marked by kindness and probity. Moreover, his Fascist affiliations
seem to me to have been made originally not in support of brute authoritarianism
and cynical contempt of the individual, but because he mistakenly supposed the
economic changes he correctly saw as necessary for a decent life would be made
under Fascism" (*PW*, 249–50).

of integrity as "man standing by his word" and sees Pound's work as informed by a "Confucian justice" that provides a sense of "just measure, awareness, disdain of fakery" (*PW*, 249). The emphasis in Pound's nonpoetic writings on "knowledge, accuracy, [and] clarity" is also important to her, though, like Duncan, she finds missing in Pound's statements an experience of the unconscious impulse she regards as an important source of her poetry. Finally, she sees in Pound's work a sense of the interrelationship of life experience and artistic creation. " 'The serious artist,' Pound says, 'will want to present as much of life as he knows.'. . . [Pound] stirs me into a sharper realization of my own sensibility." Despite Pound's lists of "essential reading," he teaches in his prose and poetry "not to accept received ideas without question, but to derive my own from concrete detail, observed and felt, from my individual experience" (*PW*, 251).

Levertov's preface to *To Stay Alive* makes Pound's *Cantos* and Williams's *Paterson* the implicit models for the form of the book. The poems in it depict "the artist as explorer in language of the experience of his or her life" and serve not as " 'confessional' autobiography, but as a document of some historical value, a record of one person's inner / outer experience of America during the 60's and the beginning of the 70's" (*SA*, 107). As in *The Cantos*, poetic material in the book becomes reusable; quotations and poems from this and other books recur in different combinations. The poems are also more allusive than most of Levertov's other work; she includes in *To Stay Alive* explanatory notes for quotes from various poets and other writers.

A reading of Part IV of the book's central section, "Staying Alive," demonstrates most clearly Levertov's adaptation of Pound's ideas and techniques. The sections of Part IV form a meditation on the relationship of the events of our daily lives to the process of history and on the possibility of reconciling even tragic personal events with the need to continue writing poetry that can enable political, social, and spiritual revolution. After a voyage in Part III to Europe and her native England—an attempt to escape the "fever" of an "anxious," strife-torn America at the height of the Vietnam War and antiwar demonstrations—

Levertov returns in Part IV to face the "tunnel of daily life." In Part III, Levertov had found an oasis in Italy; in this part her involvement with the more lyrical sections of *The Cantos* and their evocation of a mythically beautiful Mediterranean landscape is reflected in a language of calm translucence, which contrasts with the surrounding descriptions of political life in America. "Silver summer light of Trieste early morning," Part III begins, "(a silver almost gold / almost grey)" (*SA*, 166). During her stay in Italy, each movement toward peaceful and seemingly transcendent imagery is undercut by the insistent questionings of Levertov's conscience:

> Cop-out, am I,
> or merely,
>   as the day fades
>   (and Amerika
>   far away
>   tosses in fever)
> on holiday?
>   (*SA*, 167)

Such interruptions of her tranquil "holiday" return her thoughts to the pressing questions at hand and to a more engaged poetic voice. Levertov displays here a sense of the incongruity between personal and political levels in her poem; she differs from Pound in the realization that lyrical moments of aesthetic appreciation cannot be easily assimilated into an engaged political vision. Unlike Pound, who can simultaneously affirm a mystical, transcendent poetic vision and engage in political or social commentary, Levertov must choose between one mode of writing, thinking, and experiencing and the other. As the short, tentative lines in which she poses her question indicate even on a formal level, Levertov lacks a unifying vision of moral, political, and aesthetic perfection such as that which forms the basis of Pound's *Cantos*. The confused and elliptical syntax of the passage, the punctuation, and the parentheses bracketing out the now distant reality of American political life all indicate a profound sense of uncertainty.

Without a firm ethical structure such as that of sincerity or right reason and without a single evil such as *usura* to blame for all society's ills, Levertov must establish a sense of value through other means. Lacking a sense of her own "righteousness," she wavers between a desire for "oblivion" and a "hunger for revelation"; any lapse into what appears to be the realm of pure aestheticism—an expression of the "sensuous imagination"— becomes a source of guilt that destroys her immediate pleasure. Returning to England after Italy introduces another tension, this time between the "gentleness" of the "private life" still possible in England and the "anxious Amerika" of "present history." Levertov finally reconciles this conflict in the last section of Part III, deciding that the only solution is to find the "fiery stillness" that lies deep inside her own being, as in a "well." Levertov's descent into this deep well of spiritual strength is a *nekuia* "into [her] own depth as into a poem."

Levertov's meditation on the role of the individual in "present history" continues in Part IV. The final section, called simply "Report," begins with a discussion of the suicides of two friends:

> Judy ignored the world outside herself,
> Grandin was flooded by it.
> There is no suicide in our time
> unrelated to history, to whether
> each before death had listened to the living, heard
> the cry, 'Dare to struggle,
>   dare to win.'
> heard and not listened, listened and turned away.
>   (*SA*, 188)

Levertov's statement that "there is no suicide in our time / unrelated to history" reintroduces in a new context the theme of "present history." Here we have a sense of history very different from that of Modernists like Pound: it is the process of the individual taking "political" action, even within the limited realm of interpersonal solidarity, that defines history. Both "ignoring the world outside," as Levertov is herself inclined to do in her desire for "oblivion," and allowing the injustices of the world to overwhelm us are paths to suicide, to death. By understanding "history" as her "inner / outer experience of America" at a given moment in time, Levertov can come to a meaningful understanding of events—one that allows her both to help others and to strengthen herself.

Levertov moves between the personal and interpersonal levels of activity and awareness: from the attempt to interpret the suicides of others, to thoughts of her own struggle with the political rage and despair she feels, and finally to an acknowledgment of the heroic actions of her friends who are active war resisters. She prefers to speak not in the persona of Kali, the Hindu goddess of rage (one that Duncan had suggested), but in her own voice, quoting her final statement from Part II of the poem: " 'There comes / a time / when only anger / is love' " (*SA*, 188). Once again, she refuses to opt for the more mythical or "literary" solution of using a persona and thereby reasserts her own place as poet and individual in "present history." Levertov's attempt to find forms of "love" as well as "anger" in her immediate world leads her to an epiphanic vision beginning with a quote from the Russian poet Vladimir Mayakovsky and proceeding through a series of direct and indirect allusions:

'Life
       must be
              started quite anew,
       when you've changed it,
                     then
                            the singing can start up'
but he too
took his own life. Perhaps he was waiting,
not with that waiting that is itself a
                            transforming   energy—

              'Stone
              breaks stone to reveal
              STONE in stone!'—but waiting
to set all things right, (to 'rearrange all mysteries
                            in a new light')
before beginning to live? Not understanding
only conjunctions
              of song's
                     raging music

> with patient courage
> will make   a new life:
> (*SA,* 189)

Pound's presence is certainly suggested here, if not explicitly rendered. In rapid succession Levertov alludes to an inscription on a painting by the ancient Chinese artist Tao Chi ("Stone / breaks stone . . ."), she juxtaposes the phrases "set all things right" and "rearranging all mysteries in a new light" (evoking respectively Pound's notions of right reason and of the coherent splendor associated with the Eleusinian mysteries), and she re-phrases Pound's "make it new." Taken as a whole, the passage reflects Levertov's affirmation of poets like Pound whose lives reflect both intense suffering and "patient courage," both the power of "song" and the "transforming energy" to make active use of that music, that poetry. Pound is one of the writers who, as Levertov expresses it in her essay "Anne Sexton: Light Up the Cave," display both "endurance" and "love for their work." Pound certainly struggled with the same need Levertov feels to combine "song's raging music with patient courage" to "make a new life," even though he ultimately failed to accomplish his goal. Levertov has no answers either, or only incomplete ones. Rejecting the alternatives of "waiting for demolition and recon-struction" and "learning as a preparation for life," she moves through a series of metaphors for her own poetic use of "trans-forming energy": "recharge my batteries," "get my head to-gether," "knit idiom with idiom." Finally, Levertov settles on what will serve, for the moment at least, as a source of strength; again it is her own words, rather than those of Kali, that she chooses: "When the pulse rhythms / of revolution and poetry / mesh, / then the singing begins" (*SA,* 190).

Levertov's poetic diary ends, as the title of the final section suggests, with a "report": the "official" news of the invasion of Laos. "I have no virtue," she writes, "but to praise you who believe life is possible." Levertov ends by praising the Vietnam-ese people—the "you" of her apostrophe—thus finding a poetic "virtue" despite the closure-denying ellipses that end the poem (*SA,* 190). Levertov's notion of virtue as an affirmation of life is an echo of Pound's *virtù*, yet it no longer contains the same sense of artistic certainty and spiritual harmony evoked by Pound's term.

Gary Snyder's poetry can be characterized, according to Charles Molesworth, by a "sensory attention . . . and [a] sincerity lodged in the sensory realm" that are in keeping with the Imagist and Objectivist legacy of Pound.[16] Snyder's description of his own craft clearly delineates Poundian tenets such as compression, directness, and the ellipsis of unnecessary words and phrases; Snyder's notion of "sharpening the utterance down to a point where a very precise, very swift message is generated, an energy is transmitted," reminds us immediately of Pound's formulation of the image as a "vortex or cluster of fused ideas . . . endowed with energy" (*SP*, 375).

Snyder adapts other techniques that link his work with that of other poets in the Pound tradition: the use of tone leading as a musical and organizational device; the organization of pieces of knowledge, information, or experience into larger ideogrammatic units; and the attention to the visual appearance of the poem on the page. Snyder's explanation of his use of textual space makes clear his debt to both Pound and Olson: "The placement of the line on the page, the horizontal spaces and the vertical spaces are all scoring for how it is to be read and how it is to be timed. Space means time. The marginal indentations are more an indication of voice emphasis, breath emphasis—and, as Pound might have called it, logopoeia, some of the dances of ideas that are working within your syntactic field."[17]

Snyder's interest in poetic scoring reflects the combined influence of Pound's notion of logopoeia and Olson's breath-oriented practice; both predecessors contribute to Snyder's sense of the poem as a spatial field and a transcription of the oral impulse. As Thomas Parkinson observes, Snyder shares with other poets of the Pound tradition a belief in "the poem as an indicator of

---

16. Molesworth, *Gary Snyder's Vision*, 12–13.
17. Snyder, *The Real Work*, 31.

physical weight."[18] Like Olson, Duncan, or Ginsberg, Snyder views as part of the final form of the poem the "struggle" of its process and as part of that process the vicissitudes of the speaking voice.

The stylistic influence of Pound on Snyder's early poetry is almost immediately evident in his use of sound and images. Pound's presence is clear in the melody of lines and phrases such as "Pines, under pines," "Thick frost on the pine bough," "in sunlight on spiderweb," and "Pressure of sun on the rockslide"; in word combinations such as "drum-thump," "rock-fat," and "hill-flesh"; in precise image clusters such as "Rain soaks the tan stubble / Fields full of ducks" ("Hunting," poem 3); and in more sustained passages such as this one from poem 4 of "Logging":

> Cliff by Tomales Bay
> Seal's slick head
>   head shoulders breasts
>   glowing in night saltwater
> Skitter of fish, and above, behind the pines
> Bear grunts, walking the Pole-star.
>
>   (*MT*, 6)

Aside from the fact that he has transposed the scene from Pound's mythically ambiguous locale to the precise land and seascape of Tomales Bay, Snyder's description parallels fairly closely the language and imagery of the beginning of Pound's Canto II. Pound's lines, "Seal sports in the spray-whited circles of cliff-wash / sleek head, daughter of Lir" are a clear intertext for the first three lines of the quote; the walking and grunting bear can be related to the lynxes, panthers, leopards, and other "beasts" of Pound's poem (all engaged in the activities of sniffing, crouching, walking, and eating); the image of "glowing in night salt-water" picks up the various movements and colors of waves and water in this and other early Cantos; and the alliterative and onomatopoeic effects of "seal's slick head" and "skitter of fish" are strongly suggestive of similar effects throughout the early Cantos.

18. Parkinson, "The Poetry of Gary Snyder," 52–53.

Snyder also provides various kinds of internal rhyme (moving from "cliff" to "slick" to "skitter" to "fish") and effects of assonance and consonance that simulate the sonic density of Pound's writing. And the progression of vowels of a line such as "glowing in night saltwater" is a striking example of Poundian tone leading. Despite all these continuities with Pound's method, however, Snyder's use of Pound is not in the form of imitation or direct quotation; the style of the passage is not identical to Pound's. The most noticeable differences are the less mythopoeic and more naturalized vision of nature ("Bear grunts") and the more extreme parataxis of Snyder's descriptive language ("head shoulders breasts").

In addition to these linguistic and stylistic influences of Pound's writing, Snyder demonstrates throughout his work the impact of Pound's mythopoeic poetry as a means of achieving a more universal cultural framework. Snyder, like Pound and Olson, is a historian and an archaeologist as well as a poet; he is interested in exploring a history of ideas, in comparing cognitive and cultural states as they function across temporal, national, ethnic, and racial boundaries. Snyder's collection of mainly non-poetic writings, *Earth House Hold,* can be viewed in the tradition of Pound's *Guide to Kulchur* as an attempt to make the way for a regeneration of Western culture. Snyder's early volume of poems *Myths and Texts* is a cultural amalgam reminiscent of Pound's attempt to introduce cultural and historical artifacts into *The Cantos,* and his long poem *Mountains and Rivers Without End* displays certain continuities with Pound's epic in its attempt at all-inclusive form.[19] Like Pound, Snyder uses his own brand of *Kulturmorphologie* to challenge the widely accepted views of history, society, and community. But he differs

19. Woon-Ping Chin Holaday compares the structure of *Mountains and Rivers Without End* with that of Pound's epic: "As with Pound's *Cantos,* Snyder's poem revolves around the dramatic structure of a journey, but whereas Pound's is a *periplum* surveying all cultures and histories objectively, Snyder's has the specific mission of a pilgrim's wandering through the universe in search of the Truth and dedicated to the salvation of all sentient beings" ("Formlessness and Form," 44).

most radically from Pound when he espouses a form of "cultural primitivism," the attempt to derive environmental and social roots from a prehistoric epoch. Claiming that "Pound was never able to get back earlier than the Early Bronze Age" and that Olson "at least gets back to the Pleistocene," Snyder himself favors a return to even deeper roots: those of the "upper Paleolithic" (*MT,* viii).

Snyder's first two books—*Riprap* (1959) and *Myths and Texts* (1960)—are extremely divergent in style and content, and they emphasize different aspects of Pound's influence. The poems in *Riprap* exemplify an awareness of Pound's Imagist or Objectivist practice, and like Pound's early poems and translations they contain moments of contemplation or meditation on the object world. *Myths and Texts* is marked to a greater extent by the influence of Pound's *Cantos;* its three series of fragmentary poems, entitled "Logging," "Hunting," and "Burning," gather together a network of allusions and images through a method strongly influenced by Pound's ideogrammatic configurations.

Although *Myths and Texts* was not published until 1960, the poems in it were written between 1952 and 1956, thereby making the book an apprentice work for Snyder. Nevertheless, this impressive group of early poems marks Snyder from the first as an important poet in the Poundian idiom. In a sense, these short, dialogic poems function as mini-Cantos, each one developing recurring themes and images that mythologize Snyder's life experience during those years much as parts of *The Cantos* did Pound's. Snyder writes in the introduction to the book, "I tried to make my life as a hobo and worker, the questions of history and philosophy in my head, and the glimpses of the roots of religion I'd seen through meditation, peyote, and 'secret frantic rituals' into one whole thing" (*MT,* vii). Snyder's attempt to make the various levels of his experience into "one whole thing" reenacts Pound's desire to "make it cohere" in *The Cantos,* but the means by which Snyder achieves this—yogic meditation, mind-altering drugs, and religious rituals—represent an entirely different orientation from that of his predecessor.

On the level of poetic structure Snyder's poems exhibit Poundian juxtaposition, ideogrammatic linkages, collage effects, and the interplay of different voices. Often juxtaposed elements or ideograms are used, as in *The Cantos,* to express some social or economic critique or to stress the necessity of humankind's connection with nature as a means of salvaging a society in grave danger of self-annihilation. The first poem of the book is a characteristic example of Snyder's technique. He alternates allusions to *Walden* and Buddhist philosophy, and a quote from an anthropology text, with the experience of his own life in San Francisco and as a logger in the Pacific Northwest.

Snyder argues, as does Pound, that poetry is a framework of ideas within which to live, a personal mythology. Yet Snyder differentiates his own "mythological way" from that of Pound. Where Pound uses the ideogrammatic method in *The Cantos* to create idiosyncratic and often obscure connections between allusions and quotations, connections that can be made only by a reader initiated into the texts and ideas that constitute Pound's own learning, Snyder sees the interrelation of elements in his poetry as one guided by the Buddhist doctrine of "interconnectedness" or "interdependent origination." Influenced as he is by Pound's example, Snyder is nevertheless quick to see the formal problem posed by the unwieldly ideogrammatic structure of *The Cantos.* He seeks to avoid in his own work what he views as Pound's mistake: allowing long sections of his epic to become boring in their obscurity and their lack of musical and imagistic interest. For Snyder, the universal consciousness that speaks through images must make clear the connections between seemingly fragmentary poetic moments: "The ideogrammatic method is intended as a method of communication in the sense of juxtaposing apparently unrelated things automatically."[20]

A clear example of Snyder's use of the ideogrammatic method can be found in *Myths and Texts.* The second poem in "Logging" is constructed around the juxtaposition of three images of logging as a destructive force. The first is a quote from Exodus:

20. Quoted in Faas, *Towards a New American Poetics,* 133–34.

"But ye shall destroy their altars, / break their images, and cut down their groves." The second and third complete the ideogram, bringing together in a Poundian manner ancient Chinese history and contemporary Western experience:

> The ancient forests of China logged
> and the hills slipped into the Yellow Sea.
> . . . .
> San Francisco 2 × 4s
> were the woods around Seattle
> (*MT*, 3–4)

The alternative to this ideogram of human destruction is another complex of images presented in the preceding poem; stylistically and imagistically, this ideogrammatic rendering of cyclical growth and regeneration is reminiscent of Pound's sense of natural law or process:

> Green comes out of the ground
> Birds squabble
> Young girls run mad with the pine bough
> (*MT*, 3)

As in the passage from poem 3 of "Hunting" quoted previously, Snyder's lines suggest Pound while avoiding direct imitation of him. "Birds squabble," like "Bear grunts" in the previous example, is a register of nature imagery reflecting Snyder's own experience as a hiker, hobo, and logger in the Pacific Northwest, rather than Pound's more pseudomythological version.

In the last section of *Myths and Texts*, "Burning," Snyder takes on the persona of a shaman seeking personal, social, and ecological enlightenment. In the following passage from poem 14, toward the end of the book, his vision finally coincides with the righting of nature he seeks:

> Gaps between seedlings, the right year,
> Green shoots in the marshes
> Creeks in the proper directions
> Hills in proportion,
> Astrologers, go-between present
> a marriage has been.
> (*MT*, 50)

This process of spiritual and natural rebirth is made possible, as in Pound's *Cantos,* by a voyage, or *nekuia,* of the poet-hero, during which he undergoes an Ovidian and Poundian metamorphosis, taking the form of various birds, salmon, and a sea lion in a movement from the sea to the reborn land ("Hunting," poem 9). The Poundian collage continues in sections of "Burning" (poems 9, 12, and 13), though the end result of Snyder's apocalypse is of a different order from Pound's vision of "paradise" in the final Cantos. Here it is not so much a sense of certainty or right reason that prevails as it is a life wisdom comprising an amalgam of political, sexual, environmental, poetic, and spiritual elements. In one instance ("Burning," poem 7), Snyder's ideogrammatic sequence based on the female breast as an embodiment of the life force balances Pound's method with a sensual and philosophical framework that is entirely Snyder's own:

> Face in the crook of her neck
>   felt throb of vein
> Smooth skin, her cool breasts
> All naked in the dawn
>
>   "byrdes
> sing forth from every bough"
>   where are they now
> And dreamt I saw the Duke of Chou
>
> The Mother whose body is the Universe
> Whose breasts are the Sun and Moon
>   the statue of Prajna
> From Java: the quiet smile,
> The naked breasts.

(MT, 43)

In an attempt to evoke a sense of archetypal female and procreative presence Snyder juxtaposes a sensual description of his lover's body, a quotation from a Middle English lyric about the coming of spring, and a reference to a statue of a Javanese deity. Like Duncan, Snyder uses Pound's allusive technique to render a different version of feminine beauty and power.

In poem 7 of "Logging," Snyder displays another aspect of the influence of Pound's *Cantos* as he launches a brief but trenchant economic critique of the life of loggers in the early part of the century. The critique, which continues throughout "Logging," makes increasingly explicit the connection between the violent and uncaring destruction of the forests and the eventual destruction of the loggers themselves, who suffer in their economic struggle to survive. Sherman Paul comments on a Poundian scorn in Snyder's recognition of the "social fact that the spoliation of nature contributes to the spoliation of men."[21] In poem 14 of "Logging," Snyder is incensed by the lack of foresight and spirituality in Western and Christian civilization. The pine trees are "Cut down to make room for the suburbs / Bulldozed by Luther and Weyerhauser / Crosscut and chainsaw" (*MT*, 15).

Snyder's linking of economic, social, and spiritual factors in the spoliation of society is certainly consistent with Pound's overarching commentary in *The Cantos*. But Snyder's commentary on a local situation is part of a larger realm of concerns, many of which lie outside of, or serve as alternatives to, those addressed by Pound's Modernist project: Buddhist ideology as an alternative to all Western religious norms; Amerindian mythology as an alternative to Caucasian mythological systems; ecologically based theories of the planet and human species as alternatives to socioeconomic, political, and historical ones; and cultural primitivism as an alternative to a traditional understanding of Western history. Snyder and Levertov both represent a later phase of poetic postmodernism than that enacted by Olson in the early 1950s. Neither Levertov nor Snyder presents a poetics formulated primarily as a challenge to Modernist historicism in the way Olson does; instead, they are part of what Andreas Huyssen considers the postmodernism of the 1970s, which is less a decentering or deconstruction of the past than a "multi-faceted and diverse search for . . . an alternative past which, in many of its more radical manifestations, questions the

---

21. Paul, "From Lookout to Ashram," 14.

fundamental orientation of Western societies toward future growth and toward unlimited progress."[22]

Huyssen lists among the various forms such a search has taken "the feminist interest in women's history" and "the ecological search for alternatives in our relationship with nature," both of which "point to the vital need not to abandon history and the past to tradition-mongering neo-conservatives bent on reestablishing the norms of earlier industrial capitalism." He elaborates:

> There is indeed an alternative search for tradition and history going on today which manifests itself in the concern with cultural formations not dominated by logocentric and technocratic thought, in the decentering of traditional notions of identity, in the search for women's history, in the rejection of centralisms, mainstreams, and melting pots of all kinds, and in the great value put on difference and otherness.[23]

I concur with Huyssen's analysis as it applies to American poetry, but I locate the development of an alternative "radical" postmodernism in the late 1950s and the 1960s, rather than in the 1970s. The ecological and intercultural program Snyder has developed from the 1950s to the present and Levertov's sense of "present history" as a personal solution to the unique political and social circumstances of the late 1960s represent a "recuperation and reconstitution of history" that is neither completely incompatible with the avant-gardist postmodern tradition represented by Olson nor a return to the traditional or conservative notions of history and the past represented by more reactionary strains of postmodernism.[24] As is evident in the next chapter on Olson's student Edward Dorn, these explorations of alternative poetic postmodernisms continue to take new forms that challenge and revitalize the legacy of the Pound tradition.

22. Huyssen, *After the Great Divide,* 171.
23. Ibid., 172.
24. As I have argued in earlier chapters, it is a misunderstanding of Olson's project to suggest that he totally rejects the past or history, although his rhetoric sometimes goes further in that direction than that of Snyder or Levertov.

9 MIGRATING VOICES
IN THE POETRY OF EDWARD DORN

Edward Dorn is a contemporary of Robert Creeley and Allen Ginsberg, yet he seems to many readers to be of a different poetic generation from theirs. This conception arises from two factors: Dorn was a student of Charles Olson's at Black Mountain College at a time when Creeley was already a member of the faculty (in fact, he examined Dorn for his graduation exercise); and Dorn was relatively late in coming to his poetic maturity. Dorn's first book of poems, *The Newly Fallen* (1961), did not appear until five years after Ginsberg had become famous with *Howl* and nearly a decade after Creeley's writing had first been published. Dorn's long poem *Slinger,* the work for which he is best known, was not completed until the early 1970s, and it displays a different consciousness from that informing the poetry of other writers in the Pound / Williams tradition such as Olson, Duncan, and Creeley. Dorn shares with these writers the basic Poundian mode of an engaged stance and a diverse and noncanonical use of sources, but his characteristic style of digression and semantic slippage implies a structural principle that denies the clear and hierarchical presentation of values found in works by Pound, Williams, Olson, and Duncan.

In "The Pronouncement," published in the 1964 collection *Hands Up!* Dorn takes a skeptical view of what he sees as the characteristic Modernist mode of "observation," for which he turns to Olson's paradigm of writing as "exploration" as an alternative. While looking around at the landscape of New

Mexico that encircles him, Dorn reads books "of another time" by Winston Churchill, George Orwell, André Gide, and Kenneth Patchen; Dorn decides that "such a thing as humanity seems very relative, the final / adjuring of any vision." Even Pound's *Jefferson and / or Mussolini,* which Dorn "fishes out" from a "newly opened box of old books," seems to him "ceaseless prating (the unhappy function of 'style') beneath a shiny / veneer of precise common logic and raw virtue and good nature" (*CPD,* 76). Dorn finally shows his ambivalence about "pronouncements" in general, even his own; they are not sufficient to help him understand his immediate environment. Alluding to Pound's idea of literature as "news that stays news," Dorn expresses the shortcomings of a Modernist vision that has outlived its usefulness; it has "[come] down / like all news, like a curtain on a comedy" (*CPD,* 77).

If "The Pronouncement" contains Dorn's most direct poetic response to Pound and Modernism, the long poem that constitutes his third book, *From Gloucester Out* (1964), is a moving farewell to his immediate mentor Olson, celebrating both Olson's force as a "figure of outward" in Gloucester and Dorn's own movement away from the immediate sphere of Olson's influence. Dorn's next volume, *Geography* (1965), and especially its central poem, "Idaho Out," indicate a new direction in Dorn's work that will lead to Dorn's most extreme mode of writing in his four-part epic *Slinger.* The title of *Geography* and the poem's epigraph from Carl Sauer represent Dorn's homage to Olson and the legacy of his "Bibliography on America for Ed Dorn," but the poems themselves are written in a manner more clearly in reaction to Olson than in emulation of him.

The movement from Pound's *Cantos* through Olson to Dorn's poem is relatively clear. Where Pound sought his "culture" primarily in Europe, and Olson found his in the local history of the East Coast of America, Dorn makes the American West the center of his cultural interest. Olson had displayed a fascination with the western states in his plans and research for the long poem to be called "West," but he ultimately returned to the more familiar subject of Gloucester, part of New England

and of the European colonial legacy Dorn wants badly to avoid. Dorn replaces the opposition between Europe and America that had been made by poets such as Olson and Creeley with a new opposition between Far West and East Coast. As Sherman Paul comments, Dorn finds "no comfort in the old equation of America versus Europe, since . . . the only way to be an American is to . . . abrogate history and inherit (inhabit) the original geography, the space that was SPACE, because it was before the time of realtors."[1]

As Paul suggests, Dorn not only replaces Olson's geographical opposition with his own; his poetry also takes further Olson's critique of historical poetry by effecting a negation of history except as "space" — that is, except as reflected in a physical and intellectual movement through that space. As I argue, it is Dorn's new notion of "space" that allows a radically altered understanding of the ontological and linguistic processes of poetry itself, an understanding that is increasingly reflected in the form of his own poetry and more particularly in his absorption and manipulation of discourses in the fabric of his poetic writing.

Roland Barthes's *S/Z* contains a section entitled in its English translation "The Dissolve of Voices." Barthes suggests that there are moments in a text in which "it is impossible to attribute an origin, a point of view, to [a given] statement" (*SZ*, 41–42). He opposes the "classic text" (he refers specifically to the tradition of realist narrative, but his category could apply to any text containing or signaling the controlling presence of the author) to what he calls the "modern text," such as the *nouveaux romans* of Alain Robbe-Grillet, Nathalie Sarraute, and others. In the classic text, "the majority of the utterances are assigned an origin" whereas in the modern text "the voices are so treated that any reference is impossible: the discourse, or better the language speaks: nothing more." Even within the classic text, however, Barthes argues that a "plurality" of voice or origin is possible when, in the appropriation of speech from various discourses, "the [authorial] voice gets lost, as though it had

1. Paul, *Lost America of Love*, 143.

leaked through a hole in the discourse." At these moments we have what Barthes calls the "classical plural," the text as "an iridescent exchange carried on by multiple voices, on different wavelengths and subject from time to time to a sudden *dissolve,* leaving a gap which enables the utterance to shift from one point of view to another, without warning." This vocal exchange, or "dissolve," leads to a sense of "tonal instability" or even to an "atonality," which produces a text that at its most extreme is "a glistening texture of ephemeral origins" (*SZ,* 41).

What interests me about Barthes's account of textuality is not only his argument for a "classical plural" as a middle ground between the absolute authorial control of a text's origins, on the one hand, and a total instability of textual origin, on the other, but also the metaphorical terminology Barthes uses to describe this phenomenon. Here he differentiates the dissolve from what he earlier describes as the "weaving of voices," a process that he ascribes to all texts. Barthes's metaphor of a "weaving of voices" and even more dramatically his later variant of a "dissolve of voices" suggest a "dialogic" mode without clearly identifiable borders between the discourses quoted. If we consider that Barthes's original term for the translated word *dissolve* is "le *fading* des voix,"[2] the distinction between his idea and Mikhail Bakhtin's notion of heteroglossia becomes clear. Whereas Bakhtin's term connotes only a multiplicity or mixing of voices, Barthes's suggests that the boundaries between discourses themselves, and thus their origins or enunciating voices, will no longer be apparent.[3]

2. Barthes, *S/Z,* 48.
3. I rely on Barthes's terminology rather than Bakhtin's here for several reasons. First, Barthes's metaphors are more readily adaptable to my schema for reading Dorn's poetry. Second, Barthes's poststructuralist project has more theoretical and historical affinity with the postmodern context of Dorn's work and ideas than do the writings of Bakhtin. And, finally, as I read them, Bakhtin's claims for an indeterminacy of the voices and discourses composing the novel are less clearly made and less radical than those of Barthes. In *The Dialogic Imagination,* Bakhtin uses the metaphor of "orchestration" to describe the novel's adaptation of different discourses, thereby implying a more stable and consciously applied polyphony than that suggested by Barthes's notion of fading. Perhaps one could apply Bakhtin's categories to the work of more contemporary or experimental texts by distinguishing a classic heteroglossia from a modern

Let us return now to the application of these ideas to modern and contemporary American poetry in the Pound tradition. Bakhtin's paradigm of the dialogic can be usefully applied as a hermeneutic tool for understanding the work of a poet like Pound, whose ideogrammatic or collagelike juxtapositions of utterances, discourses, and languages in *The Cantos* reflect in their formal configurations the boundaries he wishes to establish between various modes of speech and writing, each of which presupposes a clear sense of origin. To a somewhat lesser extent, the dialogic or heteroglossic model is also applicable to Williams's *Paterson* and to the work of Olson and Duncan. Although Duncan's own metaphors of the poem as "dense weave" or "polyglot assemblage" resemble Barthes's weaving of voices, they do not suggest a relinquishing of authorial control or of the corresponding notions of language as a source of "truth" and an indicator of "presence."

At the other extreme is Barthes's reading of the modern text as one reflecting the complete indeterminacy, instability, and atonality of discourses allowed to speak for themselves in a text from which the controlling presence of an author—even a "planner"—is conspicuously absent. It is this sense of the modern text (more appropriately, perhaps, the postmodern text) as generated by language itself, which has as its closest parallel in American poetry today the work of the Language poets.[4] But it is in the theoretical space Barthes provides between the classic text and the modern text—the classical plural defined by the dissolve of voices, the fading, the shift in point of view, the tonal instability, the leakage in the discourse, or what I call the "slippage," the "evasion," or the "migration"—that much of Dorn's poetry is written. If the works of experimental Modernist poets such as Pound and Williams are still to be considered examples of classic

heteroglossia. The classic heteroglossia would imply the modulation of discourses or genres within the novel (or long poem) as a whole; the modern heteroglossia would include the modulation of discourses within the speech of a given character or speaker or even within a given utterance.

4. See the Conclusion for a more detailed analysis. Although the Language poets have sometimes been read as relinquishing all authorial control to the processes of language itself, this is not my understanding of their work.

texts (and according to Barthes's criteria they clearly are), and if the poetry of Olson and Duncan represents the final stage of the classic text as such, Dorn's work, especially in the later part of his career, is in a state of flux between the classic and the (post)modern.

Dorn's movement away from his predecessors begins in earnest in the volume *Geography*, despite its Olson-inspired title, and culminates in his most potent poetic work, *Slinger*, a poem that formally, linguistically, and thematically stands between the Modernist epic and the projects of more radical indeterminacy represented by the Language group. Dorn's poems maintain the sense of a subjective (poetic) voice—be it a speaker, narrator, or persona—but it is a voice that increasingly lacks a sense of authority and seems to be borrowing from other voices, rather than seeking to remain in control of its own discourse. Furthermore, the appropriation of discourse becomes a vehicle not only for making sense of the world or for establishing a directly referential meaning within the poem; it is also a way of inhabiting different spaces or, in the case of *Slinger*, of moving through different space-time matrices, each of which provides new discourses or modifies expected uses of language. What is important in the world of *Slinger* is no longer what things mean but where one has been and when one has been there. As Gunslinger (later to be called Slinger) says to the narrator "I" in Book I: "Questioner, you got some strange / obsessions, you want to know / what something *means* after you've / seen it, after you've *been* there / or were you *out* during that time?" (*S*, 27).

Dorn's poetry and nonpoetic writings continue to display an interest in space as a geographical reality—following Olson's belief in space as "the centrally important fact to man born in America."[5] But they also involve an understanding of space that is distinct from either Williams's sense of the local or Olson's methodology of place. Michael Davidson observes that Dorn's relatively early essay "What I See In *The Maximus Poems*" (1960) already "recognizes the dangers of treating 'place' as a

5. Olson, *Call Me Ishmael*, 11.

sentimental localism."[6] As both Davidson and Alan Golding point out, Dorn replaces the localism of Williams and Olson with an "inner, imaginative landscape" reflecting the mediation and cooptation of contemporary life.[7] I wish to follow up on the thoughts of these critics by examining in greater detail an aspect of Dorn's use of space neither of them has treated fully: his continual use in various guises of the trope of *movement* through space—as travel, as voyage, as migration, as "straying," as a journey across "states of mind" (*S*, 39), as a "coursing the country of our consciousness" (*S*, 48). In my analysis of the poetry, I continue to explore the relation of this central trope to Barthes's theory of a fading of discourses. As Golding and Davidson suggest, such a trope represents the absence of any firm sense of value to be found in a given locale, such as Williams finds in Paterson or Olson in Gloucester. Dorn's locale is the whole of the American West, but in his later work even that becomes insufficient because the metaphysical world Dorn creates for Slinger and his companions represents a refusal to remain within the bounds of even such a large area as the western half of the United States.

Donald Wesling identifies a movement in Dorn's works from physical space in *Geography,* to geopolitical space in *The North Atlantic Turbine* (1967), and finally to the "deconstruction of the concepts of space and place" in *Slinger*.[8] Although I agree in principle with Wesling's analysis, I also believe that what unifies Dorn's continuing conception of space in a poem such as "Idaho Out," in *Slinger,* and in Dorn's nonpoetic statements is his vision of movement through a world composed not only of places but of people, languages, discourses, signs, and codes. As he writes in a section of *North Atlantic Turbine* entitled "England, Its Latitude and Some of Its Conditions, The Seriousness of Ghosts," people live in "an ordered and endlessly transferrable place" (*CPD*, 182). Dorn's sense of contemporary man or woman not belonging in any particular place goes against the guiding beliefs

6. Davidson, "Archaeologist of Morning," 158.
7. Golding, "History, Mutation, and the Mutation of History," 11.
8. Wesling, " 'The Fire We Give Everything,' " 24.

of Williams and Olson and seems to be especially true in Dorn's view of the American West, which is "not a home" (*V*, 59) to anyone, except perhaps those Native Americans who have been forced to leave large portions of it. Instead, the West is a place of travel, of continual and restless movement: "The American West is the place men of our local civilization travel into in wide arcs to reconstruct the present version of the Greek experience.... [The West] is where you will find the Stranger so dear to our whole experience" (*V*, 58).

It is on such a "wide arc" that the various characters in *Slinger* travel on their voyage or pilgrimage — "To See / is their desire / as they wander estranged / through the lanes of the Tenders / of Objects" (*S*, 33). As in the Greek epics on which the basic form of Dorn's poem is modeled, travel brings the voyager in this "cowboy odyssey" to new places and introduces him to various "strangers" who use new kinds of language. Dorn's personal experience in the West, which he likens to a "migration," figures prominently in the form of *Slinger*.⁹ The West, he claims, has been populated and formed by a "grand migratory effect" (*V*, 14).

But it is not only people who travel, who migrate in Dorn's poems; it is often the language of the poem that migrates across semantic or stylistic borders. The characteristic slippages in Dorn's style and voice to which I alluded earlier can easily be viewed as movements or migrations; indeed, the use of such a metaphor to describe literary language is suggested by Barthes in *S/Z*: the dissolve of voices "permet a l'enonciation de *migrer* d'un point de vue a l'autre" (my emphasis).¹⁰ Barthes's term in the original French—*migrer*, "to migrate"—provides a much more vivid and concrete sense than does the English translation—"to shift"—of what is happening in such cases: the voice or point of view migrates from one place, one site in the linguis-

9. I emphasize this point partly in reaction to Marjorie Perloff and Alan Golding, both of whom argue that Dorn's central concerns in the poem have little or nothing to do with his chosen region, the American West. See Perloff, "Review of Edward Dorn's *Slinger*," 22–26; and Golding, "History, Mutation, and the Mutation of History," 10.

10. Barthes, *S/Z*, 49. In Richard Miller's translation, the dissolve of voices "enables the utterance to shift from one point of view to another" (*SZ*, 42).

tic code, to another. It has no distinct place of residence, no "home" to return to, no identifiable origin of authorship: the point of view changes spaces like a migrating subject. Such a spatial metaphor is particularly relevant to *Slinger*, an epic voyage in which the original destination of Las Vegas (a place that epitomizes the absence of home, an ironic version of Odysseus's Ithaca) is never reached.

There is convincing evidence that Dorn is aware of such a connection between travel and language. In discussing *Slinger* with Robert Bertholf in 1974, Dorn explains his use of multiple voices in the poem as a by-product of spatial considerations: "I wanted to write a poem about the penetration of the only space anybody has ever run into, and that's multiple. I mean, I don't believe [in] the lone traveler, except for short distances. But even in the mind of a lone traveler there's a multitude of dialogue" (*I*, 61–62).

If Dorn is more interested in the space organized around "the collective voice" than he is in the isolated voice of any individual speaker, he is also intrigued by the way different voices and sources interact in the mind of a single person—the poet—as he or she moves through time and space. It is in this sense, perhaps, that Dorn most closely resembles Pound, Williams, and Olson, all of whom achieve a similar synthesis of sources. But Dorn differs radically from them in his emphasis on the language randomly picked up as a material in itself, not accountable to a given source of authority. It is for this reason that anonymous sources such as AM radio play an important role in Dorn's poetics: the radio, especially when listened to in a moving car, represents a source that has no easily identifiable geographic center and that is constantly changing as the local stations *fade* in and out. The "open road" of the West, along with the radio itself, becomes a potent image for the process of poetic composition; as Dorn aptly remarks, he is "always road-testing language for a particular form of speech" (*I*, 106).

If the testing of language that would ultimately result in *Slinger* did not begin, as Dorn claims, until he was in England in the mid-1960s, he had already begun to experiment with the ironizing effects of wordplay and with the abrupt changes in diction and tone that would characterize the later style of *Slinger*. In "Idaho Out," Dorn demonstrates how far his poetic orientation has come since such earlier long poems as "Sousa" (1960) and "The Land Below" (1961). Dorn's use of language and discourse in the poem reflects a similarly changed poetic stance.

If the ironic juxtaposition of human and natural elements in "The Land Below" anticipates elements of "Idaho Out," the tone of Dorn's earlier poem finally resembles that of Williams's *Paterson* more than it does the mixture of irreverent humor and biting social and political satire characteristic of Dorn's later work. "Idaho Out," still in a sense a poem of the "local" — though a local encompassing parts of Idaho and Montana — is not primarily concerned with the localism that constitutes Dorn's earlier depiction of a small town in New Mexico, Olson's vision of Gloucester, or Williams's version of Paterson. Dorn's poem does follow Olson's attempts at a poetic embodiment of Carl Sauer's "morphology of landscape" and more particularly of Sauer's idea of a "cultural landscape" as "the impress of the works of man upon the [geographic] area."[11] But Dorn places greater emphasis than had his predecessor on humans as a destructive agent in nature, not simply participants in the natural "forces" constituting Olson's vision. Whereas Olson's poetry includes a generalized attempt to criticize the "pejorocracy" of contemporary culture, Dorn's poem has a more directly ecological and political agenda.

It is this more direct concern with a political agenda that leads Dorn to an intensified examination of the ways in which language is used by the dominant culture (through the agency of the popular media) to coopt or control human behavior and attitudes. One clear example of such a linguistic cooptation is that of the cliché, a widely disseminated belief that represents an oversimplification of reality. In "Idaho Out" a passage of geo-

---

11. Sauer, "Morphology of Landscape," 326.

graphical description slides easily into the language of cliché or, in this case, the self-conscious debunking of a cliché:

> Fort Benton
> to your right, across stretches
> of the cuts of the Blackfoot, through
> Bowman's Corner, no
> the sky
>
>   is not
>
> bigger in Montana.
>
>   (*CPD*, 115)

Dorn adopts the persona of the irreverent tour guide, first pointing out with some degree of specificity the historical and geographical highlights of the Montana landscape—"Fort Benton," "the cuts of the Blackfoot," "Bowman's Corner"—then abruptly changing registers of discourse as he refutes the seemingly unrelated cliché of Montana as a place where the sky is bigger. The tour guide figure driving around Montana and Idaho serves as another metaphor for Dorn's poetics of travel, thereby leading us through a range of discourses with uncertain origins. The cliché is an example of an utterance with no clear origin—it has been absorbed into mainstream culture as an infection of the language. In the lines that follow, he actually takes the reader across the state line as the scenic tour gives way to a darkly comic commentary on society's manipulation of natural space:

> When
> for instance you come
> from Williston
> there seems at the border a change
> but it is only because man has
> built a tavern there
> and proclaims himself of service
>   (*CPD*, 115)

Here the irony lies in the gap between the fourth line, with its sense of rising expectation, and the following lines, which state the real reason for the change—a single tavern signaling in a fairly arbitrary way the crossing of the border but having nothing whatever to do with the romanticized (and media-inspired) version of Montana as "big sky country." Dorn is interested in examining the reality behind such statements as a way of testing the referential value of language in our society. The ironic effect Dorn achieves in this passage by undermining the authority of the cliché reflects a more general skepticism about the capacity of language to be directly referential: "I've always been confused by those attempts to make language the same thing as the thing. I don't want to say again what Williams said ['No ideas but in things']—in fact I don't want to say that at all" (*I* 47). Emphasizing his own midwestern upbringing, Dorn explains his skepticism about language as similar to that of the Illinois farmer: "On the prairie there's a certain evasion—a linguistic evasion—of the word as such" (*I*, 39).

Dorn's evasion of the word as such can be seen most evidently in his frequent use of puns and wordplay. The pun, an example of words without clear borders, is an evasion of the referential meaning in favor of an unstable or migrating meaning. Wordplays such as "areal" and "Ariel" at the beginning of the poem and "newclear seance" for "nuclear science" later on anticipate the willful playfulness of *Slinger*. Dorn's persona speaks with a brand of ironic humor not present in the work of Pound, Williams, and Olson, one enacting a different relationship between language—particularly political language—and the world. The passage in which the second pun occurs is an interesting instance of Dorn's developing style, which is marked by self-conscious discursiveness:

> But I was escorting you out of Pocatello,
> sort of north.
> Perhaps past that physiographic
> menace the arco desert and
> what's there
> of the leakage of newclear seance
>   (*CPD*, 111)

In the somewhat elevated diction of "escorting," in the equivocation of "sort of north" and "perhaps," in the use of a curiously hybrid term such as "physiographic" and its juxtaposition with the more directly emotional "menace," in the lackadaisical quality of "what's there of the" followed by the vaguely threatening "leakage," and in the double pun in "newclear seance" (with its simultaneous suggestion of mysticism and propagandistic euphemism), we see an early manifestation of the characteristically playful and slippery poetry of *Slinger*. It is certainly a style already far removed from that of Pound and Olson. Later in the poem is a more sustained example of Dorn's juxtaposition of styles:

> But not to go too much into
> that ethnic shit, because
> this is geographic business
> already, in the bitterroot
> there sat snow on the tallest
> peaks and that moisture factor
> caused trees now gliding by
> from one minor drainage
> to another until we came
> to the great bitterroot
> proper and the cottonwoods
> and feather honey locusts
> lining its rushing edges.
> (*CPD*, 114)

Here the sociological comparison Dorn had made between the inhabitants of Montana and those of Idaho—"that ethnic shit"—gives way to an ecological study and finally comes to rest in a brief moment of lyrical beauty. The way in which the passage appears formally—as an uninterrupted flow of descriptive language emphasized by the ubiquitous enjambment, by the words *gliding* and *rushing*, and by the view of a landscape from the window of a passing car—disguise what is actually an unstable and shifting tonality. In Barthes's terms the "gliding by / from one minor drainage / to another" represents an instance of fading. Dorn's slippages or migrations into a new voice or discourse are not indicated by juxtaposition and fragmentation, as in Pound's writing, or by the line breaks, parentheses, or semantic spacing used by Olson. Although the two commas provide some clue to where transitions may occur within the passage, they do not account for the range of tones between "that ethnic shit" and "lining its rushing edges." Not only the boundaries between such utterances but even their sources remain uncertain in the context of the poem as a whole, and we are left to question who our narrator-guide is and what kind of tour we are being given.

Perhaps the answer to both questions is to be found in Dorn's notion of poetry as exploration; in a letter to Olson, Dorn stresses Olson's "ability to start anywhere" in a poem.[12] Dorn's own penchant for narrative digressions implies a self-conscious awareness that not all content can be made to cohere within the boundaries of a poem and that there will inevitably be places where the poem can take a different turn or be made to include other material. Despite its underlying narrative of a trip from Idaho to Montana and back, the actual progress of "Idaho Out" is a maze of startings and stoppings, twistings and turnings. Dorn even calls attention to his own digressive style by constantly reminding the reader and himself of his purpose, the "direction" of his trip, which seems to become lost in the more interesting side trips the narrator takes into different ideas and discourses: "But I was escorting you out of Pocatello," or "Let me remind you we were in Florence / Montana." After one digression that seemingly alludes to Olson and Williams—"central america and the jerseys"—Dorn makes the laconic and self-conscious comment "But we stray / we strays, as we always do" (*CPD,* 110). He finally concludes that he sought to take the reader "out on a trip / that had no point" (*CPD,* 121). In the images of straying and a trip that had no point we again see examples of authorial discourse not only in migration but in the lack of a sense of direction or telos. Like the pun, the digression is a way of sliding across boundaries, a migration in language that mirrors a migration through space. In Dorn's poetry the digression functions as an example of what Michel de Certeau calls a "rhetoric of walking" (or in this case a "rhetoric of

12. Quoted in Robert von Hallberg, "This Marvellous Accidentalism," 46–47. See von Hallberg's discussion of poetry as exploration in the same article.

driving," perhaps) in which the turns and detours of a pedestrian can be regarded as nontextual analogues for " 'turns of phrases' or 'stylistic figures.' "[13]

The final aspect of Dorn's use of discourses in "Idaho Out" that both distinguishes it from its predecessor texts and prepares the way for the writing of *Slinger* is the absorption of popular culture. At one point, after recounting a discussion with a local rancher about the relative merits of different kinds of soil, the speaker makes the seemingly irrelevant analogy "It's / like a boring popular song / all by himself he'd love / to rest his weary head / on somebody's else's shoulder / as he grows older" (*CPD*, 114). The use of pop culture extends to the description of people in the poem as well; the woman who fascinates the narrator throughout has a "jukeboxbody" and a "fabulatory build." In another passage describing the same woman, the discourse of pop-cultural sexuality is blended into that of geographical landscape to form a new sense of morphology: "she was a walking invitation / to a lovely party / her body was that tactile to the eye / or what I meant / she is part / of the morphology / the last distant place of idaho north, / already in effect Montana" (*CPD*, 112). Rather than seek to mythologize his subject in the way Olson or Pound might have done, Dorn treats her in purely sociocultural terms. Here it is the word *tactile*, with its open-ended sense of touch—sensual or scientific—that allows the sudden shift from jocular hip jargon to (apparently serious) geographical analysis.

After *Geography* Dorn's poetry increasingly foregrounds its involvement with a world of popular culture, first in political satires such as "The World Box-Score of 1966" and *The North Atlantic Turbine* and most prominently of all in *Slinger*, a poem in which Howard Hughes interacts with Parmenides, where towns have the names of television game shows (Truth or Consequences, New Mexico), and where the characters are taken

---

13. De Certeau, *The Practice of Everyday Life*, 10. De Certeau adapts a spatial perspective on discursive style from the work of Michel Foucault and Gilles Deleuze: "Style, a way of walking through a terrain, a nontextual move of attitude, organizes the text of thought" (47).

from television westerns, comic books, and 1960s drug culture. In a 1977 interview Dorn claims to rely on the *Wall Street Journal* and AM radio as well as various magazines for his primary sources. He wants above all to be a transmitter of randomly acquired but useful information:

> I never made a systematic effort to use any [particular] sources. I always just selected what was on the air, in the radio sense. . . . I've never wanted to impose my own notions on the content. Except insofar as elements enter the context of my use, but not *what* they are. I consider one thing as good as another, whether it arises from science or the so-called humanities, the newspaper or a bubblegum wrapper. All that's equal to me, as source.   (*I*, 103)

By the time of *Slinger* the supremacy of "content" has been replaced in Dorn's work by "a slick, silly, superfast, super-intelligent" radioese; Dorn's use of language in the poem, as Michael Davidson shows, seeks to incorporate all available forms of rhetoric "as semiotic systems embedded in the surface of modern American life."[14] Dorn himself characterizes language as "an active audience, with its own ideas and its own content and its own need to make its expression" apart from any "psycho-philosophical pressure [that] has nothing to do with the poem."[15]

Various commentators have noted the way in which language appears to take over the poem—either as puns that "squirm free of a speaker's grip without warning" and metaphors that "refuse to stand still" (von Hallberg) or more globally in its resistance to any unified voice or stylistic continuity (Davidson, Golding). I am interested in how *Slinger* takes further some of the processes Dorn had begun to work out in "Idaho Out" and in how it more generally foregrounds language and discourse as part of a self-conscious framework of travel narrative.

From the start *Slinger* makes clear that it is a poem concerned as much as anything with language and language use. The nar-

---

14. Davidson, "Discourse in Poetry," 149.
15. Dorn, "Strumming Language," 91.

rator of Book I, a character called simply "I," is a walking speech act. He seems, as Slinger himself tells him, to be "constructed of questions," and he is at one point accused of sounding "like the impact of a wet syllojsm." I is also, like all the characters encountered in *Slinger,* largely defined by the language he uses, by his own characteristic or predominant discourse. The form of a conversation between characters, which serves as the poem's basic structure, allows a foregrounding of discourses in a way that would not be possible within a poetic text controlled by the voice of a single speaker. I's formal and poeticizing discourse — which is marked by a penchant for classical epithets and for archaisms such as "Then sat we," "saith," and "If this be true" — is immediately contrasted with that of Lil, a stereotypical Western madame who speaks in a caricatured Western slang punctuated by such phrases as "Come up and see me anytime," "plum stumpt," and "up Boston way" and by contractions such as "outa" and "fastern." In a sense, both of these characters speak a language composed of cultural cliché.

The Gunslinger himself, the third human character present at the beginning of the poem (there is also a talking horse named Claude), appears to represent the middle ground between the speech of I and of Lil. His discourse is constantly sliding from one level to another and is thus an unlocatable hybrid of everything from slang and hip jargon, to philosophical and scientific discourse, to a language of poetic or epic grandeur. As the poem's version of the epic hero, he is a figure who not only voyages through space and time meeting "strangers" who exhibit new forms of discourse but who is himself an example of the modern polyglot, a linguistic migrant.

The opening pages of *Slinger* display a remarkable degree of self-consciousness on the part of the characters about how language is used. Lil in particular is bothered by the ridiculously high style of I: "and who is this / funny talker, you pick him up / in some sludgy seat of higher / learnin, Creeps!" Lil is offended by I's use of words such as "apogee" and "neurasthenic," but she is also capable of appropriating his discourse if she chooses; she says to Slinger, referring to I's linguistic style:

"Anyway, I remember you had / what your friend here / might call an obsession / about the man." Two pages later she is using words that sound more like I's speech than her own—"suggestive," "derisive"—and the awkward manner in which they punctuate her own discourse is indicated by a different typeface (*S*, 8–10).[16] Thus, even those characters who might be expected to represent "pure" discourses with clearly defined origins borrow from or become infected by the language of others. At the beginning of Book II, Dorn refers to the band of characters as a moving "tapestry"; they are thus not only linked but interwoven, with no clear borders between them.

I, too, is adaptable in his speech patterns, even within a single utterance. "I'm on that score not sure," he says to Slinger at one point, combining an archaically inverted syntax with a colloquial expression. Later in Book I, he describes a scene in which Slinger starts a jukebox with his gun:

> A28, Joe Turner *Early in the Mornin*
> came out and lay on the turntable
> His inquisitive .44 repeated the question
>   and B13 clicked
> Lightnin' Hopkins *Happy Blues for John Glenn*
>   and so on
> the terse trajectories of silver then
> the punctuations of his absolute .44
> without even pushing the sombrero off his eyes
>   (*S*, 21)

I narrates the scene with a sense of epic heroism, but the tone of the passage is confused: it contains a jumble of joking wordplay ("his inquisitive .44 repeated the question"), alliterative poeticism ("terse trajectories of silver"), pop-cultural parody ("*Happy Blues for John Glenn*"), and deflating understatement ("and so on").

In Book II the introduction of a new narrator, the poet/singer of the "Abso-Lute," seems to elevate the overall tone to a higher level. If a hip Western talk was the normative discourse of the

---

16. By Book IV Lil is using words such as "ameliorating" and "Etzalqualitzi" (corn and beans).

first book, here it is something more like epic or mock-epic. The Poet is particularly fond of euphemisms such as "autotheistic chemical" for cocaine; even Slinger is influenced by the Poet's speech, as he begins to quote either real or parodic lines of Shakespearean iambic pentameter: "How like a winter hath my absence been," "When most I wink then do mine eyes best see," "Like as the waves make toward the Pebbled shore," and "Thus are his cheeks the map of days outworn." The Poet's poetry, contained in several "songs," is a further destabilization of language; these songs parody various discursive modes, resulting in a chaotic mixture of styles. The epic tone invades the descriptions of Book II as well, creating a linguistic fabric that is at once parodic and out of control. The opening invocation to the book's muse deteriorates quickly, but it is nonetheless a wonderfully suggestive passage of Dornian stylistic play:

> Into the dry brilliance of the desert morning
> Along the vanes of the willow leaves
> Along the hallucination of the atmospheric realism
> Into the upper reaches of the Yggdrasillic yoga
> Over inner structure of the Human Thing
> Like Unto the formation of the pinnate ash
> in which our treehouse sways
> and the samara goes winged, Oh wild Angelica!
> Oh quickbeam! oh quake and swat into waking,
> With aspergill enter Into the future
>
> (*S*, 44–45)

If the death of the character I represents the relinquishing of the linguistic controls held in Book I by the rationalizing and normalizing ego, the Poet of Book II is at once a parodic (in)-version of the classical poet and a figure for Dorn himself, a writer who claims that his "interest in the extreme heterogeneous vocabularies of English is fanatical."[17] A later description of Lil (now Miss Lil) as she looks at herself in the mirror is another example of the linguistic excess that courses through *Slinger*. "That ancient arrangement of amaranthine flesh / the quick aniline of flawless brow" (*S*, 55) is certainly as contrived a poetic euphemism as has ever been written. The euphemism,

17. Dorn, "Strumming Language," 86.

another kind of linguistic evasion or slippage, becomes a characteristic device of this section of the poem. In describing the smell of the now decomposing body of I, the Poet proclaims, "As the Yellow Rose of Dawn climbs / he loses the light azimuthal fragrance of his arrival / and becomes a zenith / of aparticular attention" (*S*, 58). He then paraphrases his own statement in "ordinary" language: "There will be some along our way / to claim I stinks." By this point, Slinger's language seems to have assimilated that of the Poet. When asking a stranger for his name, Slinger puts the question in terms of a convoluted riddle:

> How, dreamer,
> will fate mark you
> in her index when she comes dressed
> as a crystalographer
> to religne the tumblers
> inside your genetic padlock?
>
> (*S*, 80)

As becomes ever more apparent in the even more radical permutations of language in Books III and IV, no discourse can remain pure for very long in this poem (just as Kool Everything's "uncut batch" of "'1000 percent" pure cocaine cannot remain so); Dorn's constantly migrating fabric of language demonstrates that all discourse is ultimately borrowed from somewhere, infiltrated by someone else's usage.[18] Unlike the discourses quoted by Pound and Olson, each of which has a purity and a determinate origin even within the larger heteroglossic context, the discourses that constitute Dorn's many "styles" have no single origin, belong to or in no particular place. We cannot imagine Pound's Confucius speaking the language of Baldy Bacon, but in the poetry of Edward Dorn voices migrate, leaking through the holes in their porous discourses as they pass through an indeterminate landscape.

---

18. In one of the more striking examples of such an infection or mutation, the name of Slinger himself suddenly changes to Zlinger at the beginning of Book IV and remains in that form for the rest of the poem. Two explanations suggested in the poem are "the difference between / Saying and singing" (his new name is first sung by a "chorus") and a Japanified or Hispanified pronunciation befitting his place in the new, multicultural world of the West (Slinger's "44" is now said to be "Made in Japan").

CONCLUSION

Reappropriation and Resistance:
Charles Bernstein, Language Poetry,
and Poetic Tradition

The lacunas in Pound's guides to culture have begun
to speak. . . . The present flourishing of a formally
innovative, open, investigative poetry—a poetry that
refuses to take subject matter, syntax, grammar, or
vocabulary for granted and that rejects simple and
received notions of unity of conceit, closure, and
prosody—is unprecedented in its scale in American
literature.

> Charles Bernstein,
> "Pound and the Poetry of Today"

The movement in contemporary American writing known as
Language poetry has now existed in some form for at least two
decades; but it is only recently that this language-oriented or
language-centered mode of poetic writing has begun to attract a
relatively widespread critical following. Among the more prom-
inent academic critics to have addressed the developments in
Language writing are Marjorie Perloff and Jerome McGann.
Perloff's article "The Word as Such: L=A=N=G=U=A=G=E
Poetry in the Eighties" is primarily concerned with the formal
and linguistic implications of Language poetry; she does not
attempt, except in passing, to contextualize the movement in
terms of historical tradition or literary influence.[1] McGann, in
his article "Contemporary Poetry, Alternate Routes," is almost
exclusively interested in exploring the political and historical
context out of which Language writing emerged in the 1960s
and 1970s. Writing that the primary significance of Language
poetry is "not stylistic . . . but ideological and ultimately politi-
cal," he treats Language poetry as most fundamentally a rejec-

---

1. Perloff, *Dance of the Intellect,* 215–38.

tion of "bourgeois" modes of writing—those forms of literary writing that fail to question their own ideological assumptions.[2]

I propose to read the work of the Language poets, in particular that of Charles Bernstein, in a different context from those examined by either Perloff and McGann. I consider Language poetry as a movement within the larger tradition I have defined in this book. It is my contention that Language poetry was the most vital outgrowth of this tradition in the 1970s and 1980s. Not only have the poets associated with Language writing gained the respect and support of established members of the tradition such as Robert Creeley; they have also extended in important ways the directions taken by the experimental New American Poetry movement(s) of the 1950s and 1960s. The Language poets are certainly not the only heirs to the Pound tradition who have influenced the course of American poetry over the past twenty years: poets as diverse in their orientations as Clayton Eshleman, Robert Kelly, and Diane Wakoski have made significant contributions to the tradition of Pound and Olson, and the production of Ginsberg, Creeley, Levertov, Snyder, Dorn, and other poets of their generation continues to redefine the parameters of contemporary American poetry. Nevertheless, I believe it is the Language poets who have made the most concerted, focused, and influential effort since Olson's push of the early 1950s to alter radically the way in which experimental poetry is written and understood in this country.

Like their predecessors in the Pound tradition, the Language poets are marked by an acute awareness of the poetic practices and concerns that form a context for experimental American writing and from which their own work is largely derived. In tracing the American lineage that I see as most central to Language writing, I identify the following progression(s) of poetic writing: Whitman and Dickinson to Pound, Williams, and H. D. to Zukofsky and Oppen to Olson, Duncan, and Creeley to Clark Coolidge and Michael Palmer to Language poetry.[3] Rather than

2. McGann, "Contemporary Poetry, Alternate Routes," 625.

3. As it would be highly impractical (not to mention highly problematic) to attempt listing here all the poets who are in some way allied with Language writing and to describe their various affiliations to the movement, I can at best

constituting an entirely new tradition of writing, the Language writers are the latest manifestation of a larger tradition of experimental poetic concerns with roots in the work of Pound, Williams, and Modernist / postmodernist practice. But as is also the case with Pound and his descendants, the work of Language poets cannot be understood only in reference to a narrowly defined sense of poetic tradition. The fundamentally incorporative poetics the Language poets share with the other poets in this tradition simultaneously promotes a sense of affiliation with a number of alternative traditions of poetic and nonpoetic writing, among them Russian Futurism, French Surrealism, and the New York school of John Ashbery and Frank O'Hara.

Clearly, the practices and beliefs of Bernstein and other Language writers differ significantly from those of Olson, Duncan, Creeley, and other poets of the 1950s and 1960s. The most significant change in emphasis, if not in orientation, is in a greater receptivity to the ideas generated by literary, social, and political theory.[4] Nevertheless, the Language poets have continued to look to predecessors within the Pound tradition for models of poetic composition. In many cases, direct lines of descent can be traced: from Zukofsky to Bernstein; from Olson to Barrett Watten; from Creeley to Larry Eigner, Clark

---

only suggest a means of establishing a canon for Language writing today. As it shifted from the related work of a few individuals to a "movement," then to a "school," and finally to what can best be described as a "mode" of poetic writing today, the most reliable indicator of its progress was the various affiliations that were established through journals and other publications. Ron Silliman, Barrett Watten, Bob Perelman, and Bernstein aligned themselves with Language writing largely through the magazines they edited: *Tottel's, This, Hills,* and L=A=N=G=U=A=G=E, respectively. Poets such as Bruce Andrews, Lyn Hejinian, and Steve Benson also appear to be strongly committed to language-oriented work, and the number of satellite writers with connections to the movement is in the hundreds. Silliman, who includes thirty-eight writers in his anthology *In the American Tree* (1986), claims that a "volume of absolutely comparable worth" could be constructed from the work of more than eighty other writers (xx–xxi). While this may be true, it poses a somewhat daunting task for the critic and casual reader of these poets; long gone, it seems, are the days of Black Mountain, the New York school, the San Francisco Renaissance, and the Beats, when a movement consisted of a few close friends and associates.

4. For a concise and illuminating manifesto by several members of the Language movement, see Steve Benson et al., "Aesthetic Tendency and the Politics of Poetry: A Manifesto," *Social Text* 19–20 (1988): 261–275.

Coolidge, and Robert Grenier; from Duncan to Michael Palmer; from Jack Spicer to Ron Silliman. Such lineages do not necessarily entail direct stylistic and formal influences, but they do indicate important continuities in the articulation of poetic projects and stances.

It could be argued that an equally important source for the project of Language poetry is the writing of the New York school, especially of John Ashbery and Frank O'Hara. The work of Bernstein and other Language poets shares with the early poetry of Ashbery a resistance to clarity and transparency in language and the ideological critique such a resistance implies. There is, however, a fundamental difference between Ashbery and the Language poets in their approach to both language and ideology. Where Ashbery uses the disruption of semantic clarity in his poems as a self-conscious means of revitalizing his own poetic idiom and of breaking certain habits of poetic writing, he does not appear to be deeply committed to a fundamental critique of language itself or of its operations within a social or ideological context. The Language poets, who already take such (stylistic) moves as Ashbery's for granted, are less interested in opacity per se (that is, in the way in which opacity creates or allows for a multiplicity of meanings in the poem) than in how to treat the poetic text as a field for the inclusion of different discourses that comment on each other as well as on the external events of the political and social world. Like Pound and Olson, the Language poets regard as equally important to the creation of new poetic meanings the sense of language as a social artifact that is part of larger, often nonpoetic discourses. That Ashbery's work is assimilable into a canon of American poetry such as the neo-Romantic tradition of Harold Bloom (a canon that has consistently excluded Pound, Williams, Zukofsky, Olson, Duncan, and Creeley) indicates that the intertexts making up his poems are more literary and less disruptive than those proposed by the Language poets. Whereas Ashbery generally attempts to maintain the appearance of a seamless flow of (literary) language despite the local disturbances in its semantic continuity, the Language poets follow Pound, Zukofsky, and Olson in foregrounding or disrupting the formal and syntactic as well as the semantic texture of the poem and thus in calling attention to its status as made object or artifact. Such a disruption or foregrounding is a central aspect of Bernstein's poetics, one he characterizes through the various metaphors of "maladaption," "resistance," and "antiabsorptiveness."

Even with the increasing notoriety achieved by the Language school, at this juncture it is somewhat difficult to provide a simple and overarching definition of its contours either in terms of historical origins or central participants. Ron Silliman, one of the principal practitioners of language-oriented writing, locates the "breach and [the] new movement in American writing" at the first issue of the magazine *This,* co-edited by Robert Grenier and Barrett Watten in 1971.[5] In fact, the seeds of the new movement were sown even earlier—starting with the 1964 publication of the magazine *Joglars,* co-edited by Clark Coolidge and Michael Palmer. This journal brought together in its first two issues representatives of the second generation of the Pound / Black Mountain tradition—Gary Snyder, Michael McClure, Fielding Dawson, Jonathan Williams, John Wieners, Joel Oppenheimer, Robert Kelly, Larry Eigner, and Michael Palmer as well as their Objectivist predecessors Zukofsky and Niedecker. Coolidge, Eigner, and Palmer came to be seen as the early forerunners of the Language group; they maintained a strong identification with the New American Poetry and the anticonventional sentiments of Olson's "Projective Verse," but they wished at the same time to challenge Olson's dogmatic belief in the direct referentiality of poetic expression and the "naturalness" of speech as a poetic mode.[6]

5. Silliman, *In the American Tree,* xv.
6. Coolidge (b. 1939) and Palmer (b. 1943) remain two of the most interesting poets writing in America today, and they form an important intergenerational link between the early phase of postmodernism as embodied by Olson and Duncan and the current practice of Language poetry. From their early collaboration on the editing of *Joglars,* Coolidge and Palmer have developed in different directions as poets, yet both maintain important ties to the Pound tradition. Coolidge's poetry has been associated with the project of the Language

In *Content's Dream,* an important book of critical essays, Bernstein defines the poetic practices of the Language poets in terms that reflect directly the legacy of Pound and his followers: the (inter)textual poetic space as defining a relation to other poems, poetic language, and an exterior world of social and historical particulars and the way in which this conception informs a sense of poetic "author-ity" and a concern for the poet's interaction with language and discourse. In his 1986 essay "Pound and the Poetry of Today" Bernstein locates his own work and that of other experimental American writers more specifically within the context of Pound's contributions to poetic practice. Bernstein opposes the compositional technique Pound intended for *The Cantos*—montage—with the technique of collage that he believes Pound achieved. Bernstein concurs with earlier poets that the unintended collage effect, rather than representing a "failure" in *The Cantos,* actually "opened the floodgates" for "further explorations of the unheard and unsounded in our poetry." The "free play" that is for Bernstein "the most salient feature of *The Cantos*" (*CD,* 638) creates an environment in which multiple forms of experimentations can take place.

Bernstein's 1982 statement about Language writing, "For *Change,*" situates his work and that of his colleagues in the tradition of inclusiveness proposed by the collagist work of Pound, Olson, and Duncan. The work of Language poets, Bernstein claims, is "informed not only by the synchronic activities of other active writers and the various traditions of literary writing but significantly by far larger frames of writing and art activity current and past." Furthermore, theoretical discussions by these poets include the input of those "not primarily involved with

---

writers, on whom he was an important influence and with whom the work bears certain stylistic resemblances. Palmer, who derives his characteristic style from the work of San Francisco Renaissance poets Robert Duncan and Jack Spicer, was the earliest poet to combine the two tendencies that ultimately led to Language poetry: the sense of the poem as a mysterious but latently meaningful field (as suggested by Duncan's work) and the idea of poetic discourse as arbitrary and essentially antireferential (as adapted from the work of Spicer and Ashbery). For a more detailed discussion, see Norman Finkelstein, "The Case of Michael Palmer," 532.

poetry, such as other artists, and political and cultural workers, and . . . suggest possible relationships between the poetry and recent critical and philosophical thought."[7]

Bernstein gives a more specific sense of his own range of sources in an interview with Tom Beckett. He lists Gertrude Stein, Samuel Beckett, Zukofsky, Creeley, and Laura Riding as poets in whose historical context he places his work, but he sees the more widely defined question of influence as a "byzantinely complicated matter":

> I don't feel exclusively influenced by work done in the genre of poetry, of equal importance is both nonpoetry literary and nonliterary writing. . . . As to impact, too, on my works, the other arts have been important, very formative to my thinking. Certainly looking at Pollock and Louis, say, not to mention Kandinsky or Braque or Schwitters or Gorky, etc., etc., had much more influence on my ideas than reading many poets with whom I feel an affinity. (*CD*, 390)

Bernstein's appropriation of different sources in his poems owes a great deal to Pound, Zukofsky, Olson, and Duncan, among others, who compose their works largely by using "found" or "discovered" objects as poetic material.[8] Bernstein's own adaptation of sources, however, is more closely related to that of Edward Dorn in *Slinger,* a post-Olsonian epic in which the use of radio and other media as "accidental" sources of information fills the poem with quasirandom pieces of discourse. In some respects, Bernstein goes beyond Dorn in his sense of linguistic and formal play: "made-up quotations that sound like they are from a prior text" are combined in the poem with actual quotations from various sources—poems, letters, memos, sayings (*CD*, 393–94). Sometimes Bernstein no longer remembers

7. C. Bernstein, "For *Change*," 488. These critics and philosophers include, among others, the Russian formalists, Jacques Derrida, Ludwig Wittgenstein, Félix Guattari, Gilles Deleuze, and Roland Barthes.

8. See Bernstein's discussion in "Pound and the Poetry of Today." Not only the poetry of more doctrinaire Poundians such as Zukofsky, Olson, and Duncan but also the work of various marginal or experimental writers—Blacks and Native Americans, women and gays, anthologists such as Jerome Rothenberg and George Quasha, and language-oriented poets such as Ron Silliman and Susan Howe—have all been influenced by "the visual, typographical, textually historicist [and collagist] dynamics" (638) presented in *The Cantos.*

the source of a quotation by the time it reaches the poem; thus, the Poundian notion of textual authority is almost totally undercut in Bernstein's work. Unlike Pound and Olson, Bernstein does not seek to use sources, quotations, and personae as a means of self-definition; nor does he believe in integrating the variable discourses of his "multidiscourse, polyvalent writing practice" (*CD*, 409) into a "single web," "unified field," or "one matrix" as outlined by Olson and Duncan. Instead, Bernstein takes further Olson's critique of the lyric ego by allowing language itself to shape the poem by "poking through the expected parameters" (*CD*, 38):

> In this process, the language takes on a centrifugal force that seems to trip it out of the poem, turn it out from itself, exteriorizing it. Textures, vocabularies, discourses, constructivist modes of radically different character are not integrated into a field as part of a predetermined planar architecture; the gaps and jumps compose a space within shifting parameters, types and styles of discourse constantly crisscrossing, interacting, creating new gels. (Intertextual, interstructural . . .)   (*CD*, 38–39)

Like Dorn, Bernstein uses shifting discursive parameters to subvert the expectation of a poem's "predetermined planar architecture," thus challenging habitual understandings of language use and pointing out relationships between language and ideology. Bernstein goes beyond Dorn in more actively foregrounding the various processes through which language operates—semantic, syntactic, intertextual, structural—and thus in calling even greater attention to the political acts linguistic acts unavoidably contain. It is in privileging the autonomy of language over its participation in a determined (narrative) pattern that he transgresses the poetic practices of Olson, Duncan, and even such a skillful manipulator of expected discursive formulas as Dorn. Bernstein's notion of intertextuality is clearly informed by the discussions of such theorists as Barthes and Foucault, though Bernstein is not willing to go as far as they do in dismissing the concept of authorship altogether:

> There is no question that the concept of authorship has been given much more significance than it merits, and as such is an obstacle for

reading and writing to overcome; even though I do not feel that it makes sense to carry these views to the extreme of cancelling authorship as a factor completely, making the text exclusively the product of a discourse or a period, since in crucial ways a poem is as much a resistance as a product, and for the moment at least the individual is the most salient concept with which to describe the site of this resistance. The valorization of the author function, in its current guises as persona, voice, autobiography, and self-expression, hierarchializes a complicated constellation of variables including structure, social context, genre, method, politics.   (CD, 408–9)

Thus, while the poet's interaction with different discourses may be a largely arbitrary matter, the decision to privilege certain of them in a given work establishes his or her own defining presence in the text. In his own work, Bernstein explains, he has chosen to foreground in different books varying approaches to discourse—a "sociocentric" mode in *Controlling Interests* (1980), an "idiocentric" one in *Islets / Irritations* (1983). As even the titles of the two books indicate, *Controlling Interests* is more concerned with discourses pertaining to a wider social or political realm, whereas the poems of *Islets / Irritations* are determined more by the poet's sense of his personal environment. To this extent, at least, the function of the author in Language writing remains a vital aspect of the poetry generated: the poet's role is no longer that of framing the work within a coherent or consistent lyric voice, but it continues to require the manipulation of a dialogic, heteroglossic, or intertextual fabric that reflects a social or aesthetic orientation.

As Michael Davidson suggests, Bernstein's poems can easily be understood in terms of Bakhtin's dialogic structures of literary writing. In Language writing, Davidson argues, such a discursive analysis allows us to see the way in which "the discontinuity between one line or sentence and the next is both a qualification of causal, narrative logic and an assertion of the paradigmatic nature of reference."[9] In other words, these discontinuities or lacunae serve as markers for the different assertions in the poem, each of which has a different social or

9. Davidson, "Discourse in Poetry," 146–47.

psychological context. Unlike the dialogic relationships of utter-
ances and quotations in a poem by Pound, Olson, or Snyder,
where the breaks between fragments or meaning clusters are
accompanied by clear shifts in spatial and vocal orientation, the
heteroglossia of Bernstein's poem "Baggage"—Davidson's ex-
ample from *Islets / Irritations*—is not necessarily indicated by
any visual, syntactic, or punctuational marker except the en-
jambed line ending, conventionally the moment on which we are
most accustomed to relying for a sense of semantic continuity:

> Thinking ain't doing, so really I'll
> partly I've never gotten in the habit
> you always seemed to turn
> so where begin to, where report.

Davidson demonstrates in his reading of the poem that each
attempt at assertion is undercut either by syntactic elements,
changes in tone, or qualifications and evasions. In "Part Quake,"
another poem from *Islets / Irritations,* the units of discourse are
even smaller than the partially completed statements of "Bag-
gage." Here the progression of the poem seems conditioned by
the resonances of individual words, and the gaps between iden-
tifiably meaningful utterances become more frequent:

> The restoration of slighted, by forecast thundering,
> faded aggregate sweeps plane in wanton arch
> the very lacunas discount. Preclusion of
> emphatic instability inflated within cornered
> propulsion. Militant valence, or sense of
> seen. When fills of, for, former entail
> portends an increment, adjourned at what
> is loaned, all to sudden screeching. Drop,
> instanced bodily (lozenge, prick . . .) by motor
> denotes, held in caption, ritual zone
> demark.[10]

In this complex passage lines and phrases are generated in
numerous ways: by sound and visual pattern—"fills of, for,

10. This poem is reprinted in Silliman, *In the American Tree.*

former"; by phonemic or morphological resemblance—"preclusion, propulsion, portends," "aggregate, adjourned," "instability, increment, instanced," "discount, denotes, demark"; and by recurring registers of diction. This last category, involving the semantic or intellectual interplay of words in the poem, is the most complicated level of Bernstein's composition and the most suggestive. Bernstein interweaves various patterns of discourse in the passage: weather report—"forecast thundering"; military-industrial—"cornered," "propulsion," "motor," "zone"; economic—"discount," "inflated," "increment," "loaned." Certain other words are made ambiguous by their context and could apply to more than one register of discourse at a time. "Restoration" suggests art museums but also contains other possible referents: the literature and politics of late-seventeenth-century England and the restoration of various forms of political and economic control in this century. Words such as "instability" and "caption" are similarly fluid in their denotative and connotative potential within the poem. Another group of words—"slighted," "wanton," "portends," "screeching," and "ritual"—cannot be located within any particular discourse; instead, they serve a purely connotative function, creating in their cumulative presence a disturbing emotional tonality.

In a similar way Bernstein's use of passive and participial constructions provides a unifying sense of syntactic cooperation among the various elements of the stanza and contributes to its foreboding sense of controlled panic. Just as semantic discourses cannot always be clearly located, parts of speech cannot be easily identified: are "fills," "entail," "drop," and "prick" to be read as nouns or verbs? The force of the few clearly active verbs in the passage—"sweeps," "portends," "denotes," and "demark"—is vitiated by the predominance of abstract words and prepositional phrases surrounding them. In every respect, then, the poem enacts a conflict between the possibilities of language to evade meaning and reference, on the one hand, and the activity of the poet in combining them, on the other. Bernstein's sensitivity to the phonic, semantic, and etymological qualities of words and his awareness of the various conceptual fields to which they belong counteract the seeming arbitrariness of the poem's discursive units.[11]

If such a poem as "Part Quake" is largely intertextual, it is participating in an intertext of which the individual source texts have become difficult or impossible to determine; thus, it is one much closer in kind to the universal text of Barthes or the discursive formations of Foucault than to the deliberately structured intertextual matrix of Pound or Olson. Nonetheless, like Pound and Olson before him, Bernstein is deeply concerned with the question of what constitutes the poetic "self" and the "author-ity" of a given poem. In the very act of dismantling the appearance of a coherent lyric voice in a poem like "Part Quake," Bernstein foregrounds on various levels the exercise of authorial control. For some Language writers, such as Marxist-oriented Ron Silliman, the authorial presence is completely undecidable outside its social context. Bernstein, however, takes a position between a doctrinaire materialism and a belief in the creative potential of the individual self: "Individuals are in essence that which is maladapted, idiocentric, resistant; it is in that sense that we get to know another only through the identification and appreciation of the peculiarities as particularized—mutant—and not as some generalized feature of some genre of humans" (*CD,* 410).

If the individual is no longer seen as the active historical force he or she was for the Modernists or as the "self" in the process of relating to his or her immediate environment envisioned by Olson, the concept of a clearly demarcated and particularized "individual" is still in evidence in Bernstein's writing. Bernstein's idea of a "maladaption" or "resistance" that allows spaces in the text for individual meaning echoes, though in a somewhat altered context, Olson's own use of the term *resistance* to connote

---

11. My reading of "Part Quake" emphasizes the poem's discursive and intertextual properties as opposed to the more ideological or semiotic analyses of McGann and Perloff. This is not to say that more overtly political readings of the poem or readings that emphasize the ways in which the poem comments on its own language or construction would not be equally valid and illuminating.

the physical body as the ultimate basis of our interaction with the world (see *SW*, 13–14). Bernstein invites a comparison with the physicality of Olson's conception:

> For any person, the approach to, the hearing of language is going to be different. We come at this thing we share—our language, our world, what we see, which is in common, but we come at it from different angles. We have different resistances to language that create different sounds in people's poems or speech or conceptions. . . . I mean it also in a physical sense. If I go from here to there the air is resistant. Gravity. An impedence, a weight that you're pressing against and by pressing against it you create "sound." (*CD*, 457–58).

Bernstein's more recent metaphor for the poetic act is also a physical one: that of absorptiveness. A long critical essay in the form of a poem, "Artifice of Absorption" is an intensely focused exploration into the process(es) of poetic composition. Rather than a traditional understanding of poetic texts—one that regards causal narration or thematic relevance as the unifying feature of a poetic work—Bernstein proposes a sense of the poem's ability to absorb into its "textural space" such materials as vocabulary, syntax, logic, tonality, rhythm, and reference. In doing so, the poem creates "a hyperabsorptive textual gravity in which the different originary elements are no longer isolable."[12] Absorptive works tend to hide their artifice behind an apparently seamless poetic fabric, whereas antiabsorptive works "flaunt" their techniques in such a way as to foreground the artificiality of the poetic process.

The implications of Bernstein's distinction for poetic writing and tradition are clear. Poets such as Stevens and Ashbery are fundamentally absorptive writers in whose most characteristic work any disruptions of the fabric are only "illusionistic interruptions," rather than real disjunctions. The antiabsorptive tradition in American poetry originates with Modernist writers such as Pound, Williams, Stein, Cummings, and Zukofsky, all of whose experiments with sound, visual form, typography, and

---

12. Charles Bernstein, "Artifice of Absorption," 16.

syntax have led to the current practices of Language poetry and related movements. But what interests Bernstein and his contemporaries is not merely the creation of opacity or antiabsorptiveness. Rather, it is the question of how to use "antiabsorptive means for absorptive ends"—in other words how to make the poem more, rather than less, engaging for the reader through these disruptive techniques. The challenge facing Bernstein is essentially that faced by all poets writing in the Pound tradition: how does the poet enhance the possibilities of poetic expression (in Bernstein's terms, the poem's absorptiveness) without relying on traditional techniques of transparency, meter, and causal unity or on the use of a coherent lyric voice *and* without alienating the reader? Bernstein concludes that the "thickness" of writing, that space created in the antiabsorptive text between the poem and reader, need not be an obstacle to a greater sense of connection between them. Instead, continuities of sound and diction must replace the sense of a lyric speaker or unified discourse. The formal strategies identified in my reading of "Part Quake" protect the poem from appearing utterly antiabsorptive—fragmentary, aleatory, or incoherent. The thickness of the poem will actually allow it to be reabsorbed into the world as object more easily than a conventionally absorptive poem.

Bernstein's terminology for understanding his engagement with the poetic text may seem overly scientific or technological to those who favor a more intuitive relation to the writing and understanding of poetry. But his metaphor, much like Duncan's fundamental notion of the poem as cell, is a physical and organic one; he sees the poem as a "spongy surface" that can interact with the materials available to it. In Bernstein's case it is not just the poem but the poet himself who is involved in this physical process: "I find I enact in my work an oscillating pull in both directions, cutting into & out of—en(w)rapment / resistance, enactment / delay, surfeit / lack."[13] It is this sense of the physicality of the poetic act—the poet's individual physical presence as it interacts with a shared world—that links most deeply the vari-

13. Ibid., 52.

ous poets of the Pound tradition, including a poet as different from Pound as Charles Bernstein. If Bernstein and his contemporaries no longer accept the aesthetic confidence of many of Pound's assertions or the idealism of Olson's "language as the act of the instant," they still find ways of elaborating and expanding the vision of poetry shared by Olson, Duncan, Levertov, Snyder, Zukofsky, Williams, and Pound. It is a poetry in which the internal experience of the poem constitutes the reality of the world outside it, a world still retrievable only through those sensory processes that allow us to see, hear, feel, and think it anew.

REFERENCES

Abrams, M. H. *The Mirror and the Lamp: Romantic Theory and the Critical Tradition*. New York: Norton, 1958.

Allen, Donald, ed. *The New American Poetry*. New York: Grove Press, 1960.

Altieri, Charles. *Enlarging the Temple: New Directions in American Poetry During the Sixties*. London: Associated University Press, 1979.

———. "From Symbolist Thought to Immanence: The Ground of Postmodern American Poetics." *Boundary 2* 1, no. 3 (1973): 605–42.

———. "The Objectivist Tradition." *Chicago Review* 30, no. 3 (1979): 5–26.

———. "Olson's Poetics and the Tradition." *Boundary 2* 2, nos. 1–2 (1973–74): 173–88.

Antin, David. "Modernism and Postmodernism: The Approaching Present in American Poetry." In *The Avant-Garde Tradition in Literature,* edited by Richard Kostelanetz, 216–47. Buffalo, N.Y.: Prometheus Books, 1982.

Bakhtin, M. M. *The Dialogic Imagination: Four Essays*. Edited by Michael Holquist and translated by Caryl Emerson and Michael Holquist. Austin: University of Texas Press, 1981.

Barthes, Roland. "From Work to Text." In *Textual Strategies: Perspectives in Post-Structuralist Criticism,* edited by Josué Harari, 73–81. Ithaca, N.Y.: Cornell University Press, 1979.

———. *S/Z*. Paris: Editions du Seuil, 1970. (English version: *S/Z: An Essay*. Translated by Richard Miller. New York: Farrar, Strauss and Giroux, 1974.)

Bartlett, Lee. "Gary Snyder's Han-Shan." *Sagetrieb* 2.1 (1983): 105–10.

Bate, Walter Jackson. *The Burden of The Past and the English Poet*. Cambridge, Mass.: Harvard University Press, 1970.

Beach, Christopher. Interview with Joel Oppenheimer. *Sagetrieb* 7, no. 2 (1988): 89–130.

Bernstein, Charles. "Artifice of Absorption." *Paper Air* 4, no. 1 (1987).
———. *Content's Dream: Essays, 1975–84.* Los Angeles: Sun and Moon, 1986.
———. *Controlling Interests.* New York: Roof, 1980.
———. "For *Change*." In *In the American Tree,* edited by Ron Silliman, 484–90. Orono, Maine: National Poetry Foundation, 1986.
———. *Islets / Irritations.* New York: Jordan Davies, 1983.
———. "Pound and the Poetry of Today." *Yale Review* 75, no. 4 (1986): 635–40.
Bernstein, Michael André. "Bringing It All Back Home: Derivations and Quotations in Robert Duncan and the Pound Tradition." *Sagetrieb* 1, no. 2 (1982): 176–89.
———. "Robert Duncan: Talent and the Individual Tradition." *Sagetrieb* 4, nos. 2–3 (1985): 177–90.
———. *The Tale of the Tribe: Ezra Pound and the Modern Verse Epic.* Princeton, N.J.: Princeton University Press, 1980.
Bertholf, Robert, Don Byrd, and Ian Reid, eds. *Robert Duncan: Scales of the Marvelous.* New York: New Directions, 1979.
Bloom, Harold. *The Anxiety of Influence: A Theory of Poetry.* New York: Oxford University Press, 1973.
———. *The Breaking of the Vessels.* Chicago: University of Chicago Press, 1982.
———. *Kabbalah and Criticism.* New York: Seabury, 1975.
———. *A Map of Misreading.* New York: Oxford University Press, 1975.
———. *Poetry and Repression.* New Haven, Conn.: Yale University Press, 1976.
———. *Wallace Stevens: The Poems of Our Climate.* Ithaca, N.Y.: Cornell University Press, 1977.
Bornstein, George, ed. *Ezra Pound Among the Poets.* Chicago: University of Chicago Press, 1985.
Bové, Paul. *Destructive Poetics: Heidegger and Modern American Poetry.* New York: Columbia University Press, 1980.
Breslin, James. *From Modern to Contemporary.* Chicago: University of Chicago Press, 1984.
Butterick, George. "Charles Olson and the Postmodern Advance." *Iowa Review* 11, no. 4 (1980): 4–27.
———. "Ezra Pound and the 'Truculent Ummugrunt.'" *American Poetry* 4, no. 1 (1986): 22–37.
———. *A Guide to "The Maximus Poems" of Charles Olson.* Berkeley and Los Angeles: University of California Press, 1978.
Butterick, George, ed. *Charles Olson and Robert Creeley: The Complete Correspondence.* 9 vols. to date. Santa Barbara, Calif.: Black Sparrow Press, 1980–.

Byrd, Don. *Charles Olson's* Maximus. Urbana: University of Illinois Press, 1980.

———. "The Question of Wisdom as Such." In *Robert Duncan: Scales of the Marvelous,* edited by Robert Bertholf, Don Byrd, and Ian Reid, 38–55. New York: New Directions, 1979.

Carne-Ross, D. S. *Instaurations: Essays in and out of Literature from Pindar to Pound.* Berkeley and Los Angeles: University of California Press, 1979.

Casillo, Robert. *The Genealogy of Demons: Anti-Semitism, Fascism, and the Myths of Ezra Pound.* Evanston, Ill.: Northwestern University Press, 1988.

Charters, Samuel. *Some Poems / Poets.* Berkeley: Oyez, 1971.

Christensen, Paul. *Charles Olson: Call Him Ishmael.* Austin: University of Texas Press, 1979.

Conniff, Brian. *The Lyric and Modern Poetry: Olson, Creeley, Bunting.* New York: Peter Lang, 1988.

Creeley, Robert. *Collected Essays.* Berkeley and Los Angeles: University of California Press, 1989.

———. *Collected Poems.* Berkeley and Los Angeles: University of California Press, 1984.

———. *Contexts of Poetry: Interviews 1961–71.* Edited by Donald Allen. Bolinas, Calif.: Four Seasons Press, 1973.

———. "For L. Z." *Paideuma* 7, no. 3 (1978): 383–85.

———. *A Quick Graph: Collected Notes and Essays.* Edited by Donald Allen. San Francisco: Four Seasons Press, 1970.

Davidson, Michael. "Archaeologist of Morning: Charles Olson, Edward Dorn, and the Historical Method." *ELH* 47, no. 2 (1980): 158–79.

———. "Discourse in Poetry: Bakhtin and Extensions of the Dialogical." In *Code of Signals: Recent Writings in Poetics,* edited by Michael Palmer, 143–50. Berkeley: North Atlantic, 1983.

Davie, Donald. *Ezra Pound: Poet as Sculptor.* London: Routledge and Kegan Paul, 1965.

De Certeau, Michel. *The Practice of Everyday Life.* Translated by Stephen Rendall. Berkeley and Los Angeles: University of California Press, 1984.

Dorn, Edward. *Collected Poems, 1956–1974.* Bolinas, Calif.: Four Seasons Press, 1974.

———. *Interviews.* Edited by Donald Allen. Bolinas, Calif.: Four Seasons Press, 1980.

———. *Slinger.* Berkeley: Wingbow, 1975. Republished as *Gunslinger.* Durham, N.C.: Duke University Press, 1989.

———. "Strumming Language." In *Talking Poetics from Naropa Institute: Annals of the Jack Kerouac School of Disembodied Poetics,* edited by Anne Waldman and Marilyn Webb, vol. 1, 83–96. Boulder, Colo.: Shambhala, 1978.

———. *Views*. Bolinas, Calif.: Four Seasons Press, 1980.

Duberman, Martin. *Black Mountain: An Exploration in Community*. New York: Dutton, 1972.

Duncan, Robert. *Bending the Bow*. New York: New Directions, 1968.

———. *Derivations Selected from 1950–1956*. London: Fulcrum Press, 1969.

———. *Fictive Certainties*. New York: New Directions, 1985.

———. *The First Decade: Selected Poems, 1940–1950*. London: Fulcrum Press, 1968.

———. *Ground Work: Before the War*. New York: New Directions, 1983.

———. *Ground Work II: In the Dark*. New York: New Directions, 1987.

———. "The H. D. Book," I, 3. *Coyote's Journal* 5–6 (1966): 8–31.

———. "The H. D. Book," I, 6. *Caterpillar* 1 (1967): 6–29.

———. "The H. D. Book," II, 1. *Sumac* 1 (1968): 101–46.

———. "The H. D. Book," II, 3. *Io* 6 (1969): 117–40.

———. "The H. D. Book," II, 4. *Caterpillar* 7 (1969): 27–60.

———. "The H. D. Book," II, 5. *Stony Brook* 3–4 (1969): 336–47.

———. "The H. D. Book," II, 9. *Chicago Review* 30, no. 3 (1979): 37–88.

———. Interview with Jack Cohn and Thomas O'Donnell. *Contemporary Literature* 21, no. 4 (1980): 513–48.

———. Interview with Howard Mesch. *Unmuzzled Ox* 4, no. 1 (1976): 79–96.

———. "The Lasting Contribution of Ezra Pound." *Agenda* 4 (1965): 6–14.

———. "Notes 1973: A Psycho-Physiognomy." *Maps* 6 (1974): 45–52.

———. *The Opening of the Field*. 1960. New York: New Directions, 1973.

———. "The Poetry of Unevenness": Interview with Michael Davidson and Burton Hatlen. *Sagetrieb* 4, nos. 2–3 (1985): 91–111.

———. "Reading Zukofsky." *Paideuma* 7, no. 3 (1978): 421–28.

———. *Roots and Branches*. 1964. New York: New Directions, 1969.

———. *The Years as Catches*. Berkeley: Oyez, 1966.

Edelberg, Cynthia. *Robert Creeley's Poetry: A Critical Introduction*. Albuquerque: University of New Mexico Press, 1978.

Eliot, T. S. *Selected Essays*. New York: Harcourt, Brace, Jovanovitch, 1964.

Evans, George, ed. *Charles Olson and Cid Corman: The Complete Correspondence, 1950–1964*. Vol. 1. Orono, Maine: National Poetry Foundation, 1988.

Fass, Ekbert. "Charles Olson and D. H. Lawrence: Aesthetics of the Primitive Abstract." *Boundary 2* 2, nos. 1–2 (1974): 113–26.

———. *Towards a New American Poetics: Essays & Interviews*. Santa Barbara, Calif.: Black Sparrow Press, 1978.

———. *Young Robert Duncan: Portrait of the Artist as Homosexual in Society*. Santa Barbara, Calif.: Black Sparrow Press, 1983.

Fenollosa, Ernest. *The Chinese Written Character as a Medium for Poetry*. Edited by Ezra Pound. 1936. San Francisco: City Lights, 1968.

Ferlinghetti, Lawrence, ed. *City Lights Anthology*. San Francisco: City Lights, 1974.

Finkelstein, Norman. "The Case of Michael Palmer." *Contemporary Literature* 29, no. 4 (1988): 518–37.

———. " 'Princely Manipulations of the Real' or 'A Noise in the Head of the Prince': Duncan and Spicer on Poetic Composition." *Sagetrieb* 4, nos. 2–3 (1985): 209–23.

———. "Robert Duncan: Poet of the Law." *Sagetrieb* 2 (1983): 78–88.

Foster, Hal, ed. *The Anti-Aesthetic: Essays on Postmodern Culture*. Port Townsend, Wash.: Bay Press, 1983.

Foucault, Michel. *Archaeology of Knowledge*. Translated by A. M. Sheridan Smith. New York: Tavistock, 1972.

Froula, Christine. *A Guide to Ezra Pound's Selected Poems*. New York: New Directions, 1982.

Frye, Northrop. "The Archetypes of Literature." 1951. In *The Avant-Garde Tradition in Literature*, edited by Richard Kostelanetz, 17–27. Buffalo, N.Y.: Prometheus Books, 1982.

Géfin, Laszlo. *Ideogram: History of a Poetic Method*. Austin: University of Texas Press, 1982.

Gilbert, Sandra, and Susan Gubar. *The Madwoman in the Attic: The Woman Writer and the Nineteenth-Century Literary Imagination*. New Haven, Conn.: Yale University Press, 1979.

Ginsberg, Allen. *Allen Verbatim: Lectures on Poetry, Politics, Consciousness*. Edited by Gordon Ball. New York: McGraw-Hill, 1974.

———. *Collected Poems, 1947–1980*. New York: Harper and Row, 1985.

———. *Composed on the Tongue*. Edited by Donald Allen. Bolinas, Calif.: Grey Fox, 1979.

———. "Encounters with Ezra Pound." *City Lights Anthology*, edited by Lawrence Ferlinghetti, 9–21. San Francisco: City Lights, 1974.

———. *Howl and Other Poems*. San Francisco: City Lights, 1956.

———. *Howl: Original Draft Facsimile*. Edited by Barry Miles. New York: Harper and Row, 1986.

———. *To Eberhart, from Ginsberg: Letter about "Howl," 1956*. Lincoln, Mass.: Penmaen Press, 1976.

Golding, Alan. "History, Mutation, and the Mutation of History in Edward Dorn's *Slinger*." *Sagetrieb* 6, no. 1 (1987): 7–20.

Goodwin, K. L. *The Influence of Ezra Pound*. New York: Oxford University Press, 1966.

Guillen, Claudio. *Literature as System*. Princeton, N.J.: Princeton University Press, 1973.

Guillory, John. "The Ideology of Canon-Formation: T. S. Eliot and Cleanth Brooks." *Critical Inquiry* 10, no. 1 (1983): 173–98.

Harari, Josué, ed. *Textual Strategies: Perspectives in Post-Structuralist Criticism*. Ithaca, N.Y.: Cornell University Press, 1979.

Harper, Michael. "The Sins of the Fathers: Charles Olson and Ezra Pound." *American Poetry* 4, no. 1 (1986): 38–53.

Hassan, Ihab. *The Postmodern Turn: Essays in Postmodern Theory and Culture*. Columbus: Ohio State University Press, 1987.

Hatlen, Burton. "Carroll Terrell and the Great American Poetry Wars." *Explorations* (1986): 3–15.

Hermeren, Goran. *Influence in Art and Literature*. Princeton, N.J.: Princeton University Press, 1975.

Heymann, C. David. *Ezra Pound: The Last Rower*. New York: Viking, 1976.

Holaday, Woon-Ping Chin. "Formlessness and Form in Snyder's *Mountains and Rivers Without End*." *Sagetrieb* 5, no. 1 (1986): 41–52.

Huyssen, Andreas. *After the Great Divide: Modernism, Mass Culture, Postmodernism*. Bloomington: Indiana University Press, 1986.

Hyde, Lewis. *The Gift: Imagination and the Erotic Life of Property*. New York: Random House, 1983.

Jameson, Fredric. "Postmodernism and Consumer Society." In *The Anti-Aesthetic: Essays on Postmodern Culture,* edited by Hal Foster, 111–25. Port Townsend, Wash.: Bay Press, 1983.

Jauss, Hans Robert. *Towards an Aesthetic of Reception*. Translated by Timothy Bahti. Minneapolis: University of Minnesota Press, 1982.

Johnson, Mark. "Robert Duncan's 'Momentous Inconclusions.' " *Sagetrieb* 2, no. 2 (1983): 71–84.

Kenner, Hugh. *A Homemade World: The American Modernist Writers*. New York: Knopf, 1975.

———. "The Invention of the 'Other.' " *Conjunctions* 6 (1984): 241–45.

———. *The Pound Era*. Berkeley and Los Angeles: University of California Press, 1971.

Kostelanetz, Richard, ed. *The Avant-Garde Tradition in Literature.* Buffalo, N.Y.: Prometheus Books, 1982.

Kramer, Jane. *Allen Ginsberg in America.* New York: Random House, 1969.

Krauss, Rosalind. "Sculpture in the Expanded Field." In *The Anti-Aesthetic: Essays on Postmodern Culture,* edited by Hal Foster, 31–42. Port Townsend, Wash.: Bay Press, 1983.

Krieger, Murray. *The Play and Place of Criticism.* Baltimore, Md.: Johns Hopkins University Press, 1967.

Kristeva, Julia. *Semiotiké: Recherches pour une sémanalyse.* Paris: Editions du Seuil, 1969.

Levertov, Denise. *In Her Own Province.* New York: New Directions, 1979.

———. Interview with Walter Sutton. *The Minnesota Review* 5, nos. 3–4 (1965): 305–41.

———. *Light Up the Cave.* New York: New Directions, 1981.

———. *Poems, 1960–1967.* New York: New Directions, 1983.

———. *Poems, 1968–1972.* New York: New Directions, 1984.

———. *The Poet in the World.* New York: New Directions, 1973.

Longenbach, James. *Modernist Poetics of History: Pound, Eliot and the Sense of the Past.* Princeton, N.J.: Princeton University Press, 1987.

McGann, Jerome. *The Beauty of Inflections: Literary Investigations in Historical Method and Theory.* Oxford: Clarendon Press, 1985.

———. "The *Cantos* of Ezra Pound: The Truth in Contradiction." *Critical Inquiry* 15, no. 1 (1988): 1–25.

———. "Contemporary Poetry, Alternate Routes." *Critical Inquiry* 13, no. 3 (1987): 624–47.

Mariani, Paul. *William Carlos Williams: A New World Naked.* New York: McGraw-Hill, 1982.

Molesworth, Charles. *Gary Snyder's Vision: Poetry and the Real Work.* Columbia: University of Missouri Press, 1981.

O'Conner, William van, and Edward Stone, eds. *A Casebook on Ezra Pound.* New York: Thomas Crowell, 1959.

Olson, Charles. *Additional Prose.* Edited by George Butterick. Bolinas, Calif.: Four Seasons Press, 1974.

———. *Call Me Ishmael: A Study of Melville.* London: Jonathan Cape, 1967.

———. *The Collected Poems.* Edited by George Butterick. Berkeley and Los Angeles: University of California Press, 1987.

———. *Human Universe and Other Essays.* Edited by Donald Allen. New York: Grove Press, 1967.

———. *Letters for Origin, 1950–55.* Edited by Albert Glover. London: Cape Golliard, 1970.

———. *The Maximus Poems*. Edited by George Butterick. Berkeley and Los Angeles: University of California Press, 1983.

———. *Muthologos*. Edited by George Butterick. Vol. 1. Bolinas, Calif.: Four Seasons Press, 1978.

———. *Olson*. 5 vols. Storrs, Conn.: Olson Archives, University of Connecticut, 1974–1976.

———. *Poetry and Truth: The Beloit Lectures and Poems*. Edited by George Butterick. San Francisco: Four Seasons Press, 1971.

———. *Selected Writings*. Edited by Robert Creeley. New York: New Directions, 1966.

———. *The Special View of History*. Edited by Ann Charters. Berkeley: Oyez, 1970.

Oppen, George. Interview with L. S. Dembo. *Wisconsin Studies in Contemporary Literature* 10, no. 2 (1969): 159–77.

———. *The Selected Letters*. Edited by Rachel Blau DuPlessis. Durham, N.C.: Duke University Press, 1990.

Ostriker, Alicia. "The Thieves of Language: Women Poets and Revisionist Mythmaking." In *Coming to Light: American Women Poets in the Twentieth Century*, edited by Diane Wood Middlebrook and Marilyn Yalom, 10–36. Ann Arbor: University of Michigan Press, 1985.

Palmer, Michael, ed. *Code of Signals: Recent Writings in Poetics*. Berkeley: North Atlantic, 1983.

Parkinson, Thomas. "The Poetry of Gary Snyder." *Sagetrieb* 3, no. 1 (1984): 49–61.

———. "Pound and Williams." In *Ezra Pound Among the Poets*, edited by George Bornstein, 149–67. Chicago: University of Chicago Press, 1985.

Paul, Sherman. "Clinging to the Advance: Some Remarks on 'Projective Verse.'" *North Dakota Quarterly* 47, no. 2 (1979): 7–14.

———. "From Lookout to Ashram: The Way of Gary Snyder." *Iowa Review* 1, no. 4 (1970): 70–86.

———. *Lost America of Love*. Santa Barbara, Calif.: Black Sparrow Press, 1981.

———. *Olson's Push: Origin, Black Mountain, and Recent American Poetry*. Baton Rouge: Louisiana State University Press, 1978.

Perloff, Marjorie. "Charles Olson and the 'Inferior Predecessors.'" *ELH* 40 (1973): 285–306.

———. "The Contemporary of Our Grandchildren: Pound's Influence." In *Ezra Pound Among the Poets*, edited by George Bornstein, 198–230. Chicago: University of Chicago Press, 1985.

———. *Dance of the Intellect: Studies in the Pound Tradition*. New York: Cambridge University Press, 1985.

————. *The Poetics of Indeterminacy: Rimbaud to Cage*. Princeton, N.J.: Princeton University Press, 1981.

————. "Review of Edward Dorn's *Slinger*." *The New Republic*, April 24, 1976.

Pound, Ezra. *ABC of Economics*. London: Faber, 1933.

————. *ABC of Reading*. 1934. New York: New Directions, 1960.

————. *The Cantos*. New York: New Directions, 1970.

————. *The Classic Anthology as Defined by Confucius*. Cambridge, Mass.: Harvard University Press, 1954.

————. *Guide to Kulchur*. London: Faber, 1938.

————. *Jefferson and / or Mussolini*. New York: Liveright, 1936.

————. *Literary Essays*. Norfolk, Conn.: New Directions, 1954.

————. *Make It New*. London: Faber, 1934.

————. *Personae*. 1926. New York: New Directions, 1971.

————. *Selected Letters, 1907–1941*. Edited by D. D. Paige. New York: Harcourt Brace, 1950.

————. *Selected Prose, 1909–1965*. Edited by William Cookson. New York: New Directions, 1973.

————. *The Spirit of Romance*. 1910. New York: New Directions, 1968.

Pound, Ezra, ed. *Active Anthology*. London: Faber, 1933.

Rabaté, Jean-Michel. *Language, Sexuality, and Ideology in Ezra Pound's* Cantos. Albany: State University of New York Press, 1986.

Rakoski, Carl. Interview with L. S. Dembo. *Wisconsin Studies in Contemporary Literature* 10, no. 2 (1969): 178–92.

————. "A Note on the Objectivists." *Stony Brook* 3–4 (1969): 36–46.

Reck, Michael. *Ezra Pound: A Close-Up*. New York: McGraw-Hill, 1973.

Reznikoff, Charles. Interview with L. S. Dembo. *Wisconsin Studies in Contemporary Literature* 10, no. 2 (1969): 193–202.

Riddel, Joseph. "Decentering the Image: The Project of American Poetics." In *Textual Strategies: Perspectives in Post-Structuralist Criticism*, edited by Josué Harari, 322–58. Ithaca, N.Y.: Cornell University Press, 1979.

Rosenthal, M. L. *The New Poets: American and British Poetry Since World War II*. New York: Oxford University Press, 1967.

Sauer, Carl. *Land and Life: A Selection from the Writings of Carl Ortwin Sauer*. Edited by John Leighly. Berkeley and Los Angeles: University of California Press, 1963.

Schneidau, Herbert. *Ezra Pound: The Image and the Real*. Baton Rouge: Louisiana State University Press, 1969.

————. "Wisdom Past Metaphor: Pound, Fenollosa, and Objective Verse." *Paideuma* 5 (1976): 15–29.

Seelye, Catherine, ed. *Charles Olson and Ezra Pound: An Encounter at St. Elizabeth's.* New York: Viking Press, 1975.

Silliman, Ron, ed. *In the American Tree.* Orono, Maine: National Poetry Foundation, 1986.

Smith, Lorrie. "Songs of Experience: Denise Levertov's Political Poetry." *Contemporary Literature* 27, no. 2 (1986): 213–32.

Snyder, Gary. "From Anthropologist to Informant": Interview with Nathaniel Tarn. *Alcheringa* 4 (1972): 104–13.

———. *Myths and Texts.* 1960. New York: New Directions, 1979.

———. *The Real Work: Interviews and Talks, 1964–1979.* Edited by Scott McLean. New York: New Directions, 1980.

———. *Riprap and Cold Mountain Poems.* San Francisco: Four Seasons Press, 1969.

———. *Six Sections of* Mountains and Rivers Without End. San Francisco: Four Seasons Press, 1970.

Stein, Charles. *The Secret of the Black Chrysanthemum.* Barrytown, N.Y.: Station Hill Press, 1987.

Steuding, Bob. *Gary Snyder.* New York: Twayne, 1976.

Von Hallberg, Robert. *Charles Olson: The Scholar's Art.* Cambridge, Mass.: Harvard University Press, 1978.

———. "Olson's Relation to Pound and Williams." *Contemporary Literature* 15, no. 1 (1975): 15–48.

———. "This Marvelous Accidentalism." In *Internal Resistances: The Poetry of Edward Dorn.* Edited by Donald Wesling. 45–86. Berkeley and Los Angeles: University of California Press, 1985.

Wain, John. "The Prophet Ezra v. 'The Egotistical Sublime.'" *Encounter* 33, no. 2 (1969): 63–69.

Wesling, Donald. "'The Fire We Give Everything': Dorn's Shorter Poems." In *Internal Resistances: The Poetry of Edward Dorn,* edited by Donald Wesling, 13–44. Berkeley and Los Angeles: University of California Press, 1985.

Whitehead, Alfred North. *Process and Reality: An Essay in Cosmology.* New York: Macmillan, 1930.

Whitman, Walt. *Collect and Other Prose.* Vol. 2 of *Prose Works, 1892.* Edited by Floyd Stovall. New York: New York University Press, 1964.

Wilhelm, James J. *The American Roots of Ezra Pound.* New York: Garland, 1985.

Williams, William Carlos. *Autobiography.* New York: Random House, 1951.

———. "Fistula of the Law." *Imagi* (Spring 1949): 10–11.

———. *Kora in Hell: Improvisations.* 1920. Reprinted in *Imaginations.* Edited by Webster Schott. New York; New Directions, 1970.

————. *Paterson.* New York: New Directions, 1963.

————. *Selected Essays.* New York: New Directions, 1969.

————. *The Selected Letters of William Carlos Williams.* Edited by John Thirlwall. New York: New Directions, 1957.

Zukofsky, Louis. *"A".* Berkeley and Los Angeles: University of California Press, 1978.

————. *All: The Collected Short Poems.* New York: Norton, 1965.

————. Interview with L. S. Dembo. *Wisconsin Studies in Contemporary Literature* 10, no. 2 (1969): 203–19.

————. *Prepositions: The Collected Essays.* New York: Horizon Press, 1967.

INDEX

Compositor: A-R Editions
Text: 10/13 Sabon
Printer: Thomson-Shore, Inc.
Binder: Thomson-Shore, Inc.